THE R

ITALIAN
PHRASEBOOK

Compiled by
LEXUS

ROUGH GUIDES

www.roughguides.com

Credits

Italian Phrasebook

Compiled by Lexus with Michela Masci

Lexus series editor: Sally Davies
Layout: Ajay Verma
Picture research: Rhiannon Furbear

Rough Guides Reference

Director: Andrew Lockett
Editors: Kate Berens, Tom Cabot, Tracy Hopkins, Matthew Milton, Joe Staines

Publishing information

First published in 1995
This updated edition published August 2011 by
Rough Guides Ltd, 80 Strand, London, WC2R 0RL
Email: mail@roughguides.com

Distributed by the Penguin Group:
Penguin Books Ltd, 80 Strand, London, WC2R 0RL
Penguin Group (USA), 345 Hudson Street, NY 10014, USA
Penguin Group (Australia), 250 Camberwell Road,
Camberwell, Victoria, Australia
Penguin Group (New Zealand), Cnr Rosedale and Airborne Roads, Albany,
Auckland, New Zealand

Rough Guides is represented in Canada by Tourmaline Editions Inc., 662 King
Street West, Suite 304, Toronto, Ontario, M5V 1M7

Printed in Singapore by Toppan Security Printing Pte. Ltd.
The publishers and author have done their best to ensure the
accuracy and currency of all information in the *Rough Guide Italian
Phrasebook*; however, they can accept no responsibility for any loss or
inconvenience sustained by any reader as a result of its information or advice.

A catalogue record for this book is available from the British Library.

978-1-84836-731-9

3 5 7 9 8 6 4

CONTENTS

How to use this book

The Rough Guide Italian Phrasebook is a highly practical introduction to the contemporary language. It gets straight to the point in every situation you might encounter: in bars and shops, on trains and buses, in hotels and banks, on holiday or on business. Laid out in clear A–Z style with easy-to-find, colour-coded sections, it uses key words to take you directly to the phrase you need – so if you want some help booking a room, just look up "room" in the dictionary section.

The phrasebook starts off with **Basics**, where we list some essential phrases, including words for numbers, dates and telling the time, and give guidance on pronunciation, along with a short section on the different regional accents you might come across. Then, to get you started in two-way communication, the Scenarios section offers dialogues in key situations such as renting a car, asking directions or booking a taxi, and includes words and phrases for when something goes wrong, from getting a flat tyre or asking to move apartments to more serious emergencies. You can listen to these and download them for free from www.roughguides.com/phrasebooks for use on your computer, MP3 player or smartphone.

Forming the main part of the guide is a double dictionary, first English–Italian, which gives you the essential words you'll need plus easy-to-use phonetic transliterations wherever pronunciation might be a problem. Then, in the Italian–English dictionary, we've given not just the phrases you'll be likely to hear (starting with a selection of slang and colloquialisms) but also many of the signs, labels and instructions you'll come across in print or in public places.

Scattered throughout the sections are travel tips direct from the authors of the Rough Guides guidebook series.

Finally, there's an extensive **Menu reader**. Consisting of separate food and drink sections, each starting with a list of essential terms, it's indispensable whether you're eating out, stopping for a quick drink or looking around a local food market.

Buon viaggio!
Have a good trip!

BASICS

Pronunciation

In this phrasebook, the Italian has been written in a system of imitated pronunciation so that it can be read as though it were English, bearing in mind the notes on pronunciation given below:

ay	as in may
ow	as in now
e	as in get
y	as in yes
g	always hard as in goat

Letters given in bold type indicate the part of the word to be stressed. When double consonants are given in the pronunciation such as j-j, t-t and so on, both consonants should be pronounced, for example formaggio formaj-jo, biglietto beel-yet-to.

Abbreviations

adj	adjective	*m*	masculine (nouns with il, lo)
f	feminine (nouns with la)	*mpl*	masculine plural
fpl	feminine plural		

Notes

In the English–Italian section, when two forms of the verb are given in phrases such as: '**can you...?**' puoi/può...?, the first is the familiar form and the second the polite form (see the entry for **you** in the dictionary).

In other cases when two forms are given, as in expressions like: '**a few**' alcuni/alcune, the first form is masculine and the second feminine.

Basic phrases

hello (in the daytime) buongiorno
bwonjorno

(late afternoon, in the evening)
buonasera bwonasaira

good night buonanotte
bwonanot-tay

goodbye arrivederci
ar-reevedairchee

please per favore pair favoray

yes please sì, grazie see gratzee-ay

thanks, thank you grazie
gratzee-ay

thank you very much
grazie mille meel-lay

no thanks no grazie

that's OK, don't mention it
prego praygo

how do you do? piacere
p-yachairay

how are you? come sta? komay

fine, thanks, and you? bene,
grazie e tu/lei? baynay gratzee-ay
ay too/lay?

pleased to meet you
piacere di conoscerla p-yachairay
dee konoshairla

excuse me (to get past) permesso
pairmes-so

(to get attention) mi scusi
mee skoozee

(to say sorry) chiedo scusa
k-yaydo skooza

sorry: (I'm) sorry scusa/mi scusi

skooza/mee skoozee

sorry? (didn't understand) prego?
praygo

I understand capisco

I don't understand non capisco

do you understand? capisci/
capisce? kapeeshee/kapeeshay

do you speak English?
parla inglese? eenglayzay

I don't speak Italian
non parlo italiano eetal-yano

could you say it slowly?
puoi/può dirlo più lentamente?
pwoy/pwo deerlo p-yoo lentamentay

could you repeat that?
può ripetere? pwo reepetairay

could you write it down?
può scrivermelo? pwo
skreevairmaylo

I'd like... vorrei... vor-ray

would you like...? vuoi/vuole...
vwoy/vwolay

can I have a...? vorrei... vor-ray

do you have...? avete...? avaytay

how much is it? quanto costa?
kwanto

cheers! (toast) alla salute! salootay

(thanks) grazie gratzee-ay

it is... è... ay

where is...? dov'è...? dovay

is it far from here? è lontano da
qui? ay – kwee

Dates

Use the numbers opposite to express the date, except for the first when the ordinal il primo should be used:

the first of September il primo settembre eel preemo set-tembray

the third of March il tre marzo eel tray martzo

the twenty-first of June il ventuno giugno eel ventoono yoon-yo

Days

Monday lunedì loonedee

Tuesday martedì martedee

Wednesday mercoledì mairkoledee

Thursday giovedì jovedee

Friday venerdì venairdee

Saturday sabato

Sunday domenica domayneeka

Months

January gennaio jen-na-yo

February febbraio feb-bra-yo

March marzo martzo

April aprile apreelay

May maggio maj-jo

June giugno yoon-yo

July luglio lool-yo

August agosto

September settembre set-tembray

October ottobre ot-tobray

November novembre novembray

December dicembre deechembray

Time

what time is it? che ore sono? kay oray sono

one o'clock l'una loona

two o'clock le due lay doo-ay

it's one o'clock è l'una ay loona

it's two o'clock sono le due sono lay doo-ay

it's ten o'clock sono le dieci sono lay dee-aychee

five past one l'una e cinque loona ay cheenkway

ten past two le due e dieci lay doo-ay ay dee-aychee

quarter past one l'una e un quarto loona ay oon kwarto

quarter past two le due e un quarto lay doo-ay

half past ten le dieci e mezza lay dee-aychee ay medza

twenty to ten le dieci meno venti lay dee-aychee mayno ventee

quarter to two le due meno un quarto lay doo-ay mayno oon kwarto

at eight o'clock alle otto

at half past four alle quattro e mezza al-lay kwat-tro ay medza

14.00 le quattordici
lay kwat-**tor**deechee

17.30 le diciassette e trenta
lay deechas-**set**-tay ay **tr**enta

2 a.m. le due di notte lay d**oo**-ay
dee n**o**t-tay

2 p.m. le due del pomeriggio
pomer**ee**j-jo

6 a.m. le sei del mattino lay say

6 p.m. le sei di sera dee s**ai**ra

noon mezzogiorno medz**oj**orno

midnight mezzanotte
medzan**o**t-tay

an hour un'ora **o**ra

a minute un minuto meen**oo**to

a second un secondo sek**o**ndo

a quarter of an hour un quarto
d'ora kw**a**rto d**o**ra

half an hour mezz'ora medz**o**ra

three quarters of an hour
tre quarti d'ora tray kw**a**rtee d**o**ra

Numbers

0 zero tz**ai**ro

1 uno **oo**no

2 due d**oo**-ay

3 tre tray

4 quattro kw**a**t-tro

5 cinque ch**ee**nkway

6 sei say

7 sette s**e**t-tay

8 otto **o**t-to

9 nove n**o**-vay

10 dieci dee-**ay**chee

11 undici **oo**n-deechee

12 dodici d**oh**-deechee

13 tredici tray-deechee

14 quattordici kwat-**t**or-deechee

15 quindici kw**ee**n-deechee

16 sedici s**ay**-deechee

17 diciassette deechas-s**et**-tay

18 diciotto deech**o**t-to

19 diciannove deechan-n**o**-vay

20 venti v**e**ntee

21 ventuno vent**oo**no

22 ventidue ventee-d**oo**-ay

23 ventitré ventee-tr**a**y

30 trenta tr**e**nta

31 trentuno trent**oo**no

40 quaranta kw**a**ranta

50 cinquanta cheenkw**a**nta

60 sessanta ses-s**a**nta

70 settanta set-t**a**nta

80 ottanta ot-t**a**nta

90 novanta nov**a**nta

100 cento ch**e**nto

110 centodieci chento-dee-**ay**chee

200 duecento doo-ay-ch**e**nto

300 trecento tray-ch**e**nto

1,000 mille m**ee**lay

2,000 duemila doo-ay-m**ee**la

5,000 cinquemila cheenkway-m**ee**la

5,720 cinquemilasette-centoventi
cheenkway-m**ee**la-set-tay-chento-
v**e**ntee

10,000 diecimila dee-aycheemeela

10,550 diecimilacinque-
centocinquanta dee-aycheemeela-
cheenkway-chento-cheenkwanta

20,000 ventimila venteemeela

50,000 cinquantamila
cheenkwantameela

100,000 centomila chentomeela

1,000,000 un milione oon meel-
yonay

Ordinals

In Italian, thousands are written with a full stop instead
of a comma, e.g. 1.000, 10.000.
Decimals are written with a
comma, e.g. 3.5 is 3,5 in Italian.

1st primo preemo

2nd secondo sekondo

3rd terzo tairtzo

4th quarto kwarto

5th quinto kweento

6th sesto

7th settimo set-teemo

8th ottavo ot-tavo

9th nono

10th decimo daycheemo

Regional accents

Modern standard Italian is descended from Latin and from the medieval Tuscan dialect. It is the main language of Italy and it is

❶ Piemonte & Valle d'Aosta	❻ Friuli-Venezia Giulia	❷ Abruzzo & Molise
❷ Liguria	❼ Emilia-Romagna	❸ Campania
❸ Lombardy & the lakes	❽ Tuscany	❹ Puglia
❹ Trentino-Alto Adige	❾ Umbria	❺ Basilicata & Calabria
❺ Venice & the Veneto	❿ Marche	❻ Sicily
	⓫ Rome & Lazio	⓱ Sardinia

spoken all over the country, but every region has its own accent and variations.

Many of them also retain their own dialects, some of which shade off into separate languages – the dialects of Sardinia, Sicily, Emilia-Romagna, Veneto and Piedmonte, for example. Italian dialects are quite diverse, and dialect-speakers from the north and south of Italy will have difficulty in understanding each other's speech.

But just about all speakers of local dialects also speak standard Italian, so there is no fear of not being understood, unless you

		Northern Italy, Lombardy, Piemonte, Emilia-Romagna
double consonants to single	matto	mat-to
l becomes r	molto	molto
dropping of final consonant	quando	kwand
c becomes h	casa	kaza
nd becomes nn	quando	kwando
final o becomes u	amico	ameeko

happen to be travelling in an extremely remote village in the far
south or in some hidden valley in the Alps and attempt to talk to
someone over the age of 70.

In some parts of Italy you may see signs written in more than
one language: in Trentino Alto-Adige (Italian, German and Ladin
are spoken in some areas), in Valle D'Aosta (Italian and French)
and in Friuli Venezia-Giulia (Italian and Friulan).

Here are some examples of distinctive characteristics that can
be heard in regional pronunciations of standard Italian by speakers who are influenced by the local dialect:

Veneto	Tuscany	Central-Southern Italy	Rome	Sardinia
mato	mat-to	mat-to	mat-to	mat-to
molto	molto	molto	morto	molto
kwando	kwando	kwando	kwando	kwando
kaza	haza	kaza	kaza	kaza
kwando	kwando	kwan-no	kwando	kwando
ameeko	ameeko	ameeko	ameeko	ameekoo

SCENARIOS

Download these scenarios as MP3s from
www.roughguides.com/phrasebooks

1. Accommodation

▶ Is there an inexpensive hotel you can recommend?
Mi può consigliare un albergo economico?
mee pwo konseel-yaray oon albairgo ekonomeeko

▶▶ I'm sorry, they all seem to be fully booked.
Mi dispiace, sembrano tutti al completo.
mee deesp-yachay sembrano toot-tee al komplayto

▶ Can you give me the name of a good middle-range hotel?
Mi può dare il nome di un buon albergo a prezzo medio?
mee pwo daray eel nomay dee oon bwon albairgo a pretzo mayd-yo

▶▶ Let me have a look; do you want to be in the centre?
Vediamo; vuol essere al centro?
ved-yamo vwol es-sairay al chentro

▶ If possible.
Se possibile.
say pos-seebeelay

▶▶ Do you mind being a little way out of town?
Le dà fastidio essere un po' fuori città?
lay da fasteed-yo es-sairay oon po fworee cheet-ta

▶ Not too far out.
Non troppo fuori.
non trop-po fworee

▶ Where is it on the map?
Dove si trova sulla piantina?
dovay see trova sool-la p-yanteena

▶ Can you write the name and address down?
Mi può scrivere il nome e l'indirizzo?
mee pwo skreevairay eel nomay ay leendeereetzo

▶ I'm looking for a room in a private house.
Cerco una stanza in una casa privata.
chairko oona stantza een oona kaza preevata

2. Banks

bank account	il conto bancario	konto bankar-yo
to change money	cambiare dei soldi	kamb-yaray day soldee
cheque	l'assegno	as-sen-yo
to deposit	depositare	daypozeetaray
euro	l'euro	**ay-oo**ro
pin number	il pin	peen
pound	la sterlina	stairleena
to withdraw	ritirare	reeteeraray

▶ Can you change this into euros?
Mi può cambiare questi in euro?
mee pwo kamb-yaray kwestee een **ay-oo**roo

▶▶ How would you like the money?
Come preferisce i soldi?
komay prefaireeshay ee soldee

▶ Small notes.
Banconote di piccolo taglio.
bankonotay dee peek-kolo tal-yo

▶ Big notes.
Banconote di grosso taglio.
bankonotay dee gros-so tal-yo

▶ Do you have information in English about opening an account?
Ha informazioni in inglese su come aprire un conto?
a eenformatz-yonee een eenglayzay soo komay apreeray oon konto

▶▶ Yes, what sort of account do you want?
Sì, che tipo di conto vuole?
see kay teepo dee konto vwolay

▶ I'd like a current account.
Vorrei un conto corrente.
vor-ray oon konto kor-rentay

▶▶ Your passport, please.
Il suo passaporto, per favore.
eel soo-o pas-saporto pair favoray

▶ Can I use this card to draw some cash?
Posso usare questa carta per ritirare dei soldi?
pos-so oozaray kwesta karta pair reeteeraray day soldee

▶▶ You have to go to the cashier's desk.
Deve andare alla cassa.
dayvay andaray al-la kas-sa

▶ I want to transfer this to my account at the Banco di Roma.
Voglio trasferire questi soldi nel mio conto presso il Banco di Roma.
vol-yo trasfaireeray kwestee soldee nel mee-o konto pres-so eel banko dee roma

▶▶ OK, but we'll have to charge you for the phonecall.
Va bene, ma le dobbiamo addebitare la telefonata.
va baynay ma lay dob-byamo ad-debeetaray la telefonata

3. Booking a room

payphone	telefono pubblico	telefono poob-bleeko
in the lobby	nella hall	nel-la oll
shower	la doccia	docha
telephone	telefono	telefono
in the room	in stanza	een stantza

▶ Do you have any rooms?
Avete stanze libere?
avaytay stantzay leebairay

▶▶ For how many people?
Per quante persone?
pair kwantay pairsonay

▶ For one/for two.
Per una/per due.
pair oona/pair doo-ay

▶▶ Yes, we have rooms free.
Sì, abbiamo delle stanze libere.
see ab-byamo del-lay stantzay leebairay

▶▶ For how many nights?
Per quante notti?
pair kwantay not-tee

▶ Just for one night.
Solo per una notte.
solo pair oona not-tay

▶ How much is it?
Quanto costa?
kwanto kosta

▶▶ 90 euros with bathroom and 70 euros without bathroom.
90 euro col bagno e 70 euro senza bagno.
novanta **ay-oo**ro kol ban-yo ay set-tanta **ay-oo**ro sentza ban-yo

▶ Does that include breakfast?
La colazione è compresa?
la kolatz-yonay ay komprayza

▶ Can I see a room with a bathroom?
Posso vedere una stanza col bagno?
pos-so vedairay oona stantza kol ban-yo

▶ OK, I'll take it.
Va bene, la prendo.
va baynay la prendo

▶ When do I have to check out?
Quando devo lasciare la stanza?
kwando dayvo lasharay la stantza

▶ Is there anywhere I can leave luggage?
Posso lasciare i bagagli da qualche parte?
pos-so lasharay ee bagal-yee da kwalkay partay

4. Car hire

automatic	con il cambio	kon eel kamb-yo
	automatico	owto-mateeko
full tank	il serbatoio pieno	sairbatoy-o p-yayno
manual	con il cambio	kon eel kamb-yo
	manuale	manoo-alay
rented car	l'automobile	owtomobeelay
	a noleggio	a nolej-jo

▶ I'd like to rent a car.
Vorrei noleggiare un'automobile.
vor-**ray** nolej-ja**ray** oon owtom**o**beelay

>> ▶▶ For how long?
>> Per quanti giorni?
>> pair kw**a**ntee j**o**rnee

▶ Two days.
Due giorni.
d**oo**-ay j**o**rnee

▶ I'll take the…
Prendo la…
prendo la…

▶ Is that with unlimited mileage?
Il chilometraggio è illimitato?
eel keelometra**j**-jo ay eel-leem**ee**tato

>> ▶▶ It is.
>> Sì.
>> see

>> ▶▶ Can I see your driving licence, please?
>> Mi fa vedere la patente per favore?
>> mee fa ved**ai**ray la pat**e**ntay pair fav**o**ray

>> ▶▶ And your passport.
>> E il passaporto.
>> ay eel pas-sap**o**rto

▶ Is insurance included?
l'assicurazione è compresa?
as-seekooratz-y**o**nay ay kompr**ay**za

>> ▶▶ Yes, but you have to pay the first 100 euros.
>> Sì, ma deve pagare i primi 100 euro.
>> see ma d**ay**vay pag**a**ray ee pr**ee**mee chento **ay-oo**ro

▶▶ Can you leave a deposit of 100 euros?
Può lasciare una caparra di 100 euro?
pwo lasharay oona kapar-ra dee chento ay-ooro

▶ And if this office is closed, where do I leave the keys?
E se quest'ufficio è chiuso, dove posso lasciare le chiavi?
ay say kwest oof-feecho ay k-yoozo dovay pos-so lasharay lay k-yavee

▶▶ You drop them in that box.
Le infili in quella cassetta.
lay eenfeelee een kwel-la kas-set-ta

5. Car problems

brakes	i freni	fraynee
to break down	guastarsi	gwastarsee
clutch	la frizione	freetz-yonay
diesel	il gasolio	gazol-yo
flat battery	la batteria scarica	bat-tairee-a skareeka
flat tyre	una gomma a terra	gom-ma a tair-ra
petrol	la benzina	bentzeena

▶ Excuse me, where is the nearest petrol station?
Scusi, dov'è la stazione di servizio più vicina?
skoozee dovay la statz-yonay dee sairveetz-yo p-yoo veecheena

▶▶ In the next town, about 5km away.
Nella prossima città, a circa cinque chilometri da qui.
nel-la pros-seema cheeta a cheerka cheenkway keelometree da kwee

▶ The car has broken down.
L'automobile è guasta.
lowtomobeelay ay gwasta

▶▶ Can you tell me what happened?
Può dirmi cos'è successo?
pwo deermee kozay soochays-so

▶ I've got a flat tyre.
Ho una gomma a terra.
o oona gom-ma a tair-ra

▶ I think the battery is flat.
Credo di avere la batteria scarica.
kraydo dee avairay la bat-tairee-a skareeka

▶▶ Can you tell me exactly where you are?
Può dirmi il luogo esatto dove si trova?
pwo deerme eel lwogo esat-to dovay see trova

▶ I'm about 2km outside of Pistoia on the Strada Statale 66.
Sono a circa due chilometri fuori Pistoia, sulla Strada Statale 66.
sono a cheerka doo-ay keelometree fworee peestoy-a sool-la strada statalay sessanta-say

▶▶ What type of car? What colour?
Che tipo d'automobile? Di che colore?
kay teepo dowtomobeelay, dee kay koloray

▶ Can you send a tow truck?
Può mandare un carro attrezzi?
pwo mandaray oon kar-ro at-tretzee

6. Children

baby	il bambino / la bambina	bambeeno/bambeena
boy	il ragazzo	ragatzo
child	il bambino / la bambina	bambeeno/bambeena
children	i bambini/ le bambine	bambeenee/bambeenay
cot	il lettino	let-teeno
formula	il latte in polvere	lat-tay een polvairay
girl	la ragazza	ragatza
highchair	il seggiolone	sej-jolonay
nappies (diapers)	i pannolini	pan-noleenee

▶ We need a babysitter for tomorrow evening.
Abbiamo bisogno di una babysitter per domani sera.
ab-yamo beezon-yo dee oona babysitter pair domanee saira

▶▶ For what time?
Per che ora?
pair kay ora

▶ From 7.30 to 11.00.
Dalle sette e mezza alle undici.
dal-lay set-tay ay medza al-lay oondeechee

> ▶▶ How many children? How old are they?
> **Quanti bambini? Quanti anni hanno?**
> kwantee bambeenee, kwantee an-nee an-no

▶ Two children, aged four and eighteen months.
Due bambini, uno di quattro anni e uno di diciotto mesi.
doo-ay bambeenee oono dee kwat-tro an-nee ay oono dee deechot-to mayzee

---

▶ Where can I change the baby?
Dove posso cambiare il bambino?
dovay pos-so kamb-yaray eel bambeeno

▶ Could you please warm this bottle for me?
Può scaldarmi questo biberon, per favore?
pwo skaldarmee kwesto beebairon pair favoray

▶ Can you give us a child's portion?
Può darci una porzione per bambino?
pwo darchee oona portz-yonay pair bambeeno

▶ We need two child seats.
Abbiamo bisogno di due seggiolini per bambini.
ab-yamo beezon-yo dee doo-ay sej-joleenee pair bambeenee

▶ Is there a discount for children?
C'è uno sconto per bambini?
chay oono skonto pair bambeenee

7. Communications: Internet

@, at sign	la chiocciola	k-yoch-chola
computer	il computer	computer
email	la mail	mail
Internet	Internet	eentairnet
keyboard	la tastiera	tast-yaira
mouse	il mouse	mouse

▶ Is there somewhere I can check my emails?
C'è un posto dove posso accedere alle mie mail?
chay oon posto dovay pos-so achaydairay al-lay mee-ay mail

▶ Do you have Wi-Fi?
Avete il wi-fi?
avaytay eel wifi

▶ Is there an Internet café around here?
C'è un Internet café da queste parti?
chay oon eentairnet kafay da kwestay partee

> ▶▶ Yes, there's one in the shopping centre.
> Sì, ce n'è uno nel centro commerciale.
> see chay nay oono nel chentro kom-mairchalay

> ▶▶ Do you want fifteen minutes, thirty minutes or one hour?
> Vuole quindici minuti, trenta minuti o un'ora?
> vwolay kweendeechee meenootee trenta meenootee o oon ora

▶ Thirty minutes please. Can you help me log on?
Trenta minuti, grazie. Per favore, mi può aiutare a fare il log in?
trenta meenootee gratzee-ay, pair favoray mee pwo a-yootaray a faray eel log een

> ▶▶ OK, here's your password.
> Certo, ecco la sua password.
> chairto ek-ko la soo-a password

▶ Can you change this to an English keyboard?
Si può cambiare la tastiera in britannica?
see pwo kamb-yaray la tast-yaira een breetan-neeka

▶ I'll take another quarter of an hour.
Prendo un altro quarto d'ora.
prendo oon altro kwarto dora

▶ Is there a printer I can use?
Posso accedere a una stampante?
pos-so achaydairay a oona stampantay

8. Communications: phones

mobile phone (cell phone)	il cellulare	chel-loolaray
payphone	il telefono pubblico	telayfono poob-bleeko
phone call	la telefonata	telefonata
phone card	la scheda telefonica	skayda telefoneeka
phone charger	il caricatore	kareekatoray
SIM card	la SIM card	seem kard

▶ Can I call abroad from here?
Posso telefonare all'estero da qui?
pos-so telefonaray al-lestairo da kwee

▶ How do I get an outside line?
Come si accede alla linea esterna?
komay see achayday al-la leenay-a
estairna

▶ What's the code to call the UK/US from here?
Qual è il prefisso per la Gran Bretagna/gli Stati Uniti?
kwal ay eel prefees-so pair la gran bretan-ya/l-yee statee ooneetee

zero	zero	tzairo
one	uno	oono
two	due	doo-ay
three	tre	tray
four	quattro	kwat-tro
five	cinque	cheenk way
six	sei	say
seven	sette	set-ta
eight	otto	ot-to
nine	nove	no-vay

▶ Hello, can I speak to Marco?
Salve, posso parlare con Marco?
salvay pos-so parlaray kon marco

▶▶ Yes, that's me speaking.
Sì, sono io.
see sono ee-o

▶ Do you have a charger for this?
Avete un caricatore per questo?
avaytay oon kareekatoray pair kwesto

▶ Can I buy a SIM card for this phone?
Posso comprare una SIM card per questo cellulare?
pos-so kompraray oona seem kard pair kwesto chel-loolaray

9. Directions

▶ Hi, I'm looking for the via Messina.
Salve, cerco via Messina.
salvay chairko vee-a mes-seena

▶ Hi, the via Messina, do you know where it is?
Salve, via Messina, sa dov'è?
salvay vee-a mes-seena sa dovay

▶▶ Sorry, never heard of it.
Mi dispiace, mai sentita.
mee deesp-yachay ma-ee senteeta

▶ Hi, can you tell me where the via Messina is?
Salve, mi sa dire dove si trova via Messina?
salvay mee sa deeray dovay see trova vee-a mes-seena

just after	appena dopo	ap-**pay**na **d**opo
in front of	davanti a	da**v**antee a
opposite	di fronte	dee **fr**ontay
past the...	dopo il...	**d**opo eel...
back	indietro	eend-**yay**tro
over there	lì	lee
further	più avanti	p-yoo a**v**antee
next	prossimo	pr**os**-seemo
straight ahead	sempre dritto	**s**empray dr**ee**t-to
street	strada	**str**ada
on the right	sulla destra	s**oo**l-la **d**estra
on the left	sulla sinistra	s**oo**l-la seen**ee**stra
turn off	svoltare	zvolt**ar**ay
near	vicino	veech**ee**no

▶▶ I'm a stranger here too.
Anch'io non sono di qui.
ank**ee**-o non s**o**no dee kwee

▶ Where?
Dove?
d**o**vay

▶ Which direction?
In quale direzione?
een kw**a**lay deeretz-y**o**nay

▶▶ Left at the second traffic lights.
A sinistra al secondo semaforo.
a seen**ee**stra al sek**o**ndo sem**a**foro

▶▶ Around the corner.
All'angolo.
al-langolo

▶▶ Then it's the first street on the right.
Poi è la prima strada a destra.
poy ay la preema strada a destra

10. Emergencies

accident	l'incidente	eencheedentay
ambulance	l'ambulanza	amboolantza
consul	il console	konsolay
embassy	l'ambasciata	ambashata
fire brigade	i vigili del fuoco	veejeelee del fwoko
police	la polizia	poleetzee-a

▶ Help!
Aiuto!
a-yooto

▶ Can you help me?
Può aiutarmi?
pwo a-yootarmee

▶ Please come with me! It's really very urgent.
Per favore venga con me! È davvero molto urgente.
pair favoray venga kon may, ay dav-vairo molto oorjentay

▶ I've lost my keys.
Ho perso le chiavi.
o pairso lay k-yavay

▶ My car is not working.
La mia automobile non funziona.
la mee-a owtomobeelay non foontz-yona

▶ My purse has been stolen.
Il mio borsellino è stato rubato.
eel mee-o borsel-leeno ay stato roobato

▶ I've been mugged.
Sono stata aggredita.
sono stata ag-gredeeta

▶▶ What's your name?
Come si chiama?
komay see k-yama

▶▶ I need to see your passport.
Mi può mostrare il passaporto?
mee pwo mostraray eel pas-saporto

▶ I'm sorry, all my papers have been stolen.
Mi dispiace, mi hanno rubato tutti i documenti.
mee deesp-yachay mee an-no roobato toot-tee ee dokoomentee

11. Friends

▶ Hi, how're you doing?
Ciao, come va?
chow komay va

▶▶ OK, and you?
Bene, e tu?
baynay ay too

▶ Yeah, fine.   ▶ Not bad.
Bene.   Non c'è male.
baynay   non chay malay

▶ Do you know Marco?
Conosci Marco?
konoshee marco

▶ And this is Hannah.
E questa è Hannah.
ay kwesta ay han-nah

▶▶ Yeah, we know each other.
Sì, ci conosciamo già.
see chee konosh-yamo ja

▶ Where do you know each other from?
Dove vi siete conosciuti?
dovay vee s-yaytay konoshootee

▶▶ We met at Luca's place.
Ci siamo conosciuti da Luca.
chee s-yamo konoshootee da looka

▶ That was some party, eh?
Che festa quella, vero?
kay festa kwel-la vairo

▶▶ The best.
Fantastica.
fantasteeka

▶ Are you guys coming for a beer?
Venite a prendere una birra?
veneetay a prendairay oona beer-ra

▶▶ Cool, let's go.
Grande, andiamo.
granday and-yamo

▶▶ No, I'm meeting Luisa.
No, mi vedo con Luisa.
no mee vaydo kon loo-eesa

▶ See you at Luca's place tonight.
Ci vediamo da Luca stasera.
chee ved-yamo da looka stasaira

▶▶ See you.
Ciao.
chow

12. Health

antibiotics	gli antibiotici	anteebioteechee
antiseptic ointment	la pomata antisettica	pomata anteeset-teeka
cystitis	la cistite	cheesteetay
dentist	il/la dentista	denteesta
diarrhoea	la diarrea	dee-aray-a
doctor	il dottore	dot-toray
hospital	l'ospedale	ospedalay
ill	malato/a	malato
medicine	la medicina	medeecheena
painkillers	gli analgesici	analjayseechee
pharmacy	la farmacia	farmachee-a
to prescribe	prescrivere	preskreevairay
thrush	la candida	kandeeda

▶ I'm not feeling very well.
Non mi sento bene.
non mee sento baynay

▶ Can you get a doctor?
Può chiamare un dottore?
pwo k-yamaray oon dot-toray

▶▶ Where does it hurt?
Dove le fa male?
dovay lay fa malay

▶ It hurts here.
Mi fa male qui.
mee fa malay kwee

▶▶ Is the pain constant?
Il dolore è continuo?
eel doloray ay konteenoo-o

▶ It's not a constant pain.
Non è un dolore continuo.
non ay oon doloray konteenoo-o

▶ Can I make an appointment?
Posso prendere un appuntamento?
pos-so prendairay oon ap-poontamento

▶ Can you give me something for...?
Mi può dare qualcosa per...?
mee pwo daray kwalkoza pair...

▶ Yes, I have insurance.
Sì, sono assicurato.
see sono as-seekoorato

13. Hotels

maid	la cameriera	kamair-yaira
manager	il direttore /	deeret-toray /
	la direttrice	deeret-treechay
room service	il servizio in camera	sairveetz-yo een kamaira

▶ Hello, we've booked a double room in the name of Cameron.
Salve, abbiamo prenotato una camera doppia a nome Cameron.
salvay ab-yamo praynotato oona kamaira dop-ya a nomay cameron

▶▶ That was for four nights, wasn't it?
Era per quattro notti, vero?
aira pair kwat-tro not-tee vairo

▶ Yes, we're leaving on Saturday.
Sì, ripartiamo sabato.
see reepart-yamo sabato

▶▶ Can I see your passport please?
Posso vedere il suo passaporto, per favore?
pos-so vedairay eel soo-o pas-saporto pair favoray

▶▶ There you are, room 321 on the third floor.
Ecco a voi, camera trecentoventuno al terzo piano.
ek-ko a voy kamaira tray-chento-ventoono al tairtzo p-yano

▶ I can't get this keycard to work.
Non riesco ad usare la mia keycard.
non ree-aysko ad oozaray la mee-a keycard

▶▶ Sorry, I need to reactivate it.
Mi spiace, gliela devo riattivare.
mee spee-achay l-yee-ayla dayvo ree-at-teevaray

▶ What time is breakfast?
A che ora è la colazione?
a kay ora ay la kolatz-yonay

▶ There aren't any towels in my room.
Nella mia camera non ci sono asciugamani.
nel-la mee-a kamaira non chee sono ashoogamanee

▶ My flight isn't until this evening, can I keep the room a bit longer?
Il mio aereo non parte fino a stasera, posso ancora tenere la camera?
eel mee-o a-airay-o non partay feeno a stasaira pos-so ankora tenairay la kamaira

▶ Can I settle up? Is this card ok?
Posso saldare il conto? Accettate questa carta di credito?
pos-so saldaray eel konto, achet-tatay kwesta karta dee kraydeeto

14. Language difficulties

▶▶ Your credit card has been refused.
La sua carta di credito è stata respinta.
la soo-a karta dee kraydeeto ay stata respeenta

▶ What, I don't understand; do you speak English?
Come, non capisco; parla inglese?
komay non kapeesko parla eenglayzay

▸▸ This isn't valid.
Non è valida.
non ay valeeda

▸ Could you say that again?
Può ripetere?
pwo reepetairay

▸ Slowly.
Lentamente.
lentamentay

▸ I understand very little Italian.
Capisco solo un po' d'italiano.
kapeesko solo oon po deetal-yano

▸ I speak Italian very badly.
Parlo italiano molto male.
parlo eetal-yano molto malay

▸▸ You can't use this card to pay.
Non può usare questa carta per pagare.
non pwo oozaray kwesta karta pair pagaray

▸▸ Do you understand?
Capisce?
kapeeshay

▸ Sorry, no.
No, mi dispiace.
no mee deesp-yachay

▸ Is there someone who speaks English?
C'è qualcuno che parla inglese?
chay kwalkoono kay parla eenglayzay

▸ Oh, now I understand.
Oh, ora capisco.
oh ora kapeesko

▸ Is that ok now?
Va bene ora?
va baynay ora

15. Meeting people

a few words	qualche parola	kwalkay parola
interpreter	l'interprete	eentairpretay
to translate	tradurre	tradoor-ray

▶ Hello.
Salve.
salvay

▶▶ Hello, my name's Anna.
Salve, mi chiamo Anna.
salvay mee k-yamo an-na

▶ Graham, from England, Thirsk.
Io sono Graham, di Thirsk, in Inghilterra.
ee-o sono graham dee thirsk een eengeeltair-ra

▶▶ Don't know that, where is it?
Non conosco questo posto, dove si trova?
non konosko kwesto posto dovay see trova

▶ Not far from York, in the North; and you?
Non lontano da York, nel nord; e lei di dov'è?
non lontano da york nel nord ay lay dee dovay

▶▶ I'm from Milan; here by yourself?
Io sono di Milano; è qui da solo?
ee-o sono dee meelano ay kwee da solo

▶ No, I'm with my wife and two kids.
No, sono qui con mia moglie e i miei due figli.
no sono kwee kon mee-a mol-yay ay ee m-yay-ee doo-ay feel-yee

▶ What do you do?
Che lavoro fa?
kay lavoro fa

▶▶ I'm in computers.
Mi occupo di computer.
mee ok-koopo dee computer

▶ Me too.
Anch'io.
ankee-o

▶ Here's my wife now.
Ecco mia moglie.
ek-ko mee-a mol-yay

▶▶ Nice to meet you.
Piacere.
p-yachairay

16. Nightlife

heavy metal	heavy metal	heavy metal
folk	folk	folk
jazz	jazz	jetz
hip-hop	hip-hop	eep-op
electro	electro	elektro
rock	rock	rok

▶ What's a good club for...?
Qual è un buon locale dove suonano musica...?
kwal ay oon bwon lokalay dovay swonano moozeeka

▶▶ There's going to be a great gig at the Globo tomorrow night.
Domani sera ci sarà un bel concerto al Globo.
domanee saira chee sara oon bel konchairto al globo

▶ Where can I hear some local music?
Dove posso ascoltare musica locale?
dovay pos-so askoltaray moozeeka lokalay

▶ What's a good place for dancing?
Qual è una buona discoteca?
kwal ay oona bwona deeskotayka

▶ Can you write down the names of the best bars around here?
Può scrivermi i nomi dei bar migliori in quest'area?
pwo skreevairmee ee nomee day bar meel-yoree een kwest-aray-a

▶▶ That depends what you're looking for.
Dipende da quello che cerca.
deependay da kwel-lo kay chairka

▶ The place where the locals go.
Dove va la gente del posto.
dovay va la jentay del posto

▶ A place for a quiet drink.
Un locale tranquillo.
oon lokalay trankweel-lo

▶▶ The casino across the bay is very good.
Il casinò dall'altra parte della baia è molto bello.
eel kaseeno dal-altra partay del-la ba-ya ay molto bel-lo

▶ I suppose they have a dress code.
Immagino bisogna vestirsi in un certo modo.
im-majeeno bizon-ya vesteersee een oon chairto modo

▶▶ You can wear what you like.
Può vestirsi come preferisce.
pwo vesteersee komay prefaireeshay

▶ What time does it close?
A che ora chiude?
a kay ora k-yooday

17. Post offices

airmail	la posta aerea	posta a-airay-a
post card	la cartolina	kartoleena
post office	la posta	posta
stamp	il francobollo	frankobol-lo

▶ What time does the post office close?
Che ora chiude la posta?
a kay ora k-yooday la posta

▶▶ Five o'clock weekdays.
Alle cinque dal lunedì al venerdì.
al-lay cheenkway dal loonedee al venairdee

▶ Is the post office open on Saturdays?
La posta è aperta il sabato?
la posta ay apairta eel sabato

▶▶ Until midday.
Fino a mezzogiorno.
feeno a medzojorno

▶ I'd like to send this registered to England.
Vorrei spedire questo in Inghilterra per raccomandata.
vor-ray spedeeray kwesto een eengeeltair-ra pair rak-komandata

▶▶ Certainly, that will cost 10 euros.
Sì, sono 10 euro.
see sono dee-aychee ay-ooro

▶ And also two stamps for England, please.
E anche due francobolli per l'Inghilterra, per favore.
ay ankay doo-ay frankobol-lee pair leengeeltair-ra pair favoray

▶ Do you have some airmail stickers?
Ha degli adesivi di posta aerea?
a dayl-yee adeseevee dee posta a-airay-a

▶ Do you have any mail for me?
C'è posta per me?
chay posta pair may

ESTERO	international
PACCHI	parcels
FERMO POSTA	poste
	restante

18. Restaurants

bill	il conto	konto
menu	il menù	menoo
table	il tavolo	tavolo

▶ Can we have a non-smoking table?
Vorremmo un tavolo per non fumatori.
vor-raym-mo oon tavolo pair non foomatoree

▶ There are two of us.
Siamo in due.
s-yamo een doo-ay

▶ There are four of us.
Siamo in quattro.
s-yamo een kwat-tro

▶ What's this?
Questo cos'è?
kwesto kozay

▶▶ It's a type of fish.
È un tipo di pesce.
ay oon teepo dee peshay

▶▶ It's a local speciality.
È una specialità del posto.
ay **oo**na spech-yal**ee**ta del **po**sto

▶▶ Come inside and I'll show you.
Entri e le faccio vedere.
entree ay lay **fa**cho ved**ai**ray

▶ We would like two of these, one of these, and one of those.
Vorremmo due di questi, uno di questi, e uno di questi.
vor-**ray**m-mo d**oo**-ay dee kw**e**stee **oo**no dee kw**e**stee ay **oo**no dee kw**e**stee

▶▶ And to drink?
E da bere?
ay da b**ai**ray

▶ Red wine.   ▶ White wine.
Vino rosso.   Vino bianco.
v**ee**no r**o**s-so   v**ee**no b-y**a**nko

▶ A beer and two orange juices.
Una birra e due succhi d'arancia.
oona b**ee**r-ra ay d**oo**-ay s**oo**k-kee dar**a**ncha

▶ Some more bread please.
Ancora pane, per favore.
ank**o**ra p**a**nay pair fav**o**ray

> **▶▶ How was your meal?**
> È andata bene?
> ay andata baynay

▶ Excellent! Very nice!
Ottimo! Molto buono!
ot-teemo molto bwono

> **▶▶ Will there be anything else?**
> Desiderano altro?
> dezeederano altro

▶ Just the bill, thanks.
Solo il conto, grazie.
solo eel konto gratzee-ay

19. Self-catering accommodation

air-conditioning	l'aria condizionata	aree-a kondeetz-yonata
apartment	l'appartamento	ap-partamento
cooker	la cucina	koocheena
fridge	il frigo	freego
heating	il riscaldamento	reeskaldamento
hot water	l'acqua calda	akwa kalda
lightbulb	la lampadina	lampadeena
toilet	il gabinetto	gabeenet-to

▶ The toilet's broken, can you get someone to fix it?
Il gabinetto è guasto, può mandare qualcuno ad aggiustarlo?
eel gabeenet-to ay gwasto pwo mandaray kwalkoono ad aj-joostarlo

▶ There's no hot water.
Non c'è l'acqua calda.
non chay lakwa kalda

▶ Can you show me how the air-conditioning works?
Può mostrarmi come funziona l'aria condizionata?
pwo mostrarmee komay foontz-yona laree-a kondeetz-yonata

> **▶▶ OK, what apartment are you in?**
> Certo, in quale appartamento siete?
> chairto een kwalay ap-partamento s-yaytay

▶ We're in number five.
Siamo al numero cinque.
s-yamo al noomairo cheenkway

▶ Can you move us to a quieter apartment?
Può trasferirci in un appartamento più tranquillo?
pwo trasfaireerchee een oon ap-partamento p-yoo trankweel-lo

▶ Is there a supermarket nearby?
C'è un supermercato qui vicino?
chay oon soopair-mairkato kwee veecheeno

▶▶ Have you enjoyed your stay?
Avete avuto una buona permanenza?
avaytay avooto oona bwona pairmanentza

▶ Brilliant holiday, thanks!
Una vacanza splendida, grazie!
oona vakantza splendeeda gratzee-ay

20. Shopping

▶▶ Can I help you?
Posso esserle d'aiuto?
pos-so es-sairlay da-yooto

▶ Can I just have a look around?
Posso dare uno sguardo?
pos-so daray oono zgwardo

▶ Yes, I'm looking for...
Sì, cerco...
see chairko...

APERTO	open
CAMBIARE	to exchange
LA CASSA	cash desk
CHIUSO	closed
SVENDITA	sale

▶ How much is this?
Quanto costa questo?
kwanto kosta kwesto

▶▶ Thirty-two euros.
Trentadue euro.
trentadoo-ay ay-ooro

▶ OK, I think I'll have to leave it; it's a little too expensive for me.
Lasciamo stare; è un po' troppo caro per me.
lash-yamo staray ay oon po trop-po karo pair may

▶▶ How about this?
E questo?
ay kwesto

▶ Can I pay by credit card?
Posso pagare con una carta di credito?
pos-so pagaray kon oona karta dee kraydeeto

▶ It's too big.
È troppo grande.
ay trop-po granday

▶ It's too small.
È troppo piccolo.
ay trop-po peek-kolo

▶ It's for my son – he's about this high.
È per mio figlio: è alto più o meno così.
ay pair mee-o feel-yo ay alto p-yoo o mayno kozee

▶▶ Will there be anything else?
Altro?
altro

▶ That's all thanks.
È tutto, grazie.
ay toot-to gratzee-ay

▶ Make it twenty euros and I'll take it.
Se me lo dà a venti euro, lo prendo.
say may lo da a ventee ay-ooro lo prendo

▶ Fine, I'll take it.
Bene lo prendo.
baynay lo prendo

21. Shopping for clothes

to alter	modificare	modeefeekaray
bigger	più grande	p-yoo granday
just right	perfetto	pairfet-to
smaller	più piccolo	p-yoo peek-kolo
to try on	provare	provaray

▶▶ Can I help you?
Posso esserle d'aiuto?
pos-so es-sairlay da-yooto

▶ No, thanks, I'm just looking.
No, grazie, do solo un'occhiata.
no gratzee-ay doh solo oon ok-yata

▶▶ Do you want to try that on?
Vuole provarlo?
vwolay provarlo

▶ Yes, and I'll try this one too.
Sì, e provo anche questo.
see ay provo ankay kwesto

▶ Do you have it in a bigger size?
Avete una taglia più grande?
avaytay oona tal-ya p-yoo granday

▶ Do you have it in a different colour?
Avete un altro colore?
avaytay oon altro koloray

▶▶ That looks good on you.
Le sta bene.
lay sta baynay

▶ Can you shorten this?
Può accorciarlo?
pwo ak-korcharlo

▶▶ Sure, it'll be ready on Friday, after 12.00.
Certo, sarà pronto venerdì, dopo mezzogiorno.
chairto sara pronto venairdee dopo medzojorno

22. Sightseeing

art gallery	la galleria d'arte	gal-lairee-a dartay
bus tour	la gita in autobus	jeeta een owtobooss
city centre	il centro della città	chentro del-la cheet-ta
closed	chiuso	k-yoozo
guide	la guida	gweeda
museum	il museo	moozay-o
open	aperto	apairto

▶ I'm interested in seeing the old town.
Mi piacerebbe vedere la città vecchia.
mee p-yachaireb-bay vedairay la cheet-ta vek-ya

▶ Are there guided tours?
Ci sono visite guidate?
chee sono veezeetay gweedatay

►► I'm sorry, it's fully booked.
Mi dispiace, siamo al completo.
mee deesp-yachay s-yamo al komplayto

► How much would you charge to drive us around for four hours?
Quanto vorrebbe per portarci in giro in automobile per quattro ore?
kwanto vor-reb-bay pair portarchee een jeero een owtomobeelay pair kwat-tro oray

► Can we book tickets for the concert here?
Possiamo prenotare qui i biglietti per il concerto?
pos-yamo prenotaray kwee ee beel-yet-tee pair eel konchairto

►► Yes, in what name?   ►► Which credit card?
Sì, a che nome?   Quale carta di credito?
see a kay nomay   kwalay karta dee kraydeeto

► Where do we get the tickets?
Dove possiamo ritirare i biglietti?
dovay pos-yamo reeteeraray ee beel-yet-tee

►► Just pick them up at the entrance.
Potete ritirarli all'entrata.
potaytay reeteerarlee al-lentrata

▶ Is it open on Sundays?
Apre la domenica?
apray la domayneeka

▶ How much is it to get in?
Quanto costa l'ingresso?
kwanto kosta leengres-so

▶ Are there reductions for groups of 6?
Ci sono sconti per gruppi di 6 persone?
chee sono skontee pair groop-pee dee say pairsonay

▶ That was really impressive!
Era davvero straordinario!
aira dav-vairo stra-ordeenaree-o

23. Taxis

▶ Can you get us a taxi?
Può chiamarci un taxi?
pwo k-yamarchee oon taxee

▶▶ For now? Where are you going?
Lo volete subito? Dove andate?
lo volaytay soobeeto, dovay andatay

▶ To the town centre.
In centro città.
een chentro cheet-ta

▶ I'd like to book a taxi to the airport for tomorrow.
Vorrei prenotare un taxi per l'aeroporto, per domani.
vor-ray prenotaray oon taxee pair la-airoporto pair domanee

▶▶ Sure, at what time? How many people?
Certo, per che ora? Quante persone?
chairto pair kay ora, kwantay pairsonay

▶ How much is it to Piazza Repubblica?
Quanto costa fino a Piazza Repubblica?
kwanto kosta feeno a p-yatza repoob-bleeka

▶ Right here is fine, thanks.
Va bene qui, grazie.
va baynay kwee gratzee-ay

▶ Can you wait here and take us back?
Può aspettarci qui e poi riportarci indietro?
pwo aspet-tarchee kwee ay poy reeportarchee eend-yaytro

▶▶ How long are you going to be?
Quanto vi fermate?
kwanto vee fairmatay

24. Trains

to change trains	cambiare	kamb-yaray
platform	il binario	beenaree-o
return	andata e ritorno	andata ay reetorno
single	sola andata	sola andata
station	la stazione	statz-yonay
stop	la fermata	fairmata
ticket	il biglietto	beel-yet-to

▶ How much is...?
Quanto costa...?
kwanto kosta...

▶ A single, second class to...
Un biglietto di seconda classe, di sola andata per...
oon beel-yet-to dee sekonda klas-say dee sola andata pair...

▶ Two returns, second class to...
Due biglietti di seconda classe, andata e ritorno per...
doo-ay beel-yet-tee dee sekonda klas-say andata ay reetorno pair...

▶ For today.
Per oggi.
pair oj-jee

▶ For tomorrow.
Per domani.
pair domanee

▶ For next Tuesday.
Per martedì prossimo.
pair martedee pros-seemo

▶▶ There's a supplement for the Intercity.
C'è un supplemento per l'Intercity.
chay oon soop-plemento pair leentairseetee

▶▶ Do you want to make a seat reservation?
Vuole prenotare un posto?
vwolay prenotaray oon posto

▶▶ You have to change at Bologna.
Deve cambiare a Bologna.
dayvay kamb-yaray a bologna

▶ Is this seat free?
È libero questo posto?
ay leebairo kwesto posto

▶ Excuse me, which station are we at?
Scusi, che stazione è questa?
skoozee kay statz-yonay ay kwesta

▶ Is this where I change for Pisa?
È qui che devo cambiare per Pisa?
ay kwee kay dayvo kamb-yaray pair pisa

ENGLISH
→ ITALIAN

A

a, an uno/una **oo**no/**oo**na

about: about 20 circa venti cheerka

it's about 5 o'clock sono le cinque circa

a film about Italy un film sull'Italia

above di sopra

above… sopra a…

abroad all'estero al-lestairo

absolutely (I agree) senz'altro sentzaltro

accelerator l'acceleratore m achelairat**o**ray

accept accettare achet-taray

accident l'incidente m eencheed**ay**ntay

there's been an accident c'è stato un incidente chay

accommodation l'alloggio m al-l**o**j-jo

accurate accurato ak-koor**a**to

ache (verb) fare male faray malay

my back aches mi fa male la schiena

across: across the road dall'altra parte della strada partay

adapter il riduttore reed**oo**t-toray

address l'indirizzo m eendeer**ee**tzo

what's your address? qual è il suo indirizzo? kwalay ay eel s**oo**-o

address book la rubrica

admission charge il prezzo d'ingresso pretzo deengr**e**s-so

Adriatic il mare Adriatico maray

adult l'adulto m ad**oo**lto

advance: in advance in anticipo een ant**ee**cheepo

aeroplane l'aeroplano m a-airopl**a**no

after dopo

after you dopo di lei lay

after lunch dopo pranzo

afternoon il pomeriggio pomair**ee**j-jo

in the afternoon nel pomeriggio

this afternoon questo pomeriggio

aftershave il dopobarba

aftersun cream la crema doposole dopos**o**lay

afterwards dopo

again di nuovo dee nw**o**vo

against contro

age l'età f **a**yta

ago: a week ago una settimana fa

an hour ago un'ora fa

agree: I agree sono d'accordo

AIDS l'aids m a-eeds

air l'aria f

by air per via aerea pair vee-a a-**a**iray-a

air-conditioning l'aria condizionata kondeetz-yon**a**ta

airmail: by airmail per via aerea a-**a**iray-a

airmail envelope la busta per posta aerea b**oo**sta pair

airport l'aeroporto m a-airop**o**rto

to the airport, please all'aeroporto, per favore pair fav**o**ray

airport bus l'autobus dell'aeroporto m l**ow**toboos

aisle seat il posto vicino al corridoio veech**ee**no al kor-reed**o**-yo

alarm clock la sveglia zv**e**l-ya

Albania l'Albania f

Albanian (adj) albanese alban**ay**zay

alcohol l'alcool m alk**o**l

alcoholic alcolico alk**o**leeko

all: all the boys tutti i ragazzi t**oo**t-tee ee

all the girls tutte le ragazze t**oo**t-tay lay

all of it tutto t**oo**t-to

all of them tutti

that's all, thanks è tutto, grazie ay – gr**a**tzee-ay

allergic: I'm allergic to... sono allergico a... al-l**ai**rjeeko

allowed: is it allowed? è permesso? ay pairm**e**s-so

all right (I agree) va bene, d'accordo b**e**nay

I'm all right sto bene

are you all right? stai/sta bene? sty/sta

almond la mandorla

almost quasi kw**a**zee

alone s**o**lo

alphabet l'alfabeto m

a a	**j** ee-l**oo**nga	**s** es-say
b bee	**k** kap-pa	**t** tee
c chee	**l** el-lay	**u** oo
d dee	**m** em-may	**v** voo
e ay	**n** en-nay	**w** voo d**o**p-yo
f ef-fay	**o** o	**x** eeks
g jee	**p** pee	**y** **ee**pseelon
h ak-ka	**q** koo	**z** tz**ay**-ta
i ee	**r** air-ray	

Alps le **A**lpi

already già ja

also anche **a**nkay

although anche se say

altogether in tutto een t**oo**t-to

always sempre s**e**mpray

am: I am s**o**no

a.m.: at seven a.m. alle s**e**tte del mattino **a**l-lay

amazing (surprising) sorprendente sorprend**e**ntay

(very good) eccezionale echetz-yon**a**lay

ambulance l'ambulanza f ambool**a**ntza

call an ambulance! chiamate un'ambulanza! k-yam**a**tay

America l'America f am**ai**reeka

American americano amaireek**a**no

I'm American (male/female) sono americano/american**a**

among tra, fra

amount la quantit**à**

(money) la s**o**mma

amp: a 13 amp fuse un fusibile da tredici ampere foo**zee**beelay da – amp**ai**ray

amphitheatre l'anfiteatro *m* anfeetay-**a**tro

ancient antico

and e ay

angry arrabbiato ar-rab-**ya**to

animal l'animale *m* anee**ma**lay

ankle la caviglia kav**ee**l-ya

anniversary (wedding) l'anniversario di matrimonio *m*

annoy: this man's annoying me quest'uomo mi sta importunando kwest**wo**mo mee sta eemportoon**a**ndo

annoying seccante sek-**ka**ntay

another un altro, un'altra oon

can we have another room? potremmo avere un'altra stanza? av**ai**ray

another beer, please ancora una birra, per favore

antibiotics gli antibiotici anteebee-**o**teechee

antifreeze l'antigelo *m* antee**je**lo

antihistamine l'antistaminico *m*

antique: is it an antique? è un pezzo d'antiquariato? ay oon petzo danteekwar-**ya**to

antique shop il negozio di antiquariato ne**go**tz-yo dee

antiseptic l'antisettico *m*

any: have you got any bread/ tomatoes? avete del pane/dei pomodori? av**e**tay del – /day

do you have any change? ha degli spiccioli? a d**a**yl-yee sp**ee**ccholee

sorry, I don't have any mi dispiace, non ne ho mee deesp-**ya**chay non nay o

anybody qualcuno kwalk**oo**no

does anybody speak English? c'è qualcuno che parla inglese? chay – kay parla eengl**a**yzay

there wasn't anybody there non c'era nessuno lì non ch**ai**ra nes-**soo**no

anything qualcosa kwalk**o**za

anything else? altro?
nothing else, thanks nient'altro, grazie n-yent**a**ltro
would you like anything to drink? vuole qualcosa da bere? vw**o**lay kwalk**o**za da b**ai**ray
I don't want anything, thanks non voglio niente, grazie non v**o**l-yo n-y**e**ntay

apart from a parte part**a**y

apartment l'appartamento *m*

aperitif l'aperitivo *m* apaireet**ee**vo

apology le scuse sk**oo**zay

Apennines gli Appennini

appendicitis l'appendicite *f* ap-pendeech**ee**tay

appetizer l'antipasto *m*

apple la mela m**a**yla

appointment l'appuntamento *m* ap-poontam**e**nto

good morning, how can I help you? buongiorno, mi dica

I'd like to make an appointment vorrei fissare un appuntamento vor-**ray** fees-**sar**ay

what time would you like? per che ora? pair kay

three o'clock le tre

I'm afraid that's not possible; is four o'clock all right? mi dispiace, non è possibile: va bene alle quattro? mee deesp-**yach**ay, non ay pos-**see**beelay: va **bay**nay

yes, that will be fine sì, va bene

the name was...? il suo nome, per favore? **soo**-o **no**may

---

apricot l'albicocca f albeek**ok**-ka

April aprile apr**ee**lay

are: we are siamo s-**ya**mo

  you are siete s-**yay**tay

  they are sono **so**no

area la zona

area code il prefisso

arm il braccio **bra**cho

arrange: will you arrange it for us? può organizzarlo per noi? pwo organeetz**ar**lo pair noy

arrival l'arrivo m ar-**ree**vo

arrive arrivare ar-reev**ar**ay

  when do we arrive? quando arriviamo? kwando ar-reev-**ya**mo

has my fax arrived yet? è arrivato il mio fax?

we arrived today siamo arrivati oggi s-**ya**mo

art l'arte f **ar**tay

art gallery la galleria d'arte gal-lair**ee**-a

artist l'artista m/f

as: as big as (così) grande come koz**ee** grand**ay ko**may

  as soon as possible al più presto possibile p-yoo – pos-**see**beelay

ashtray il portacenere portachen**air**ay

ask chiedere k-**yay**dairay

  I didn't ask for this non ho chiesto questo non o k-**ye**sto **kwe**sto

  could you ask him to...? può chiedergli di...? pwo k-**yay**dairl-yee dee

asleep: she's asleep dorme **dor**may

aspirin l'aspirina f

asthma l'asma f

astonishing stupefacente stoopay-fach**en**tay

at: at the hotel in albergo

  at the station alla stazione

  at six o'clock alle sei al-**lay**

  at Giovanni's da Giovanni

@, at sign la chiocciola k-**yoch**-chola

ATM il bancomat

athletics l'atletica f atl**ay**teeka

attractive attraente at-tra-**en**tay

aubergine la melanzana

melantzana

August agosto

aunt la zia tzee-a

Australia l'Australia *f* owstral-ya

Australian australiano owstral-
yano

I'm Australian (*male/female*)
sono australiano/australiana

Austria l'Austria *f* owstree-a

Austrian austriaco owstree-ako

automatic automatico
owtomateeko

(car) l'automobile con il cambio
automatico *f* owtomobeelay kon
eel kamb-yo

automatic teller il bancomat

autumn l'autunno *m* owtoon-no

in the autumn in autunno

avenue il viale vee-alay

average (not good) mediocre
med-yokray

(ordinary) ordinario ordeenar-yo

on average in media mayd-ya

awake: is he awake? è sveglio?
ay zvayl-yo

away: go away! vattene!
vat-tenay

is it far away? è lontano?

awful terribile tair-reebeelay

axle l'asse *m* as-say

B

baby (*male/female*) il bambino,
la bambina

baby food gli alimenti per
bambini

baby's bottle il biberon

baby-sitter il/la baby-sitter

back (of body) la schiena sk-yayna

(back part) la parte posteriore
partay postair-yoray

at the back dietro d-yetro

**can I have my money
back?** posso riavere i miei
soldi? ree-avairay ee mee-yay
soldee

to come/go back tornare
tornaray

backache il mal di schiena
sk-yayna

bacon la pancetta panchet-ta

bad cattivo kat-teevo

a bad headache un brutto
mal di testa broot-to

badly male malay

bag la borsa

(handbag) la borsetta

(suitcase) la valigia valeeja

baggage i bagagli bagal-yee

baggage check il deposito
bagagli

baggage claim il ritiro bagagli

bakery la panetteria panet-
tairee-a, il panificio paneefeecho

balcony il balcone balkonay

a room with a balcony
una stanza con balcone

bald calvo

ball (large) la palla

(small) la pallina

ballet il balletto

banana la banana

band (musical) il gruppo groop-po

bandage la fasciatura fashatoora

Bandaids i cerotti chairot-tee

bank (money) la banca

bank account il conto in banca

bar il bar

   a bar of chocolate una tavoletta di cioccolato chok-kolato

barber's il barbiere barb-yairay

basket il cestino chesteeno

   (in shop) il cestello chestel-lo

bath il bagno ban-yo

   can I have a bath? posso fare un bagno? faray

bathroom il bagno, la stanza da bagno stantza

   with a private bathroom con bagno

bath towel l'asciugamano da bagno *m* ashoogamano

bathtub la vasca da bagno

battery la batteria bat-tairee-a

bay la baia ba-ya

be essere es-sairay

beach la spiaggia spee-aj-ja

beach mat la stuoia stwo-ya

beach umbrella l'ombrellone *m* ombrel-lonay

beans i fagioli fajolee

   French beans i fagiolini fajoleenee

   broad beans le fave favay

beard la barba

beautiful bello

because perché pairkay

   because of... a causa di... kowza

bed il letto

   I'm going to bed vado a letto

bed and breakfast camera con prima colazione preema kolatz-yonay

bedroom la camera da letto

beef il manzo mandzo

beer la birra beer-ra

   two beers, please due birre, per favore doo-ay beer-ray

before prima di preema

begin cominciare komeencharay

   when does it begin? quando comincia? kwando komeencha

beginner il/la principiante preencheep-yantay

beginning: at the beginning all'inizio al-eeneetz-yo

behind dietro (a) d-yetro

   behind me dietro di me may

beige beige

believe credere kraydairay

bell (church) la campana

   (doorbell) il campanello

below sotto (a)

belt la cintura cheentoora

bend (in road) la curva koorva

berth la cuccetta koochet-ta

beside: beside the... accanto a... ak-kanto

best il migliore meel-yoray

better meglio mayl-yo

   are you feeling better? ti senti/si sente meglio? see sentay

between tra, fra

beyond oltre oltray

bicycle la bicicletta beecheeklet-ta

big grande gra**n**day

  too big troppo grande

  it's not big enough
  non è abbastanza grande
  ay ab-ba**s**tantza

bike la bici b**ee**chee

  (motorbike) la moto(cicletta)
  motoche**e**klet-ta

bikini il bik**i**ni

bill il c**o**nto

  could I have the bill,
  please? il conto, per favore

bin la pattumiera pat-toom-y**ai**ra

bin liners i sacchetti per la
  pattumiera sak-k**e**t-tee pair la
  pat-toom-y**ai**ra

binding (ski) l'att**a**cco *m*

bird l'uccello *m* ooch**e**l-lo

biro la b**i**ro

birthday il compleanno
  kompl**a**y-an-no

  happy birthday! buon
  compleanno! bwon

biscuit il bisc**o**tto

bit: a little bit un po'

  a big bit un grosso pezzo p**e**tzo

  a bit of… un pezzetto di…
  petz**e**t-to dee

  a bit expensive un po' caro

bite (by insect) la puntura
  poont**oo**ra

  (by dog) il morso

bitter amaro

black nero n**ai**ro

blanket la coperta kop**ai**rta

blast! accidenti! acheed**e**ntee

bleach (for toilet) la varechina
  varek**ee**na

bless you! salute! sal**oo**tay

blind cieco chee-**ay**ko

blinds gli avvolgibili
  av-voljee**bee**lay

blister la vescica vesh**ee**ka

blocked (road, pipe) blocc**a**to

  (sink) intasato eentaz**a**to

block of apartments
  il caseggiato kasej-j**a**to

blond biondo b-y**o**ndo

blood il sangue s**a**ngway

  high blood pressure la
  pressione alta press-y**o**nay

blouse la camicetta kameech**e**t-ta

blow-dry l'asciugatura col fon *f*
  ashoogat**oo**ra

  I'd like a cut and blow-dry
  vorrei taglio e piega con il fon
  vor-r**ay** tal-yo ay p-y**ay**ga

blue blu bloo

  blue eyes gli occhi azzurri
  ok-kee adz**oo**r-ree

blusher il fard

boarding house la pensione
  pens-y**o**nay

boarding pass la carta
  d'imbarco eemb**a**rko

boat la barca

  (for passengers) il batt**e**llo

body il c**o**rpo

boil (*verb*: of water) bollire
  bol-l**ee**ray

  (water, potatoes etc) far bollire

boiled egg l'uovo sodo *m* w**o**vo

boiler lo scaldabagno skaldaban-yo

bone l'osso *m*

bonnet (of car) il cofano

book il libro

(*verb*) prenotare prenotaray

can I book a seat?
posso prenotare un posto?

I'd like to book a table for two vorrei prenotare un tavolo per due vor-**ray** prenotaray – pair doo-ay

what time would you like it booked for? per che ora lo vuole? kay – vwolay

half past seven per le sette e mezza

that's fine va bene baynay

and your name? il suo nome, per favore soo-o nomay

bookshop/bookstore la libreria leebrairee-a

boot (footwear) lo stivale steevalay

(of car) il bagagliaio bagal-ya-yo

border (of country) il confine konfeenay

bored: I'm bored mi sto annoiando an-noy-ando

boring noioso noy-ozo

born: I was born in Manchester sono nato/nata a Manchester

I was born in 1960 sono nato/nata nel millenove-centosessanta

borrow prendere a prestito prendairay

may I borrow...? posso prendere a prestito...?

both tutti e due toot-tee ay doo-ay, tutte e due toot-tay

bother: sorry to bother you mi scusi il disturbo skoozee eel deestoorbo

bottle la bottiglia bot-teel-ya

a bottle of house red una bottiglia di (vino) rosso della casa

bottle-opener il apribottiglie apreebot-teel-yay

bottom (of person) il sedere sedairay

at the bottom of... (hill etc) ai piedi di... a-ee p-yaydee (street, sea etc) in fondo a...

box la scatola

(wooden) la cassetta

box office il botteghino bot-tegeeno

boy il ragazzo ragatzo

boyfriend il ragazzo

bra il reggiseno rej-jeesayno

bracelet il braccialetto brachalet-to

brake il freno frayno

brandy il brandy

bread il pane panay

white bread il pane bianco b-yanko

brown bread il pane nero nairo

wholemeal bread il pane integrale eentegralay

break (*verb*) rompere rompairay

I've broken the... ho rotto il/la... o r**o**t-to

I think I've broken my wrist credo di essermi rotto il p**o**lso kr**a**ydo dee es-s**ai**rmee

break down (car) rimanere in panne reeman**a**iray een pan-nay

I've broken down sono rim**a**sto in panne

breakdown il guasto gw**a**sto

breakdown service il servizio riparazioni sairv**ee**tz-yo reeparatz-y**o**nee

breakfast la (pr**i**ma) colazione kolatz-y**o**nay

break-in: I've had a break-in mi s**o**no entr**a**ti i l**a**dri in c**a**sa

breast il seno s**a**yno, il p**e**tto

breathe respirare respeer**a**ray

breeze la brezza br**e**tza

bridge (over river) il ponte p**o**ntay

brief breve br**a**yvay

briefcase la cart**e**lla

bright (light etc) brillante breel-l**a**ntay

bright red r**o**sso acceso ach**a**yzo

brilliant (idea, person) brillante breel-l**a**ntay

bring portare port**a**ray

I'll bring it back later lo riporter**ò** pi**ù** t**a**rdi reeport**a**iro

Britain la Gran Bretagna bret**a**n-ya

British brit**a**nnico

brochure l'op**u**scolo *m* op**oo**skolo

broken rotto r**o**t-to

bronchitis la bronchite bronk**ee**tay

brooch la sp**i**lla

broom la sc**o**pa

brother il frat**e**llo

brother-in-law il cognato kon-y**a**to

brown marrone mar-**ro**nay

  brown hair i capelli castani

  brown eyes gli occhi castani
ok-kee

bruise il livido

brush (for hair) la spazzola sp**a**tzola

  (artist's) il pennello

  (for cleaning) la scopa

bucket il secchio s**e**k-yo

buffet car il vagone ristorante
vag**o**nay reest**o**rantay

buggy (for child) il passeggino
pas-sej-j**ee**no

building l'edificio m edeef**ee**cho

bulb (light bulb) la lampadina

bumper il paraurti para-**oo**rtee

bunk la cuccetta koochet-ta

bureau de change l'agenzia di
cambio f ajentz**ee**-a dee kamb-yo

burglary il furto f**oo**rto

burn la bruciatura broochat**oo**ra

  (*verb*) bruciare broochar**ay**

burnt: this is burnt questo è
bruciato kw**e**sto ay brooch**a**to

burst: a burst pipe una
tubatura scoppiata toobat**oo**ra
skop-y**a**ta

bus l'autobus m **ow**toboos

  **what number bus is it
to...?** che numero va a...? kay
n**oo**mairo

  when is the next bus to...?
quando parte il prossimo
autobus per...? kwando part**ay**

  what time is the last bus? a
che ora parte l'ultimo autobus?

  could you let me know

when we get there? mi può
dire quando siamo arrivati?
pwo d**ee**ray kwando s-yamo

business gli affari

  does this bus go to...?
questo autobus va a...?
kw**e**sto

  no, you need a number...
no, deve prendere il...
d**ay**vay pr**e**ndairay

bus station la stazione degli
autobus statz-y**o**nay dayl-yee
owtoboos

bus stop la fermata dell'autobus
fairm**a**ta

bust il busto b**oo**sto

busy (restaurant etc) animato

  I'm busy tomorrow domani
ho da fare o da far**ay**

but ma

butcher's il macellaio
machel-la-yo

butter il burro b**oo**r-ro

button il bottone bot-t**o**nay

buy comprare kompra-ray

  where can I buy...?
dove vendono...?

by: by bus/car in autobus/
macchina een

  written by... scritto da...

  by the window vicino al
finestrino veech**ee**no

  by the sea sul mare sool

  by Thursday per giovedì pair

bye ciao chow

C

cabbage il cavolo

cabin (on ship) la cabina

cable car la funivia fooneevee-a

café il caffè kaf-**fay**

cagoule la giacca a vento jak-ka

cake la torta

cake shop la pasticceria
pasteechai**ree**-a

call (verb) chiamare k-yamaray

(to phone) telefonare telefonaray

  what's it called? come si
  chiama? komay see k-yama

  he/she/it is called…
  si chiama…

  please call the doctor
  chiamate un medico, per favore
  k-yama**tay** oon maydeeko

  **please give me a call at
  7.30 a.m. tomorrow** domani
  mattina, mi svegli alle sette e
  mezza, per favore mee zvayl-yee
  al-lay

  please ask him to call me
  gli chieda di chiamarmi, per
  favore l-yee kee-yayda dee

call back: I'll call back later

  (phone back) richiamerò più
  tardi reek-yamairo p-yoo

**call round: I'll call round
  tomorrow** passerò domani

camcorder la videocamera

camera la macchina fotografica
mak-keena

camera shop il negozio del
fotografo negotz-yo del

camp (verb) campeggiare
kampej-jaray

  can we camp here?
  possiamo accamparci qui? pos-
  yamo ak-kamparchee kwee

camping gas il gas liquido
leekweedo

campsite il campeggio kampej-jo

can la lattina

  a can of beer una lattina di
  birra

can: can you…? puoi/può…?
pwoy/pwo

  can I have…? posso avere…?
  avairay

  I can't… (am not able to)
  non posso…

  (don't know how to) non so…

Canada il Canada

Canadian canadese kanadayzay

  I'm Canadian sono canadese

canal il canale kanalay

cancel annullare an-nool-laray

candies le caramelle karamel-lay

candle la candela kandayla

canoe la canoa kano-a

canoeing la canoa

can opener l'apriscatole m
apreeskatolay

cap (hat) il berretto bair-ret-to

  (of bottle) il tappo

car la macchina mak-keena,
l'auto(mobile) f owtomobeelay

  by car in macchina

carafe la caraffa

  **a carafe of house white,
  please** una caraffa di (vino)

bianco della casa, per favore kaza

caravan la roulotte roolot

caravan site il campeggio per roulotte kampej-jo pair

carburettor il carburatore karbooratoray

card (birthday etc) il biglietto beel-yet-to

my (business) card il mio biglietto da visita veezeeta

cardigan il cardigan

cardphone il telefono a scheda telayfono a skayda

careful attento

be careful! fa'/faccia attenzione! facha at-tentz-yonay

caretaker il portinaio porteena-yo

car ferry la nave traghetto navay

car hire l'autonoleggio m owtonolej-jo

carnival il carnevale karnevalay

car park il parcheggio parkej-jo

carpet il tappeto tap-payto

(wall to wall) la moquette moket

carriage (of train) la carrozza kar-rotza

carrier bag il sacchetto sak-ket-to

carrot la carota

carry portare portaray

carry-cot il porte-enfant port-onfan

carton il tetrapack, la scatola di cartone

carwash l'autolavaggio m owtolavaj-jo

case (suitcase) la valigia valeeja

cash il contante kontantay

(verb) riscuotere reeskwotairay

will you cash this cheque for me? mi cambia questo assegno? kwesto as-sen-yo

cash desk la cassa

cash dispenser il bancomat

cashier (male/female) il cassiere kas-yairay, la cassiera

cassette la cassetta

cassette recorder il registratore a cassette rejeestratoray a kas-set-tay

castle il castello

casualty department il pronto soccorso

cat il gatto

catch (verb) prendere prendairay

where do we catch the bus to…? dove prendiamo l'autobus per…? dovay prend-yamo

cathedral la cattedrale kat-tedralay, il duomo dwomo

Catholic cattolico

cauliflower il cavolfiore kavolf-yoray

cave la grotta

ceiling il soffitto

celery il sedano saydano

cellar (for wine) la cantina

cell phone il telefonino telayfoneeno

cemetery il cimitero cheemeetairo

Centigrade centigrado chenteegrado

centimetre il centimetro chenteemetro

central centrale chentralay

central heating il riscaldamento autonomo owtonomo

centre il centro chentro

how do we get to the city centre? come si arriva in centro? komay

cereal i cereali chairay-alee

certainly certamente chairtamentay

certainly not certamente no

chair la sedia sayd-ya

chair lift la seggiovia sej-jovee-a

change (money) gli spiccioli speecholee

(verb: money, trains) cambiare kamb-yaray

can I change this for...? posso cambiarlo con...? kamb-yarlo

I don't have any change non ho spiccioli o

can you give me change for a 50 euro note? mi può cambiare cinquanta euro? mee pwo – cheenkwanta ay-ooro

DIALOGUE

do we have to change (trains)? dobbiamo cambiare? dob-yamo

yes, change at Rome/ no it's a direct train sì, cambiate a Roma/no, è diretto kamb-yatay – ay

changed: to get changed cambiarsi kamb-yarsee

chapel la cappella

charge il prezzo pretzo

(verb) far pagare pagaray

what is the charge per night? quantè a notte? kwantay

charge card la carta di addebito

cheap a buon mercato bwon mairkato

do you have anything cheaper? ha qualcosa di meno caro? kwalkoza

check (verb) controllare kontrol-laray

(US: noun) l'assegno m as-sen-yo

see **cheque**

(US: bill) il conto

see **bill**

could you check the..., please? può controllare..., per favore? pwo

checkbook il libretto degli assegni dayl-yee as-sen-yee

check-in il check-in

check in (at airport) fare il check-in faray

where do we have to check in? dove dobbiamo fare il check-in? dovay dob-yamo

cheek la guancia gwancha

cheerio! ciao! chow

cheers! (toast) alla salute! salootay

cheese il formaggio formaj-jo

chemist's la farmacia farmachee-a

cheque l'assegno m as-sen-yo

do you take cheques?
accettate assegni? achet-tatay
as-sen-yee

cheque book il libretto degli
assegni dayl-yee

cheque card la carta assegni

cherry la ciliegia cheel-yay-ja

chess gli scacchi skak-kee

chest il petto

chewing gum il chewing gum

chicken il pollo

chickenpox la varicella
varee-chel-la

child (*male/female*) il bambino,
la bambina

child minder la bambinaia
bambeena-ya

children's pool la piscina per
bambini peesheena pair

children's portion la porzione
per bambini portz-yonay

chin il mento

china la porcellana porchel-lana

Chinese cinese cheenayzay

chips le patatine fritte patateenay
freet-tay

chocolate il cioccolato
chok-kolato

milk chocolate il cioccolato
al latte al lat-tay

plain chocolate il cioccolato
fondente fondentay

a hot chocolate
una cioccolata calda

choose scegliere shayl-yairay

Christian name il nome di
battesimo nomay dee bat-
tayzeemo

Christmas il Natale natalay

Christmas Eve la vigilia di
Natale veejeel-ya

Merry Christmas! Buon
Natale! bwon

church la chiesa k-yayza

Travel tip Rules for visiting churches, cathedrals
and religious buildings are
much the same as they are
all over the Mediterranean
and are strictly enforced
everywhere: dress modestly,
which means no shorts (not
even Bermuda-length ones)
and covered shoulders
for women. Try to avoid
wandering around during a
service.

---

cider il sidro

cigar il sigaro

cigarette la sigaretta

cigarette lighter l'accendino *m*
achendeeno

cinema il cinema cheenema

circle il cerchio chairk-yo

(in theatre) la galleria

city la città cheet-ta

city centre il centro chentro

clean (*adj*) pulito pooleeto

**can you clean these for
me?** me li/le può pulire?
may lee/lay pwo pooleeray

cleaning solution (for contact
lenses) la soluzione per la
pulizia delle lenti a contatto
solootz-yonay pair la pooleetzee-a

cleansing lotion la lozione detergente lotz-yonay detairjentay

clear chiaro k-yaro

clever intelligente eentel-leejentay

cliff la scogliera skol-yaira

climbing l'alpinismo m

cling film la pellicola trasparente trasparentay

clinic la clinica

cloakroom il guardaroba gwardaroba

clock l'orologio m orolojo

close (*verb*) chiudere k-yoodairay

DIALOGUE

what time do you close? a che ora chiudete? kay – k-yoodaytay

we close at 8 pm chiudiamo alle otto k-yood-yamo

do you close for lunch? chiudete per pranzo?

yes, between 1 and 3.30 pm sì, dall'una alle tre e mezza

closed chiuso k-yoozo

cloth (fabric) la stoffa
(for cleaning etc) lo straccio stracho

clothes gli abiti

clothes line la corda del bucato

clothes peg la molletta da bucato

cloud la nuvola noovola

cloudy nuvoloso noovolozo

clutch la frizione freetz-yonay

coach (bus) la corriera kor-yaira, il pullman
(on train) la carrozza kar-rotza

coach station la stazione dei pullman statz-yonay day

coach trip la gita in pullman jeeta

coast la costa
on the coast sulla costa sool-la

coat (long coat) il cappotto
(jacket) la giacca jak-ka

coat hanger la gruccia groocha

cockroach lo scarafaggio skarafaj-jo

cocoa il cacao kaka-o

code (for telephoning) il prefisso prayfees-so
what's the (dialling) code for Florence? qual è il prefisso di Firenze? kwalay

coffee il caffè kaf-fay
two coffees, please due caffè, per favore

coin la moneta monayta

Coke la Coca-Cola

cold (*adj*) freddo
I'm cold ho freddo o
I have a cold ho il raffreddore raf-fred-doray

collapse: he's collapsed ha avuto un collasso a avooto

collar il colletto

collect prendere prendairay
I've come to collect... sono venuto a prendere...

collect call la telefonata a carico

del destinatario

college l'istituto superiore *m*
eesteet**oo**to soopair-y**o**ray

colour il colore kol**o**ray

**do you have this in other
colours?** ce l'ha in altri colori?
chay la

colour film la pellicola a colori

comb il pettine pet-t**ee**nay

come venire ven**ee**ray

where do you come from?
di dov'è? dee dov**ay**

I come from Edinburgh
sono di Edimburgo

come back ritornare reetorn**a**ray

I'll come back tomorrow
tornerò domani tornair**o**

come in entrare entr**a**ray

comfortable comodo

compact disc il compact disc

company (business) la ditta

compartment (on train)
lo scompartimento

compass la bussola b**oo**s-sola

complain lamentarsi

complaint il reclamo rekl**a**mo

I have a complaint voglio
fare un reclamo v**o**l-yo f**a**ray

completely completamente
kompletam**e**ntay

computer il computer

concert il concerto konch**ai**rto

concussion la commozione
cerebrale kom-motz-y**o**nay
chairay-br**a**lay

conditioner (for hair) il balsamo

condom il preservativo
prezairvat**ee**vo

conference la conferenza
konfair**e**ntza

confirm dare conferma
daray konf**ai**rma

congratulations!
congratulazioni!
kongratoolatz-y**o**nee

connecting flight la coincidenza
ko-eenchee-d**e**ntza

connection la coincidenza

conscious cosciente kosh**e**ntay

constipation la stitichezza
steeteek**e**tza

consulate il consolato

contact mettersi in contatto con

contact lenses le lenti a
contatto

contraceptive il contraccettivo
kontrachet-t**ee**vo

convenient comodo

that's not convenient
non (mi) va bene b**ay**nay

cook (*verb*) cucinare koocheen**a**ray

it's not cooked non è
abbastanza cotto ay ab-bast**a**nza

cooker la cucina kooch**ee**na

cookie il biscotto

cooking utensils gli utensili da
cucina kooch**ee**na

cool fresco

cork il tappo

corkscrew il cavatappi

corner: on the corner
all'angolo

in the corner nell'angolo

cornflakes i fiocchi di granturco f-**yok**-kee dee grant**oor**ko

correct (right) es**a**tto

corridor il corridoio kor-reed**o**-yo

cosmetics i cosmetici kosm**e**teechee

cost costare kost**a**ray

   how much does it cost?
   quanto c**o**sta? kw**a**nto

cot il lett**i**no

cotton il cotone kot**o**nay

cotton wool l'ovatta f

couch (sofa) il div**a**no

couchette la cuccetta kooch**e**t-ta

cough la tosse t**o**s-say

cough medicine lo sciroppo per la tosse sheer**o**p-po pair

could: could you…? potr**e**sti/ potr**e**bbe…? potr**a**yb-bay

   could I have…? vorr**e**i… vor-r**a**y

   I couldn't… (wasn't able to) non ho potuto… o pot**oo**to

country il paese pa-**a**yzay
   (countryside) la campagna kamp**a**n-ya

couple (two people) la coppia k**o**p-ya

   a couple of… un paio di… p**a**-yo dee

courgette il zucchino zook-k**ee**no

courier la guida turistica gw**ee**da

course (main course etc) la port**a**ta

   of course naturalmente natooralm**e**ntay

   of course not no di certo dee ch**a**irto

cousin (male/female) il cugino kooj**ee**no, la cug**i**na

cow la mucca m**oo**k-ka

crab il granchio grank-yo

cracker il cracker kr**e**kair

craft shop il negozio di artigianato nay-g**o**tz-yo dee arteejan**a**to

crash l'incidente m eencheed**e**ntay

   I've had a crash ho avuto un incidente o av**oo**to

crazy pazzo p**a**tzo

cream (on milk, in cake) la p**a**nna
   (lotion) la crema kr**a**yma
   (colour) crema

crèche l'asilo nido m

credit card la carta di credito kr**a**ydeeto

   do you take credit cards?
   prendete carte di credito? prend**a**ytay kart**a**y

credit crunch la stretta del credito *stret-ta del kraydeeto*

crisps le patatine *patateenay*

crockery il vasellame *vazel-lamay*

crossing (by sea) la traversata *travair-sata*

crossroads l'incrocio *m* *eenkrocho*

crowd la folla

crowded affollato

crown (on tooth) la capsula *kapsoola*

cruise la crociera *krochaira*

crutches le stampelle *stampel-lay*

cry (*verb*) piangere *p-yanjairay*

cucumber il cetriolo *chetree-olo*

cup la tazza *tatza*

    a cup of..., please una tazza di..., per favore

cupboard l'armadio *m armad-yo* (in kitchen) la credenza *kredentza*

cure la cura *koora*

curly riccio *reecho*

current la corrente *kor-rentay*

curtains le tende *tenday*

cushion il cuscino *koosheeno*

custom il costume *kostoomay*

Customs la dogana

cut il taglio *tal-yo*
    (*verb*) tagliare *tal-yaray*

    I've cut myself mi sono tagliato *tal-yato*

cutlery le posate *pozatay*

cycling il ciclismo *cheekleesmo*

cyclist il/la ciclista *cheekleesta*

D

dad il papà

daily ogni giorno *on-yee jorno*
    (*adj*) quotidiano *kwoteed-yano*

damage (*verb*) danneggiare
dan-nej-jaray

damaged danneggiato
dan-nej-jato

I'm sorry, I've damaged this
mi dispiace, l'ho danneggiato
mee deesp-yachay lo

damn! accidenti! acheedentee

damp (*adj*) umido **oo**meedo

dance il ballo

(*verb*) ballare bal-**la**ray

would you like to dance?
balla?

dangerous pericoloso
paireekolo**zo**

Danish danese dana**y**zay

dark (*adj*: colour) scuro sk**oo**ro

(hair) bruno br**oo**no

it's getting dark si sta
facendo buio fachendo b**oo**-yo

date: what's the date today?
che giorno è oggi? kay j**o**rno
ay **o**j-jee

let's make a date for next
Monday possiamo fissare
un appuntamento per lunedì
prossimo? pos-**ya**mo fees-**sa**ray
oon ap-poontamento

dates (fruit) i datteri d**a**t-tairee

daughter la figlia fee**l**-ya

daughter-in-law la nuora nw**o**ra

dawn l'alba *f*

at dawn all'alba

day il giorno j**o**rno

the day after il giorno d**o**po

the day after tomorrow
dopodom**a**ni

the day before
il giorno pr**i**ma

the day before yesterday
l'altroieri *m* altro-y**ai**ree

every day **o**gni giorno **o**n-yee

all day? t**u**tto il giorno?

in two days' time tra d**u**e
gi**o**rni

have a nice day! bu**o**na
giornata! bw**o**na jornata

day trip la gita (di un giorno)
j**ee**ta dee oon j**o**rno

dead m**o**rto

deaf s**o**rdo

deal (business) l'affare *m* af-f**a**ray

it's a deal affare f**a**tto

death la morte m**o**rtay

decaffeinated coffee
il caffè decaffeinato
kaf-f**ay** dekaf-fee-ayn**a**to

December dicembre
deechembray

decide decidere dech**ee**dairay

we haven't decided yet non
abbiamo anc**o**ra deciso ab-y**a**mo
– dech**ee**zo

decision la decisione
decheez-y**o**nay

deck (on ship) il ponte (di
coperta) p**o**ntay dee kop**ai**rta

deckchair la sedia a sdraio
s**a**yd-ya a zdra-yo

deep prof**o**ndo

definitely certamente
chairtam**e**ntay

definitely not assolutamente
no as-soolootam**e**ntay

degree (qualification) la laurea
  lowray-a

delay il ritardo

deliberately volutamente
  volo"otamentay

delicatessen (shop)
  la gastronomia

delicious delizioso deleetz-yozo

deliver consegnare konsen-yaray

delivery (of mail) la consegna
  konsen-ya

Denmark la Danimarca

dental floss il filo interdentale
  eentairdentalay

dentist il/la dentista

it's this one here è questo
  qui ay kwesto kwee

this one? questo?

no that one no, quello
  kwel-lo

here? qui?

yes sì

dentures la dentiera dent-yaira

deodorant il deodorante
  day-odorantay

department il reparto

department store il grande
  magazzino granday magatzeeno

departure la partenza partentza

departure lounge la sala
  d'attesa (delle partenze)
  at-tayza del-lay partentzay

depend: it depends dipende
  deependay

it depends on...
  dipende da...

deposit (on bottle) la cauzione
  kowtz-yonay
  (for reservation) la caparra
  (as part payment) l'acconto *m*

description la descrizione
  deskreetz-yonay

dessert il dessert des-sair

destination la destinazione
  desteenatz-yonay

develop sviluppare
  zveeloop-paray

diabetic (*male/female*) il diabetico
  dee-abayteeko, la diabetica
    diabetic foods gli alimenti
    per diabetici dee-abayteechee

dial (*verb*) comporre il numero
  (di...) kompor-ray eel
  noomairo dee

dialling code il prefisso
  telefonico prefees-so

diamond il diamante
  dee-amantay

diarrhoea la diarrea dee-aray-a

diary (business etc) l'agenda *f*
  ajenda
  (for personal experiences) il diario
  dee-ar-yo

dictionary il dizionario
  deetz-yonario

didn't
  see **not**

die morire moreeray

diesel il gasolio gazol-yo

diet la dieta d-yayta
    I'm on a diet sono a dieta

**I have to follow a special
diet** devo seguire una dieta
speciale *dayvo segweeray –
spechalay*

difference la differenza
deef-fairentza

what's the difference?
qual è la differenza? *kwalay*

different diverso *deevairso*

this one is different questo è
diverso *kwesto ay*

a different table un altro
tavolo

difficult difficile *deef-feecheelay*

difficulty la difficoltà

dinghy il gommone *gommonay*

dining room la sala da pranzo
prandzo

dinner (evening meal) la cena
chayna

to have dinner cenare
chenaray

direct (adj) diretto *deeret-to*

is there a direct train?
c'è un treno diretto? *chay*

direction la direzione *deeretz-
yonay*

which direction is it? in
quale direzione è? *kwalay – ay*

is it in this direction? è in
questa direzione? *ay een kwesta*

directory enquiries
informazioni elenco abbonati
eenformatz-yonee

dirt lo sporco

dirty sporco

disabled invalido

**is there access for the
disabled?** c'è un accesso per
gli invalidi? *chay oon aches-so
pair*

disappear scomparire
skompareeray

it's disappeared è sparito *ay*

disappointed deluso *deloozo*

disappointing deludente
deloodentay

disaster il disastro

disco la discoteca

discount lo sconto

is there a discount? c'è uno
sconto? *chay*

disease la malattia *malat-tee-a*

disgusting (taste, food) disgustoso
deesgoostozo

dish (meal) il piatto *p-yat-to*

(bowl) la scodella

dishes i piatti

dishcloth lo strofinaccio per i
piatti *strofeenacho pair*

disinfectant il disinfettante
deeseenfet-tantay

disk (for computer) il dischetto
deesket-to

disposable nappies (diapers)
i pannolini (usa e getta) *ooza
ay jet-ta*

distance la distanza *deestantza*

in the distance in lontananza
lontanantza

distilled water l'acqua distillata
f akwa

district la zona

disturb disturbare *deestoorbaray*

diversion (detour) la deviazione
  dev-yatz-yo**nay**

diving board il trampolino

divorced divorziato deevortz-**ya**to

dizzy: I feel dizzy mi gira la
  testa mee **jee**ra

do fare **fa**ray

  what shall we do? che
  facciamo? kay fa**cha**mo

  how do you do it? come si
  fa? **ko**may

  will you do it for me? lo può
  fare lei per me? pwo **fa**ray lay
  pair may

DIALOGUE

  how do you do? piacere
  p-ya**cha**iray

  nice to meet you molto
  lieto l-**yay**to

  what do you do? (work)
  che lavoro fa? kay

  I'm a teacher, and you?
  sono insegnante, e lei?
  eensen-**yan**tay, ay lay

  I'm a student sono studente
  stoo**den**tay

  **what are you doing this
  evening?** che cosa fa
  questa sera? kay **ko**za fa
  kwesta **sai**ra

  **we're going out for a
  drink; do you want to
  join us?** andiamo a bere
  qualcosa: vuole venire
  con noi? and-**ya**mo a **bai**ray
  kwal**ko**za: **vwo**lay ve**nee**ray
  kon noi

DIALOGUE

  do you want cream? con
  panna?

  I do, but she doesn't per
  me sì, ma non per lei pair
  may – lay

doctor il medico **ma**ydeeko

  we need a doctor
  abbiamo bisogno di un
  medico ab-**ya**mo beez**on**-yo
  dee

  please call a doctor può
  chiamare un medico, per
  fav**o**re? pwo k-ya**ma**ray

DIALOGUE

  where does it hurt? dove le
  fa male? **do**vay lay fa **ma**lay

  right here proprio qui kwee

  does that hurt more? così
  le fa male di più? lay – **ma**lay
  dee p-yoo

  yes sì

  take this to a chemist
  porti questo in farmacia
  kwesto een farma**chee**-a

document il documento
  doko**om**ento

dog il cane **ka**nay

doll la bambola

domestic flight il volo nazionale
  natz-yo**na**lay

donkey l'asino *m*

don't!: don't do that! non farlo!
  see **not**

door (of room) la porta
  (of train, car) lo sportello

doorman il portiere port-yairay

double doppio dop-yo

double bed il letto a due piazze doo-ay p-yatzay

double room la camera doppia dop-ya

doughnut il krapfen

down giù joo

down here quaggiù kwaj-joo

put it down over there lo/la metta giù lì

it's down there on the right è giù di lì sulla destra

it's further down the road è più avanti su questa strada ay p-yoo – soo kwesta

downhill skiing la discesa libera deeshayza leebaira

download (verb) scaricare skareekaray

downmarket (restaurant etc) scadente skadentay

downstairs di sotto

dozen la dozzina dodzeena

half a dozen mezza dozzina medza

drain lo scarico

draught beer la birra alla spina beer-ra

draughty: it's draughty c'è corrente chay kor-rentay

drawer il cassetto

drawing il disegno deesayn-yo

dreadful terribile tair-reeb-beelay

dream il sogno son-yo

dress il vestito

dressed: to get dressed (oneself) vestirsi

dressing (for cut) la fasciatura fasha-toora

salad dressing il condimento

dressing gown la vestaglia vestal-ya

drink (alcoholic) la bevanda alcolica

(non-alcoholic) la bibita analcolica

(verb) bere bairay

a cold drink una bevanda fredda

can I get you a drink? posso offrirti qualcosa da bere? kwalkoza da bairay

what would you like (to drink)? cosa vuoi bere? koza vwoy

no thanks, I don't drink no, grazie, non bevo alcolici bayvo alkoleechee

I'll just have a drink of water posso avere solo un po' d'acqua? avairay – dakwa

drinking water l'acqua potabile akwa potabeelay

is this drinking water? è potabile quest'acqua? ay – kwest

drive (verb) guidare gweedaray

can you drive? sa guidare?

we drove here siamo venuti in macchina s-yamo venootee een mak-keena

I'll drive you home ti/la accompagno a casa in macchina ak-kompan-yo

driver (of car) l'autista *m/f* owteesta

(of bus) il/la conducente kondoochentay

driving licence la patente patentay

drop: just a drop, please (of drink) solo una goccia gocha

drug la medicina medeecheena

drugs (narcotics) la droga

drunk (adj) ubriaco oobree-ako

drunken driving la guida in stato di ebbrezza gweeda – eb-bretza

dry (adj) asciutto ashoot-to

(wine) secco

dry-cleaner il lavasecco

duck l'anatra *f*

due: he was due to arrive yesterday doveva arrivare ieri dovayva ar-reevaray

when is the train due? a che ora dovrebbe arrivare il treno? a kay ora dovreb-bay

dull (pain) sordo

(weather) uggioso uj-joso

(boring) noioso noy-ozo

dummy (baby's) il succhiotto sook-yot-to

during durante doorantay

dust la polvere polvairay

dustbin la pattumiera pat-toom-yaira

dusty polveroso

duty-free (goods) merci esenti da dazio mairchee esentee da datz-yo

duty-free shop il duty free

duvet il piumone p-yoo-monay

DVD il DVD dee-voo-dee

E

each (every) ciascuno chaskoono

how much are they each? quanto vengono l'uno/una? kwanto

ear l'orecchio *m* orek-yo

earache: I have earache ho mal d'orecchi o mal dorek-kee

early presto

early in the morning di mattina presto

I called by earlier sono passato/passata prima

earrings gli orecchini orek-keenee

east l'est *m*

in the east ad est

Easter la Pasqua paskwa

easy facile facheelay

eat mangiare manjaray

we've already eaten, thanks abbiamo già mangiato, grazie ab-yamo ja manjato

eau de toilette l'eau de toilette *f*

EC la CE chay

economy class la classe turistica klas-say

Edinburgh Edimburgo

egg l'uovo *m* wovo

eggplant la melanzana melantzana

Eire la Repubblica d'Irlanda repoob-bleeka deerlanda

either: either... or... o... o...

   either of them o l'uno/l'una o l'altro/l'altra

elastic l'elastico *m*

elastic band l'elastico *m*

elbow il gomito

electric elettrico

electrical appliances gli elettrodomestici elet-trodomesteechee

electric fire la stufa elettrica stoofa

electrician l'elettricista *m* elet-treecheesta

electricity l'elettricità *f* elet-treecheeta

elevator l'ascensore *m* ashensoray

else: something else qualcos'altro kwalkoz

   somewhere else da qualche altra parte kwalkay – partay

   would you like anything else? altro?

   no, nothing else, thanks nient'altro, grazie n-yentaltro

e-mail una mail

   (*verb:* person) mandare una mail a mandaray

   (text, file) inviare via mail eenv-yaray vee-a

embassy l'ambasciata *f* ambashata

emergency l'emergenza *f* emairjentza

   this is an emergency!

è un'emergenza! ay

emergency exit l'uscita di sicurezza *f* oosheeta dee seekooretza

empty vuoto vwoto

end la fine feenay

   (*verb*) finire feeneeray

   at the end of the street in fondo alla strada

   when does it end? quando finisce? kwando feeneeshay

engaged (toilet, telephone) occupato ok-koopato

   (to be married) fidanzato feedantzato

engine (car) il motore motoray

England l'Inghilterra *f* eengeeltair-ra

English inglese eenglayzay

   I'm English sono inglese

   do you speak English? parla inglese?

enjoy: to enjoy oneself divertirsi

   how did you like the film? ti/le è piaciuto il film? lay ay p-yachooto

   I enjoyed it very much; did you enjoy it? mi è piaciuto molto; e a te/lei? ay a tay/lay

enjoyable piacevole p-yachayvolay

enlargement (of photo) l'ingrandimento *m*

enormous enorme enormay

enough abbastanza ab-bast**a**ntza

  there's not enough… non c'è
  abbastanza… non chay

  it's not big enough non è
  grande abbastanza ay

  that's enough basta

entrance l'entrata *f*

envelope la busta b**oo**sta

epileptic epilettico

equipment l'attrezzatura *f*
  at-trezzat**oo**ra

error l'errore *m* er-r**o**ray

especially specialmente
  spech**a**lmentay

essential essenziale
  es-sentz-y**a**lay

  it is essential that…
  è essenziale che… ay – kay

EU l'UE *f* oo ay

euro l'euro *m* **a**y-**oo**ro

Eurocheque l'eurocheque *m*
  ay-**oo**rochek

Eurocheque card la carta
  eurocheque

Europe l'Europa *f* ay-**oo**ropa

European europeo ay-ooropay-o

even perfino pairf**ee**no

  even if… anche se… **a**nkay say

evening la sera s**ai**ra

  this evening questa sera
  kw**e**sta

  in the evening di sera

evening meal la cena ch**a**yna

eventually alla fine feen**a**y

ever mai my

DIALOGUE

**have you ever been to
Padua?** è mai stato a
Padova? ay

**yes, I was there two years
ago** sì, ci sono stato due
anni fa chee

every ogni **o**n-yee

  every day ogni giorno

everyone ognuno on-y**oo**no

everything tutto t**oo**t-to

everywhere dappertutto
  dap-pairt**oo**t-to

exactly! esattamente!
  esat-tam**e**ntay

exam l'esame *m* esam**a**y

example l'esempio *m* esemp-yo

  for example per esempio pair

excellent eccellente echel**e**ntay

  excellent! ottimo!

except eccetto echet-to

excess baggage il bagaglio in
  eccesso bagal-yo een eches-so

exchange rate il tasso di
  cambio k**a**mb-yo

exciting emozionante
  emotz-yon**a**ntay

excuse me (to get past) permesso
  pairm**e**s-so

  (to get attention) mi scusi
  mee sk**oo**zee

  (to say sorry) chiedo scusa
  k-y**a**ydo sk**oo**za

exhaust (pipe) il tubo di
  scappamento t**oo**bo

exhausted (tired) esausto es**ow**sto

exhibition la mostra

exit l'uscita *f* oosheeta

  where's the nearest exit?
  dov'è l'uscita più vicina?
  dovay – p-yoo veecheena

expect aspettare aspet-taray

expensive caro

experienced esperto espairto

explain spiegare sp-yegaray

  can you explain that? me lo
  puoi/può spiegare? may lo pwoy/
  pwo

express (mail, train) l'espresso *m*

extension (telephone) l'interno *m*
eentairno

  extension 221, please
  interno duecentoventuno, per
  favore

extension lead la prolunga

**extra: can we have an extra
one?** possiamo averne uno/
una in più? pos-yamo avairnay
– p-yoo

  **do you charge extra for
that?** si paga in più per
questo? pair kwesto

extraordinary straordinario stra-ordeenar-yo

extremely estremamente estrema-mentay

eye l'occhio *m* ok-yo

   will you keep an eye on my suitcase for me? mi tiene d'occhio la valigia, per favore? mee t-yaynay

eyebrow pencil la matita per le sopracciglia pair lay sopra-cheel-ya

eye drops il collirio kol-leer-yo

eyeglasses gli occhiali ok-yalee

eyeliner l'eye-liner *m*

eye make-up remover lo struccante per gli occhi strook-kantay pair l-yee ok-kee

eye shadow l'ombretto *m*

F

face la faccia facha

factory la fabbrica

Fahrenheit Fahrenheit

faint (*verb*) svenire sveneeray

   she's fainted è svenuta ay svenoota

   I feel faint mi sento venir meno mayno

fair (funfair) il luna park loona

   (trade) la fiera f-yaira

   (*adj*) giusto joosto

fairly abbastanza ab-bastantza

fake il falso

fall l'autunno *m* owtoon-no

fall (*verb*) cadere kadairay

   she's had a fall è caduta ay kadoota

false falso

family la famiglia fameel-ya

famous famoso

fan (electrical) il ventilatore venteelato-ray

   (hand held) il ventaglio vental-yo

   (sports: *male/female*) il tifoso, la tifosa

fan belt la cinghia della ventola cheeng-ya

fantastic fantastico

far lontano

DIALOGUE

   is it far from here? è lontano da qui? ay – kwee

   no, not very far no, non è molto lontano

   well how far? quant'è lontano? kwantay

   it's about 20 kilometres circa venti chilometri cheerka

fare il prezzo del biglietto pretzo del beel-yet-to

farm la fattoria fat-toree-a

fashionable di moda

fast veloce velochay

fat (person) grasso

   (on meat) il grasso

father il padre padray

father-in-law il suocero swochairo

faucet il rubinetto

fault il difetto

   sorry, it was my fault mi dispiace, è stata colpa mia mee deesp-yachay ay – mee-a

   it's not my fault non è colpa mia

faulty difettoso deefet-tozo

favourite preferito prefaireeto

fax il fax

   (*verb:* person) mandare un fax a mandaray

   (document) mandare per fax

February febbraio feb-bra-yo

feel sentire senteeray

   I feel hot sento caldo

   I feel unwell non mi sento bene baynay

   I feel like going for a walk ho voglia di fare una passeggiata o vol-ya dee faray oona pas-sej-jata

   how are you feeling? come si sente? komay see sentay

   I'm feeling better mi sento meglio mayl-yo

felt-tip (pen) il pennarello

fence lo steccato

fender il paraurti para-oortee

ferry il traghetto traget-to

festival (music, arts) il festival

fetch (andare a) prendere prendairay

   I'll fetch him vado a prenderlo prendairlo

   will you come and fetch me later? passi/passa a prendermi più tardi? prendairmee p-yoo

feverish febbricitante feb-breecheetantay

few: a few alcuni/alcune alkoonee/alkoonay

   a few days alcuni giorni

fiancé il fidanzato feedantzato

fiancée la fidanzata

field il campo

fight la lite leetay

figs i fichi feekee

file il file

fill riempire r-yempeeray

fill in riempire

   do I have to fill this in? devo riempire questo? dayvo – kwesto

fill up fare il pieno faray eel p-yayno

   fill it up, please il pieno, per favore favoray

filling (in cake, sandwich) il ripieno reep-yayno

   (in tooth) l'otturazione *f* ot-tooratz-yonay

film (movie) il film feelm

   (for camera) la pellicola

filthy lurido looreedo

find (*verb*) trovare trovaray

   I can't find it non lo/la trovo

   I've found it l'ho trovato/trovata

find out scoprire skopreeray

   could you find out for me? può informarsi per me? pwo – pair may

fine (weather) bello

   (punishment) la multa

how are you? come sta?
ko**may**

I'm fine, thanks bene, grazie
bay**nay** grat**zee**-ay

is that OK? va bene?

that's fine, thanks va bene,
grazie

finger il dito

finish (*verb*) finire feen**ee**ray

I haven't finished yet non ho
an**co**ra fin**i**to o

when does it finish? quando
finisce? kwando feen**ee**shay

fire: fire! al fuoco! f**wo**ko

can we light a fire here?
si **po**ssono ac**ce**ndere fuochi
qui? ach**e**ndairay fw**o**kee kwee

it's on fire è in fiamme ay een
f-yam-may

fire alarm l'allarme antincendio
m al-**lar**may anteench**e**nd-yo

fire brigade i vigili del fuoco
vee**jee**lee del fw**o**ko

fire escape l'uscita di sicurezza
oosh**ee**ta dee seek**oo**retza

fire extinguisher l'estintore *m*
esteen-**to**ray

first primo pr**ee**mo

I was first c'ero prima io ch**air**o
– **ee**-o

at first all'inizio een**eetz**-yo

the first time la prima volta

first on the left la prima a
sin**i**stra

first aid il pronto soc**co**rso

first aid kit la cassetta del pronto
soccorso

first class (travel etc) in prima
classe klas-**say**

first floor (UK) il primo piano
(US) il piano terra t**air**-ra

first name il nome di battesimo
nomay dee bat-**tay**seemo

fish il pesce p**e**shay

fishing village il villaggio di
pesc**a**tori veel-**laj**-jo

fishmonger's la pescheria
peskair**ee**-a

fit (attack) l'attacco *m*

it doesn't fit me non mi sta

fitting room il camerino di prova

fix (*verb*) riparare reepar**a**ray
(arrange) fissare fees-**sa**ray

can you fix this? può
ripar**ar**lo? pwo

fizzy frizzante freetz**a**ntay

flag la bandiera band-**yai**ra

flannel la pezza di spugna
petza dee sp**oo**n-ya

flash (for camera) il flash

flat (*noun*: apartment)
l'appartamento *m*
(*adj*) piatto p-yat-to

I've got a flat tyre ho una
gomma a terra o – t**air**-ra

flavour il sapore sap**o**ray

flea la pulce p**oo**lchay

flight il volo

flight number il numero del
volo n**oo**mairo

flippers le pinne p**ee**n-nay

flood l'inondazione *f*
eenondatz-**yo**nay

floor (of room) il pavim**e**nto
(of building) il pi**a**no
on the floor sul pavim**e**nto
sool

Florence Firenze feer**e**ntzay

Florentine (*adj*) fiorent**i**no

florist il fior**a**io f-y**o**ra-yo

flour la far**i**na

flower il fi**o**re f-y**o**ray

flu l'influ**e**nza *f*

**fluent: he speaks fluent
Italian** p**a**rla l'itali**a**no
correntem**e**nte eetal-y**a**no
kor-rentem**e**ntay

fly la m**o**sca
(*verb*) vol**a**re vol**a**ray

fly in arriv**a**re in a**e**reo ar-reev**a**ray
een a-**ai**ray-o

fly out part**i**re in a**e**reo part**ee**ray

fog la n**e**bbia

foggy: it's foggy c'è n**e**bbia chay

folk dancing le d**a**nze folk
d**a**ntzay

folk music la m**u**sica folk
m**oo**zeeka

follow segu**i**re segw**ee**ray
follow me mi s**e**gua
mee s**a**y-gwa

food il c**i**bo ch**ee**bo

food poisoning l'intossicazi**o**ne
aliment**a**re *f* eentos-seekatz-
y**o**nay ali-ment**a**ray

food shop/store il neg**o**zio di
g**e**neri aliment**a**ri neg**o**tz-yo dee
j**ay**nairee

foot il pi**e**de p-y**ay**day
on foot a pi**e**di

football il c**a**lcio k**a**lcho
(ball) il pall**o**ne pal-l**o**nay

football match la part**i**ta di c**a**lcio

for per pair, da
**do you have something
for…?** (headache/diarrhoea
etc) av**e**te qualc**o**sa c**o**ntro…?
av**ay**tay kwalk**o**za

who's the ice cream for?
per chi è il gel**a**to?
pair kee ay

that's for me è per me may

and this one? e qu**e**sta?
ay kw**e**sta

that's for her qu**e**lla è per lei
kw**e**l-la – lay

**where do I get the bus
for San Pietro?** d**o**ve si
pr**e**nde l'**a**utobus per San
Pi**e**tro? d**o**vay see pr**e**nday
l**ow**-toboos pair

**the bus for San Pietro
leaves from Termini
Station** l'**a**utobus per San
Pi**e**tro p**a**rte d**a**lla Stazi**o**ne
T**e**rmini p**a**rtay – statz-y**o**nay

**how long have you been
here for?** da qu**a**nto è qui?
kw**a**nto ay kwee

**I've been here for two days,
how about you?** s**o**no qui da
d**u**e gi**o**rni, e lei? j**o**rnee, ay lay

I've been here for a week
s**o**no qui da **u**na settim**a**na

forehead la fronte fr**o**ntay

foreign straniero stran-y**a**iro

foreigner (*male/female*)
lo straniero stran-y**a**iro,
la strani**e**ra

forest la for**e**sta

forget dimenticare
deementeek**a**ray

I forget non ric**o**rdo

I've forgotten ho dimentic**a**to

fork la forchetta fork**e**t-ta

(in road) la biforcazione
beeforkatz-y**o**nay

form (document) il modulo
m**o**doolo

formal (dress) da cerimonia
chaireem**o**n-ya

fortnight quindici giorni
kweend**ee**chee j**o**rnee

fortunately fortunatamente
fortoonata-m**e**ntay

**forward: could you forward
my mail?** potrebbe inoltrare la
mia corrispondenza?
potreb-bay eenoltr**a**ray la m**ee**-a
kor-reespond**e**ntza

forwarding address il nuovo
recapito nw**o**vo

foundation cream il fondot**i**nta

fountain la fontana

foyer (of hotel) l'atrio *m*

(theatre) il foyer

fracture la frattura frat-t**oo**ra

France la Francia fr**a**ncha

free libero l**ee**bairo

(no charge) gratuito grat**oo**-eeto

is it free (of charge)?
è gratis?

freeway l'autostrada *f* owtostr**a**da

freezer il freezer fr**ee**tzair

French francese franch**a**yzay

French fries le patatine fritte
patat**ee**-nay fr**ee**t-tay

frequent frequente frekw**e**ntay

**how frequent is the bus to
Perugia?** ogni quanto passa
l'autobus per Perugia? **o**n-yee
kw**a**nto – pair

fresh fresco

fresh orange juice il succo
d'arancia s**oo**k-ko dar**a**ncha

Friday venerdì venaird**ee**

fridge il frigo

fried fritto

fried egg l'uovo al tegamino
m w**o**vo

friend (*male/female*) l'amico *m*,
l'amica *f*

friendly cordiale kord-y**a**lay

from da

**when does the next train
from Rome arrive?**
quando arriva il prossimo
treno da Roma? kw**a**ndo

from Monday to Friday
dal lunedì al venerdì

from next Thursday
da giovedì pr**o**ssimo

---

where are you from?
di dov'è? dov**a**y

I'm from Slough sono di
Slough

DIALOGUE

front il davanti

  in front davanti

  in front of the hotel davanti all'albergo

  at the front sul davanti sool

frost il gelo jaylo

frozen ghiacciato g-yachato

frozen food i cibi surgelati cheebee soor-jelatee

fruit la frutta froot-ta

fruit juice il succo di frutta sook-ko dee froot-ta

fry friggere freej-jairay

frying pan la padella

full pieno p-yayno

  it's full of... è pieno/piena di... ay

  I'm full sono pieno/piena

full board la pensione completa pens-yonay komplayta

fun: it was fun è stato divertente deevairtentay

funeral il funerale foonairalay

funny (strange) strano

  (amusing) buffo boof-fo

furniture i mobili

further più avanti p-yoo

  it's further down the road è più avanti su questa strada

DIALOGUE

how much further is it to San Gimignano? quanto manca a San Gimignano? kwanto

about 5 kilometres circa cinque chilometri cheerka – keelometree

fuse il fusibile foozeebeelay

  the lights have fused sono saltate le valvole saltatay lay valvolay

fuse box i fusibili foozeebeelee

fuse wire il filo fusibile -beelay

future il futuro footooro

  in future in futuro

G

gallon il gallone gal-lonay

game (cards etc) il gioco jo-ko

  (match) la partita

  (meat) la selvaggina selvaj-jeena

garage (for fuel) il distributore di benzina deestreebootoray dee bentzeena

  (for repairs) l'autofficina f owtof-feecheena

  (for parking) l'autorimessa f owtoreemes-sa

garden il giardino jardeeno

garlic l'aglio m al-yo

gas il gas

gas cylinder (camping gas) la bombola del gas

gas permeable lenses le lenti semirigide semeereejeeday

gasoline (US) la benzina bentzeena

gas station la stazione di servizio statz-yonay dee sairveetz-yo

gate il cancello kanchel-lo

  (at airport) l'uscita f oosheeta

gay gay

gay bar il bar gay

gear la marcia marcha

gearbox la scatola del cambio kamb-yo

gear lever la leva del cambio

general generale jenairalay

Genoa Genova jaynova

gents (toilet) la toilette (degli uomini) twalet dayl-yee wo-meenee

genuine (antique etc) autentico owtenteeko

German (adj) tedesco

German measles la rosolia

Germany la Germania

get (fetch) prendere prendairay

  will you get me another one, please? me ne porta un altro/un'altra, per favore? may nay

  how do I get to…? come si arriva a…? komay

  do you know where I can get them? sa dove posso trovarli/trovarle? dovay – trovarlay

can I get you a drink? posso offrirle qualcosa da bere? of-freerlay kwalkoza da bairay

no, I'll get this one, what would you like? no, offro io questa volta, cosa prende? ee-o kwesta – koza prenday

a glass of red wine un bicchiere di vino rosso beek-k-yairay

get back (return) tornare tornaray

get in (arrive) arrivare ar-reevaray

get off scendere shendairay

  where do I get off? dove devo scendere? dovay dayvo

get on (to train etc) salire saleeray

get out (of car etc) scendere shendairay

get up (in the morning) alzarsi altzarsee

gift il regalo

gift shop il negozio di articoli da regalo negotz-yo

gin il gin

  a gin and tonic, please un gin tonic, per favore

girl la ragazza ragatza

girlfriend la ragazza

give dare daray

  can you give me some change? mi può dare degli spiccioli? mee pwo – dayl-yee

  I gave it to him l'ho dato a lui lo – loo-ee

will you give this to…?
puoi/può dare questo a…?
pwoy/pwo – kwesto

DIALOGUE

**how much do you want
for this?** quanto vuole per
questo? kwanto vwolay pair
kwesto

20 euros venti euro ventee
ay-ooro

I'll give you 10 euros gliene
do dieci l-yee-aynee – dee-
ay-chee

give back restituire resteetweeray
glad contento
glass (material) il vetro
(tumbler) il bicchiere beek-yairay
(wine glass) il bicchiere da vino
a glass of wine un bicchiere
di vino
glasses (spectacles) gli occhiali
ok-yalee
gloves i guanti gwantee
glue la colla
go (verb) andare andaray
**we'd like to go to the
Roman Forum** vorremmo
andare al Foro Romano
vor-rem-mo
where are you going?
dove stai andando? dovay sty
where does this bus go?
dove va questo autobus?
dovay va kwesto
let's go! andiamo! and-yamo
she's gone (left) se n'è andata
say nay

where has he gone? dov'è
andato? dovay
I went there last week
ci sono andato la settimana
scorsa chee
pizza to go una pizza da
portare via portaray vee-a
go away andare via andaray
go away! vattene! vat-tenay
go back (return) tornare tornaray
go down (the stairs etc) scendere
shendairay
go in entrare entraray
go out (in the evening) uscire
oosheeray
**do you want to go out
tonight?** vuoi/vuole uscire
stasera? vwoy/vwolay
go through attraversare
at-travairsaray
go up (stairs) salire saleeray
goat la capra
goats' cheese il caprino
God Dio dee-o
goggles (for skiing) gli occhiali da
sci ok-yalee da shee
(for swimming) gli occhiali da
nuoto nwoto
gold l'oro m
golf il golf
golf course il campo di golf
gondola la gondola
gondolier il gondoliere gondol-
yairay
good buono bwono
good! bene! baynay
it's no good non va bene

goodbye arrivederci
 ar-reevedairchee

good evening buonasera
 bwonasaira

Good Friday Venerdì Santo
 venairdee santo

good morning buongiorno
 bwonjorno

good night buonanotte
 bwonanot-tay

goose l'oca *f*

got: we've got to leave
 dobbiamo partire dob-yamo
 parteeray

  have you got any...?
 avete...? avaytay

government il governo govairno

gradually gradualmente
 gradoo-almentay

grammar la grammatica

gram(me) il grammo

granddaughter la nipote
 neepotay

grandfather il nonno

grandmother la nonna

grandson il nipote neepotay

grapefruit il pompelmo

grapefruit juice il succo di
 pompelmo sook-ko

grapes l'uva *f* oova

grass l'erba *f* airba

grateful grato

gravy il sugo soogo

great (excellent) fantastico

  that's great! magnifico!

  a great success un gran
 successo sooches-so

Great Britain la Gran Bretagna
bretan-ya

Greece la Grecia grecha

greedy goloso

Greek (adj) greco

green verde vairday

green card (car insurance)
la carta verde

greengrocer's il fruttivendolo
froot-teevendolo

grey grigio greejo

grill la griglia greel-ya

grilled alla griglia

grocer's il negozio di alimentari
negotz-yo

ground la terra tair-ra

on the ground per terra pair

ground floor il piano terra tair-ra

group il gruppo groop-po

guarantee la garanzia
garantzee-a

is it guaranteed?
è garantito? ay

guest l'ospite m/f ospeetay

guesthouse la pensione
pens-yonay

guide la guida gweeda

guidebook la guida

guided tour la visita guidata
veezeeta gweedata

guitar la chitarra keetar-ra

gum (in mouth) la gengiva jen-jeeva

gun il fucile foocheelay

gym la palestra

H

hair i capelli

hairbrush la spazzola per capelli
spatzola pair

haircut il taglio di capelli tal-yo

hairdresser (men's) il barbiere
barb-yairay

(male/female) il parrucchiere
par-rook-yairay, la parrucchiera

hairdryer il fon

hair gel il gel per capelli jel pair

hairgrips i fermacapelli

hair spray la lacca per capelli

half la metà

half an hour mezz'ora medzora

half a litre mezzo litro medzo

about half that una metà di
quello kwel-lo

half board la mezza pensione
medza pens-yonay

half bottle mezza bottiglia
bot-teel-ya

half fare mezzo biglietto
medzo beel-yet-to

half price metà prezzo pretzo

ham il prosciutto proshoot-to

hamburger l'hamburger m
amboorgair

hammer il martello

hand la mano

handbag la borsetta

handbrake il freno a mano
frayno

handkerchief il fazzoletto
fatzolet-to

handle (on door, suitcase)
la maniglia man**ee**l-ya
(on handbag) il m**a**nico

hand luggage il bagaglio a
mano bag**a**l-yo

hang-gliding il deltaplano

hangover i p**o**stumi d**e**lla
sbornia zb**o**rn-ya

  I've got a hangover s**o**ffro
  per i postumi di una sbornia

happen succedere sooch**ay**dairay

  what's happening?
  che succede? kay sooch**ay**day

  what has happened? che è
  successo? ay sooch**ay**s-so

happy felice fel**ee**chay

  I'm not happy about this
  non ne s**o**no conv**i**nto nay

harbour il p**o**rto

hard duro d**oo**ro
(difficult) difficile deef-f**ee**cheelay

hard-boiled egg l'uovo s**o**do
m w**o**vo

hard lenses le lenti rigide
r**ee**jeeday

hardly a mala pena
  hardly ever quasi mai
  kw**a**zee my

hardware shop il neg**o**zio di
ferramenta neg**o**tz-yo dee
fair-ram**e**nta

hat il capp**e**llo

hate (*verb*) detestare detest**a**ray

have avere av**a**iray

  can I have…? vorrei… vor-r**ay**
  do you have…? hai/ha…?
  a-ee/a

what'll you have?
cosa prendi/prende? k**o**za
pr**e**ndee/pr**e**nday

I have to leave now
devo andarmene ad**e**sso
d**ay**vo andarm**e**nay

do I have to…? d**e**vo…?

can we have some…?
vorremmo un po' di…
vor-r**e**m-mo

hayfever la febbre da fieno
feb-bray da f-y**ay**no

hazelnuts le nocciole noch**o**lay

he lui loo-ee

head la t**e**sta

headache il mal di testa

headlights i fari

headphones la cuffia k**oo**f-ya

health food shop il neg**o**zio
di cibi natur**a**li neg**o**tz-yo dee
ch**ee**bee

healthy s**a**no

hear sentire sent**ee**ray

hearing aid l'apparecchio
acustico *m* ap-par**e**k-yo
ak**oo**steeko

heart il cu**o**re kw**o**ray

heart attack l'inf**a**rto *m*

heat il c**a**ldo

heater (in room) il radiat**o**re
rad-yat**o**ray

(in car) il riscaldamento

heating il riscaldamento

heavy pesante pezantay

heel (of foot) il tallone tal-lonay

(of shoe) il tacco

could you heel these? può rifare i tacchi a queste scarpe? pwo reefaray ee tak-kee a kwestay skarpay

heelbar riparazione scarpe reeparatz-yonay

height l'altezza faltetza

helicopter l'elicottero m eleekot-tairo

hello (in the daytime) buongiorno bwonjorno

(late afternoon, in the evening) buonasera bwonasaira

(answer on phone) pronto

helmet (for motorcycle) il casco

help l'aiuto m a-yooto

(verb) aiutare a-yootaray

help! aiuto!

can you help me? mi può aiutare? pwo

thank you very much for your help grazie dell'aiuto gratzee-ay

helpful disponibile deesponeebeelay

hepatitis l'epatite fepateetay

her: I haven't seen her non l'ho vista lo

to her a lei lay, le lay

with her con lei, con sé say

for her per lei

that's her è lei

that's her towel è il suo asciugamano ay eel soo-o

herbal tea la tisana teezana

herbs le erbe airbay

here qui kwee

here is/are... ecco...

here you are ecco a te/lei tay/lay

hers: that's hers quello è suo kwel-lo ay soo-o

hey! ehi! ay-ee

hi! (hello) ciao! chow, salve! salvay

hide (verb) nascondere naskondairay

high alto

highchair il seggiolone sej-jolonay

highway l'autostrada fowtostrada

hill la collina

him: I haven't seen him non l'ho visto lo

to him a lui loo-ee, gli l-yee

with him con lui, con sé say

for him per lui pair

that's him è lui ay

hip il fianco f-yanko

hire noleggiare nolej-jaray

for hire a nolo

where can I hire a bike? dove posso noleggiare una bicicletta? dovay

his: it's his car è la sua macchina ay la soo-a

that's his quello è suo kwel-lo ay soo-o

hit (verb) colpire kolpeeray

hitch-hike fare l'autostop faray lowtostop

hobby l'hobby m
hockey l'hockey m
hold (*verb*) tenere tenairay
hole il buco booko
holiday la vacanza vakantza
  on holiday in vacanza
home la casa kaza
  at home (in my house etc) a casa
  (in my country) in patria
  we go home tomorrow
  torniamo in patria domani
  torn-yamo
honest onesto
honey il miele m-yaylay
honeymoon la luna di miele
  loona dee
hood (US; of a car) il cofano
hope la speranza spairantza
  I hope so spero di sì spairo
  I hope not spero di no
hopefully se tutto va bene
  say toot-to va baynay
horn (of car) il clacson
horrible orribile or-reebeelay
horse il cavallo
horse riding l'equitazione f
  ekweetatz-yonay
hospital l'ospedale m ospedalay
hospitality l'ospitalità f
  thank you for your
  hospitality grazie
  dell'ospitalità
hot caldo
  (spicy) piccante peek-kantay
  I'm hot ho caldo o
  it's hot today fa caldo oggi
  oj-jee

hotel l'albergo m albairgo
hotel room la camera d'albergo
hour l'ora f
house la casa kaza
house wine il vino della casa
hovercraft l'hovercraft m
how come komay
  how many? quanti? kwantee
  how much? quanto?

  how are you? come stai/sta?
  komay sty
  fine, thanks, and you? bene,
  grazie, e lei? baynay – ay lay

  how much is it? quanto
  costa? kwanto
  ... euros... euro ay-ooro
  I'll take it lo/la prendo

humid umido oomeedo
humour l'umorismo m
  oomoreezmo
hungry: I'm hungry ho fame
  o famay
  are you hungry? ha fame? a
hurry (*verb*) sbrigarsi
  I'm in a hurry ho fretta o
  there's no hurry non c'è fretta
  non chay
  hurry up! sbrigati! zbreegatee
hurt far male malay
  it really hurts mi fa proprio
  male
husband il marito mareeto
hydrofoil l'aliscafo m
hypermarket l'ipermercato m

I io **ee**-o

ice il ghiaccio g-**ya**cho

  with ice con ghiaccio

  no ice, thanks niente
  ghiaccio, grazie n-**ye**ntay

ice cream il gelato je**la**to

ice-cream cone il cono gelato

iced coffee il caffè freddo
  kaf-**fay**

ice lolly il ghiacciolo g-yacho**lo**

ice rink la pista di pattinaggio
  (sul ghiaccio) pat-teena**j**-jo sool
  g-**ya**cho

ice skates i pattini da ghiaccio

idea l'idea f ee**day**-a

idiot l'idiota m/f eed-**yo**ta

if se say

ignition l'accensione m
  achens-**yo**nay

ill malato

  I feel ill mi sento male ma**lay**

illness la malattia malat-**tee**-a

imitation (leather etc) l'imitazione
  f eemeetatz-**yo**nay

immediately immediatamente
  eem-med-yata**men**tay

important importante
  eempor**tan**tay

  it's very important è molto
  importante ay

  it's not important non ha
  importanza non a eempor**tan**tza

impossible impossibile
  eempos-**see**beelay

impressive notevole no**tay**-volay

improve migliorare meel-yo**ra**ray

  **I want to improve my
  Italian** voglio migliorare il mio
  italiano **vol**-yo – eel **mee**-o

in: it's in the centre
  è in centro een **chen**tro

  in my car con la mia
  macchina

  in Florence a Firenze

  in two days from now
  tra due giorni

  in five minutes tra cinque
  minuti

  in May a maggio

  in English in inglese

  in Italian in italiano

  is he in? c'è? chay

inch il pollice pol-**lee**chay

include comprendere
  kompren**dai**ray

  does that include meals?
  sono compresi i pasti?
  kompra**yzee**

  is that included? questo è
  compreso? **kwes**to ay

inconvenient scomodo

incredible incredibile
  eenkred**ee**beelay

Indian indiano eend-**ya**no

indicator la freccia **fre**cha

indigestion l'indigestione f
  eendeejest-**yo**nay

indoor pool la piscina coperta
  pee-**shee**na ko**pair**ta

indoors all'interno een**tair**no

inexpensive a buon mercato
  bwon mair**ka**to

see **cheap**

infection l'infezione *f*
eenfetz-yonay

infectious contagioso kontajozo

inflammation l'infiammazione *f*
eenf-yam-matz-yonay

informal informale eenformalay

information l'informazione *f*
eenformatz-yonay

  **do you have any
information about…?**
ha informazioni su…?

information desk il banco
(delle) informazioni del-lay

injection l'iniezione *f*
een-yetz-yonay

injured ferito faireeto

  she's been injured è rimasta
ferita ay

in-laws i suoceri swochairee

inner tube (for tyre) la camera
d'aria

innocent innocente een-
nochentay

insect l'insetto *m*

insect bite la puntura d'insetto
poon-toora

  **do you have anything for
insect bites?** ha qualcosa per
le punture d'insetto? a kwalkoza
pair lay poon-tooray

insect repellent l'insettifugo *m*
eenset-teefoogo

inside dentro

  inside the hotel nell'albergo

  let's sit inside sediamoci
dentro sed-yamochee

insist insistere eenseestairay

I insist insisto

insomnia l'insonnia *f*

instant coffee il caffè solubile
kaf-fay soloobeelay

instead invece eenvaychay

  give me that one instead
mi dia quello, invece kwel-lo

  instead of… invece di…

insulin l'insulina *f* eensooleena

insurance l'assicurazione *f*
as-seekooratz-yonay

intelligent intelligente
eentel-leejentay

**interested: I'm interested
in…** mi interesso di… mee
eentaires-so

interesting interessante
eentaires-santay

  that's very interesting
è molto interessante ay

international internazionale
eentairnatz-yonalay

Internet Internet eentairnet

interpret interpretare
eentairpretaray

interpreter l'interprete *m/f*
eentairpretay

intersection l'incrocio *m*
eenkrocho

interval (at theatre) l'intervallo *m*
eentairval-lo

into in

  I'm not into…
non m'interesso di…

introduce presentare presentaray

  may I introduce…? posso
presentarle…? presentarlay

invitation l'invito *m*

invite invitare eenveetaray

Ireland l'Irlanda *f* eerlanda

Irish irlandese eerlandayzay

I'm Irish sono irlandese

iron (for ironing) il ferro da stiro
fair-ro

can you iron these for me?
me li può stirare? may lee pwo
steeraray

is è ay

island l'isola *f* eezola

it esso

it is... è... ay

is it...? è...?

where is it? dov'è? dovay

it's him è lui loo-ee

it was... era... aira

Italian (*adj*) italiano eetal-yano

(language, man) l'italiano *m*

(woman) l'italiana *f*

the Italians gli Italiani

Italy l'Italia *f* eetal-ya

itch: it itches mi prude prooday

J

jack (for car) il cric

jacket la giacca jak-ka

jar il vasetto

jam la marmellata

jammed: it's jammed si è
inceppato ay eenchep-pato

January gennaio jen-na-yo

jaw la mascella mashel-la

jazz il jazz jetz

jealous geloso jelozo

jeans i jeans

jellyfish la medusa medooza

jersey la maglia mal-ya

jetty il molo

Jewish ebreo ebray-o

jeweller's la gioielleria
joy-el-lairee-a

jewellery i gioielli joy-el-lee

job l'impiego *m* eemp-yaygo

jogging il jogging

to go jogging andare a fare
jogging andaray a faray

joke lo scherzo skairtzo

(story) la barzelletta bartzel-let-ta

journey il viaggio vee-aj-jo

have a good journey!
buon viaggio! bwon

jug la brocca

a jug of water una brocca
d'acqua dakwa

juice il succo sook-ko

July luglio lool-yo

jump (*verb*) saltare saltaray

jumper il maglione mal-yonay

jump leads il cavo per collegare
due batterie pair kol-legaray doo-
ay bat-tairee-ay

junction il bivio beev-yo

June giugno joon-yo

just (only) solo

just two soltanto due

just for me solo per me pair may

just here proprio qui kwee

not just now non ora

we've just arrived siamo
appena arrivati s-yamo
ap-payna

keep tenere ten**ai**ray

keep the change tenga il r**e**sto

can I keep it? p**o**sso tenerlo? ten-**ai**rlo

please keep it puoi/può tenerlo pwoy/pwo

ketchup il ketchup

kettle il bollitore bol-leet**o**ray

key la chiave k-y**a**vay

the key for room 201, please (la chiave del) duecentuno, per fav**o**re

key ring il portachiavi portak-**ya**vee

kidneys (in body) i reni r**a**ynee

(food) il rognone ron-y**o**nay

kill (verb) uccidere ooch**ee**dairay

kilo il chilo k**ee**lo

kilometre il chilometro keel**o**metro

how many kilometres is it to…? a quanti chilometri da qui è…? kw**a**ntee – kwee ay

kind (generous) gentile jent**ee**lay

that's very kind of you è m**o**lto gentile da parte tua/sua ay – partay t**oo**-a/s**oo**-a

which kind do you want? che t**i**po vuole? kay – vw**o**lay

I want this/that kind questo/quel tipo kw**e**sto/kwel

king il re ray

kiosk il chiosco kee-**o**sko

(selling newspapers) l'edicola f

kiss il bacio b**a**cho

(verb) baciare bach**a**ray

kitchen la cucina kooch**ee**na

kitchenette il cucinino koocheen**ee**no

Kleenex i fazzolettini di c**a**rta fatzolet-t**ee**nee

knee il ginocchio jeen**o**k-yo

knickers le mutande moot**a**nday

knife il coltello

knitwear la maglieria mal-yee-air**ee**-a

knock (verb: on door) bussare boos-s**a**ray

knock down: he's been knocked down è stato invest**i**to ay

knock over (object) far cadere kad**ai**ray

(pedestrian) investire eenvest**ee**ray

know (somebody, a place) conoscere kon**o**shairay

(something) sapere sap**ai**ray

I don't know non lo so

I didn't know that non lo sapevo sap**ay**vo

do you know where I can find…? sai/sa dove posso trovare…? s**a**-ee/sa d**o**vay p**o**s-so trov**a**ray

L

label l'etichetta f eteek**e**t-ta

ladies' (toilets) la toilette (delle donne) tw**a**let d**e**l-lay d**o**n-nay

ladies' wear l'abbigliamento da
donna *m* ab-beel-yamento
lady la signora seen-yora
lager la birra chiara beer-ra k-yara
lake il lago
lamb l'agnello *m* an-yel-lo
lamp la lampada
lane (motorway) la corsia
(small road) la stradina
language la lingua leengwa
language course il corso di
lingua
laptop il computer portatile
computer portateelay
large grande granday
last ultimo oolteemo
**what time is the last train to
Trieste?** a che ora parte l'ultimo
treno per Trieste? kay – partay
last week la settimana scorsa
last Friday venerdì scorso

last night la notte scorsa
late tardi
sorry I'm late mi scuso del
ritardo mee skoozo
the train was late il treno era
in ritardo
we must go – we'll be late
dobbiamo andare – altrimenti
faremo tardi dob-yamo andaray
– faraymo
it's getting late si sta facendo
tardi fachendo
later più tardi p-yoo
I'll come back later
torno più tardi
see you later ci vediamo
dopo chee ved-yamo
later on più tardi
latest ultimo oolteemo
**by Wednesday at the
latest...** entro mercoledì al più
tardi p-yoo

laugh (*verb*) ridere r**ee**dairay

launderette la lavanderia automatica lavand**ee**ra-a owto-mat**ee**ka

laundromat la lavanderia automatica

laundry (clothes) il buc**a**to

(place) la lavand**e**ria

lavatory il gabin**e**tto

law la legge l**e**j-jay

lawn il pr**a**to all'ingl**e**se eengl**a**yzay

lawyer l'avvoc**a**to *m*

laxative il lassat**i**vo

lazy p**i**gro

lead (electrical) il f**i**lo

(*verb*) condurre kond**oo**r-ray, guid**a**re gweed**a**ray

where does this lead to? dove p**o**rta questo? d**o**vay – kw**e**sto

leaf la foglia f**o**l-ya

leaflet il dépliant daypli-**a**n

leak la perdita p**a**irdeeta

(*verb*) perdere p**a**irdairay

the roof leaks gocciola acqua dal tetto g**o**chola **a**kwa

learn imparare eempar**a**ray

least: not in the least per niente n-y**e**ntay

at least come minimo k**o**may

leather il cuoio kw**o**-yo, la pelle p**e**l-lay

leave (*verb*: depart) partire part**ee**ray

(leave behind) lasciare lash**a**ray

I am leaving tomorrow p**a**rto dom**a**ni

he left yesterday è partito ieri ay – y**a**iree

may I leave this here? p**o**sso lasciarlo qui? lash**a**rlo kwee

I left my coat in the bar ho lasci**a**to il capp**o**tto al bar o

when does the bus for Venice leave? a che **o**ra parte l'autobus per Ven**e**zia kay – part**a**y l**ow**toboos pair

leek il p**o**rro

left la sinistra seen**ee**stra

on the left, to the left a sinistra

turn left giri a sinistra j**ee**ree

there's none left non ce nè più nessuno/nessuna chay nay p-yoo nes-s**oo**no

left-handed mancino manch**ee**no

left luggage (office) il dep**o**sito bagagli bag**a**l-yee

leg la gamba

lemon il limone leem**o**nay

lemonade la gassosa gas-s**o**za

lemon tea il tè al limone tay al leem**o**nay

lend prestare prest**a**ray

will you lend me your... ? può prest**a**rmi il suo/la sua...? pwo – s**oo**-o/s**oo**-a

lens (of camera) l'obiettivo *m* ob-yet-t**ee**vo

lesbian la l**e**sbica

less meno m**a**yno

less than meno di

less expensive più a buon mercato p-yoo

lesson la lezione letz-y**o**nay

let (allow) permettere pairmet-tairay

will you let me know? mi faccia sapere mee facha sapairay

I'll let you know ti/le farò sapere lay

let's go for something to eat andiamo a mangiare qualcosa and-yamo a manjaray kwalkoza

let off far scendere shendairay

will you let me off at...? può farmi scendere a...? pwo

letter la lettera let-taira

do you have any letters for me? ci sono lettere per me? chee sono let-tairay pair may

letterbox la buca delle lettere booka del-lay

lettuce la lattuga lat-tooga

lever la leva layva

library la biblioteca beeblee-otayka

licence il permesso pairmes-so

lid il coperchio kopairk-yo

lie (verb: tell untruth) mentire menteeray

lie down stendersi stendairsee

life la vita

lifebelt il salvagente salvajentay

lifeguard (male/female) il bagnino ban-yeeno, la bagnina

life jacket il giubbotto di salvataggio joob-bot-to dee salva-taj-jo

lift (in building) l'ascensore m ashensoray

could you give me a lift? mi puoi/può dare un passaggio?

mee pwoy/pwo daray oon pas-saj-jo

would you like a lift? vuoi/vuole un passaggio? vwoy/vwolay

lift pass lo skipass

a daily/weekly lift pass uno skipass giornaliero/settimanale

light la luce loochay

(not heavy) leggero lej-jairo

do you have a light? (for cigarette) puoi/può farmi accendere? pwoy/pwo farmee achendairay

light green verde chiaro k-yaro

light bulb la lampadina

I need a new light bulb ho bisogno di una lampadina nuova o beezon-yo dee

lighter (cigarette) l'accendino m achen-deeno

lightning il fulmine foolmeenay

like (verb) piacere p-yachairay

I like it mi piace mee pee-achay

I like going for walks mi piace fare passeggiate

I like you mi piaci pee-achee

I don't like it non mi piace

do you like...? ti/le piace...? tee/lay

I'd like a beer vorrei una birra vor-ray

I'd like to go swimming vorrei andare a fare una nuotata andaray

would you like a drink? vuoi/vuole qualcosa da bere? vwoy/vwolay kwalkoza da bairay

would you like to go for a walk? ti/le va di fare una passeggiata?

what's it like? comè? komay

like this così kozee

I want one like this ne voglio uno/una come questo/questa nay vol-yo – komay kwesto/kwesta

lime il lime la-eem

line la linea leen-ay-a

could you give me an outside line? mi dà la linea, per favore?

lips le labbra

lip salve la pomata per le labbra pair lay

lipstick il rossetto

liqueur il liquore leekworay

listen ascoltare askoltaray

litre il litro

a litre of white wine un litro di vino bianco

little piccolo

just a little, thanks solo un po', grazie

a little milk un po' di latte

a little bit more ancora un po'

live (verb) vivere veevairay

we live together conviviamo konveev-yamo

where do you live? dove abita? dovay

I live in London abito a Londra

lively (person, town) pieno di vita p-yayno dee veeta

liver il fegato faygato

loaf la pagnotta pan-yot-ta

lobby (in hotel) l'atrio m

lobster l'aragosta f

local locale lokalay

can you recommend a local wine/restaurant? mi può consigliare un vino/un ristorante del posto? mee pwo konseel-yaray

lock la serratura sair-ratoora

(verb) chiudere a chiave k-yoodairay a k-yavay

it's locked è chiuso a chiave ay k-yoozo

lock in chiudere dentro

lock out chiudere fuori fwooree

I've locked myself out mi sono chiuso/chiusa fuori k-yoozo

locker (for luggage etc) l'armadietto m armad-yet-to

lollipop il lecca-lecca

Lombardy la Lombardia

London Londra

long lungo loongo

how long will it take to fix it? quanto ci vuole per accomodarlo? kwanto chee vwolay pair

how long does it take? quanto tempo ci vuole?

a long time tanto tempo

one day/two days longer ancora un giorno/due giorni

long-distance call l'inter-urbana f eentairoorbana

look: I'm just looking, thanks sto solo dando un'occhiata, grazie ok-yata

you don't look well hai/ha una brutta cera a-ee/a oona broot-ta chaira

look out! attenzione! at-tentz-yonay

can I have a look? posso dare un'occhiata? daray

look after badare a badaray

look at guardare gwardaray

look for cercare chairkaray

I'm looking for... sto cercando... chairkando

look forward to non vedere l'ora di vedairay

I'm looking forward to it non vedo l'ora vaydo

loose (handle etc) che si sta staccando kay

lorry il camion kam-yon

lose perdere pairdairay

I'm lost, I want to get to... mi sono perso/persa, voglio andare a... pairso – vol-yo andaray

I've lost my bag ho perso la borsa o

lost property (office) l'ufficio oggetti smarriti m oof-feecho oj-jet-tee zmar-reetee

lot: a lot, lots molto

not a lot non molto

a lot of Parmesan molto parmigiano

a lot of sauce molta salsa

a lot of people molta gente jentay

a lot of boys molti ragazzi

a lot of drinks molte bevande

a lot bigger molto più grande p-yoo

I like it a lot mi piace molto mee pee-achay

lotion la lozione lotz-yonay

loud forte fortay

lounge (in house, hotel) il salone salonay

(in airport) la sala d'attesa at-tayza

love l'amore m amoray

(verb) amare amaray

I love Italy mi piace molto l'Italia mee p-yachay

lovely bello

(meal) delizioso deleetz-yozo

low basso

luck la fortuna fortoona

good luck! buona fortuna! bwona

luggage i bagagli bagal-yee

luggage trolley il carrello

lump (on body) il gonfiore gonf-yoray

lunch il pranzo prandzo

lungs i polmoni

luxurious lussuoso loos-soo-ozo

luxury il lusso loos-so

M

machine la macchina mak-keena

mad (insane) pazzo patzo

(angry) furioso fooree-ozo

magazine la rivista

maid (in hotel) la cameriera
  kamair-**ya**ira

maiden name il cognome da
  nubile kon-**yo**may da n**oo**beelay

mail la p**o**sta
  see **post**
  (*verb*) impostare eempost**a**ray
  is there any mail for me?
  c'è p**o**sta per me? chay – may

mailbox la buca delle lettere
  b**oo**ka del-lay l**e**t-tairay

main principale preench**ee**palay

main course la port**a**ta
  principale

main post office l'ufficio
  postale centrale *m* oof-f**ee**cho
  post**a**lay chentr**a**lay

main road (in town) la str**a**da
  principale preench**ee**palay
  (in country) la strada maestra
  m**y**stra

mains switch l'interruttore
  generale *m* eentair-root-t**o**ray
  jenair**a**lay

make fare f**a**ray
  (*noun:* brand name) la m**a**rca
  I make it 50 euros secondo
  i miei calcoli s**o**no cinquanta
  euro cheenkw**a**nta **ay-oo**ro
  what is it made of? di che
  cosa è f**a**tto/f**a**tta? kay k**o**za

make-up il trucco tr**oo**k-ko

man l'uomo *m* w**o**mo

manager il direttore deeret-t**o**ray
  can I see the manager?
  p**o**sso parlare con il direttore?
  parl**a**ray

manageress la direttrice
  deeret-tr**ee**chay

manual (car with manual gears)
  la macchina con il cambio
  manuale mak-keena kon eel
  k**a**mb-yo manoo-**a**lay

many m**o**lti/molte m**o**ltay
  not many non molti/molte

map (city plan) la pianta p-y**a**nta
  (road map, geographical) la
  cart**i**na

March marzo m**a**rtzo

margarine la margarina
  margar**ee**na

market il mercato mairk**a**to

marmalade la marmellata
  d'arance dar**a**nchay

married: I'm married (said by
  a *male/female*) s**o**no spos**a**to/
  spos**a**ta
  are you married? (said to a
  male/female) è spos**a**to/spos**a**ta?
  ay

mascara il masc**a**ra

match (football etc) la part**i**ta

matches i fiammiferi f-yam-
  m**ee**fairee

material (fabric) la st**o**ffa

matter: it doesn't matter
  non imp**o**rta
  what's the matter? che c'è?
  kay chay

mattress il mater**a**sso

May maggio m**a**j-jo

**may: may I have another
  bottle?** potrei avere
  un'altra bott**i**glia? potr**ay** av**a**iray

may I come in? posso
entrare? entr**a**ray

may I see it? posso vederlo/
vederla? ved**ai**rlo/ved**ai**rla

may I sit here? posso sedere
qui? sed**ai**ray kwee

maybe forse f**o**rsay

mayonnaise la maionese
ma-yon**ay**zay

me: that's for me è per me
ay pair may

send it to me m**a**ndalo/lo
m**a**ndi a me

me too anch'io ank**ee**-o

meal il p**a**sto

did you enjoy your meal?
le è piaciuto? lay ay
p-yach**oo**to

**it was excellent, thank
you** era **o**ttimo, gr**a**zie **ai**ra

mean (*verb*) significare
seen-yeefeek**a**ray

what do you mean? che
cosa intendi/intende? kay k**o**za
eent**e**ndee/eent**e**nday

**what does this word
mean?** cosa significa
questa parola? k**o**za seen-
yeef**ee**ka kw**e**sta

it means… in English in
inglese significa… eengl**ay**zay

measles il morbillo morb**ee**l-lo

meat la carne k**a**rnay

mechanic il meccanico mek-
k**a**neeko

medicine la medicina
medeech**ee**na

Mediterranean il Mediterraneo
medeetair-r**a**nay-o

medium (*adj:* size) medio m**a**yd-yo

medium-dry semis**e**cco

medium-rare non tr**o**ppo c**o**tto

medium-sized di taglia media
t**a**l-ya m**a**yd-ya

meet (someone) incontrare
eenkontr**a**ray

(each other) incontr**a**rsi

nice to meet you piacere
di conoscerla p-yach**ai**ray dee
kon**o**shair-la

where shall I meet you?
dove ci incontriamo? d**o**vay
chee

meeting la riunione r-yoon-y**o**nay

meeting place il luogo
d'incontro lw**o**go

melon il melone mel**o**nay

memory stick il chiavetta
k-yav**e**t-ta

men gli uomini wo-m**ee**nee

mend riparare reepar**a**ray

**could you mend this for
me?** me lo può riparare?
may – pwo

menswear l'abbigliamento da
uomo *m* ab-beel-yam**e**nto da
w**o**mo

mention (*verb*) nominare
nomeen**a**ray

don't mention it prego pr**a**ygo

menu il menù men**oo**

**may I see the menu,
please?** mi dà il menù,

per favore?

see page 229 for Menu reader

message il messaggio mes-saj-jo

are there any messages for me? ci sono messaggi per me? chee – pair may

I want to leave a message for... vorrei lasciare un messaggio per... vor-**r**ay lasharay

metal il metallo

metre il metro

microwave (oven) il forno a microonde meekro-**o**nday

midday mezzogiorno medzoj**o**rno

at midday a mezzogiorno

middle: in the middle nel mezzo m**e**dzo

in the middle of the night in piena notte p-**yay**na

the middle one quello/quella in mezzo kw**e**l-lo

midnight mezzanotte medzan**o**t-tay

at midnight a mezzanotte

might: I might (not) go può darsi che io (non) ci vada pwo – kay **ee**-o non chee

I might want to stay another day forse dovrò fermarmi ancora un giorno f**o**rsay

migraine l'emicrania *f* emeekr**a**n-ya

Milan Milano meel**a**no

mild (taste) leggero lej-**ja**iro

(weather) mite m**ee**tay

mile il miglio m**ee**l-yo

milk il latte l**a**t-tay

milkshake il frappé frap-p**ay**

millimetre il millimetro

minced meat la carne macinata k**a**rnay macheen**a**ta

mind: never mind non fa niente n-y**e**ntay

I've changed my mind ho cambiato idea o kamb-y**a**to eed**ay**-a

do you mind if I open the window? le dispiace se apro la finestra? lay deesp-y**a**chay say

no, I don't mind no, faccia pure f**a**cha p**oo**ray

DIALOGUE

mine: it's mine è mio/mia ay

mineral water l'acqua minerale *f* **a**kwa meenair**a**lay

minibar il frigobar

mints le mentine ment**ee**nay

minute il minuto meen**oo**to

in a minute in un attimo

just a minute un attimo

mirror lo specchio sp**e**k-yo

Miss (la) signorina seen-yor**ee**na

miss: I missed the bus ho perso l'autobus o p**a**irso

missing smarrito

one of my... is missing non trovo uno/una dei miei/delle mie... day mee-**yay**/del-lay mee-ay

there's a suitcase missing manca una valigia

mist la nebbiolina neb-yol**ee**na

mistake lo sbaglio zbal-yo

I think there's a mistake credo ci sia un errore kraydo chee see-a oon air-roray

sorry, I've made a mistake chiedo scusa, mi sono sbagliato/sbagliata k-yaydo skooza mee – sbal-yato

misunderstanding l'equivoco m ekwee-voko

mix-up: sorry, there's been a mix-up mi dispiace, è successa un po' di confusione mee deesp-yachay ay sooches-sa – konfooz-yonay

mobile phone il telefonino telayfoneeno

modern moderno modairno

modern art gallery la galleria d'arte moderna gal-lairee-a dartay

moisturizer l'idratante m ee-dratantay

moment: I won't be a moment (won't be long) faccio in un attimo facho

monastery il monastero monastairo

Monday lunedì loonedee

money i soldi

month il mese mayzay

monument il monumento monoomento

moon la luna loona

moped il motorino

more più p-yoo

can I have some more

water, please? vorrei ancora acqua, per favore vor-ray

more expensive/interesting più caro/interessante

more than 50 più di cinquanta

more than that di più

a lot more molto di più

morning la mattina

this morning questa mattina kwesta

in the morning di mattina

mosquito la zanzara tzantzara

mosquito repellent l'insettifugo m eenset-teefoogo

most: I like this one most of all questo/questa mi piace più di tutti/tutte kwesto – mee p-yachay p-yoo dee toot-tee/ toot-tay

most of the time la maggior parte del tempo maj-jor partay

most tourists la maggior parte dei turisti day

mostly per lo più pair lo p-yoo

mother la madre madray

motorbike la motocicletta moto-cheeklet-ta

motorboat il motoscafo

motorway l'autostrada *f* owtostrada

mountain la montagna montan-ya

　in the mountains in montagna

mountaineering l'alpinismo *m*

mouse il topo

moustache i baffi

mouth la bocca

mouth ulcer la stomatite stomateetay

move (*verb*) muovere mwovairay

　he's moved to another room si è trasferito in un'altra stanza see ay trasfaireeto

　could you move your car? potrebbe spostare la macchina? potreb-bay spostaray

　could you move up a little?

si può spostare un po' più in là? see pwo – p-yoo

　where has it been moved to? dove è stato trasferito? dovay ay

movie il film feelm

movie theater il cinema cheenema

MP3 format il formato emme-pi-tre formato em-may pee tray

Mr (il) signor seen-yor

Mrs (la) signora seen-yora

Ms (la) signora

much molto

　much better/worse molto meglio/peggio mayl-yo/pej-jo

　much hotter molto più caldo p-yoo

　not much non molto

　not very much non molto

　I don't want very much non voglio molto vol-yo

mud il fango

mug (for drinking) il bicchierone beek-yaironay

I've been mugged sono stato aggredito ag-gredeeto

mum la mamma

mumps gli orecchioni orek-yonee

museum il museo moozay-o

mushrooms i funghi foongee

music la musica moozeeka

musician il/la musicista moozeecheesta

Muslim (adj) musulmano

mussels le cozze kotzay

must: I must devo dayvo

I mustn't drink alcohol non devo bere alcol bairay

mustard la senape saynapay

my il mio, la mia, (plural) i miei mee-yay, le mie lay mee-ay

myself: I'll do it myself lo farò da me may

by myself da solo

N

nail (finger) l'unghia f oong-ya
(metal) il chiodo k-yodo

nail varnish lo smalto per le unghie pair lay oong-yay

name il nome nomay

my name's John mi chiamo John k-yamo

what's your name? come ti chiami/si chiama? komay tee k-yamee/see k-yama

what is the name of this

street? come si chiama questa strada? kwesta

napkin il tovagliolo toval-yolo

Naples Napoli

nappy il pannolino

> **Travel tip** Supplies for babies and small children, such as nappies and milk formula, can be pricey. Nappy changing facilities are few and far between.

narrow (street) stretto

nasty (person) antipatico
(weather, accident) brutto broot-to

national nazionale natz-yonalay

nationality la nazionalità natz-yonaleeta

natural naturale natooralay

nausea la nausea nowzay-a

navy (blue) blu marino

Neapolitan (adj) napoletano

near vicino a veecheeno

is it near the city centre? è vicino al centro della città? ay

do you go near the Colosseum? passa vicino al Colosseo?

where is the nearest...? dov'è il... più vicino? dovay eel... p-yoo

nearby vicino veecheeno

nearly quasi kwazee

necessary necessario neches-sar-yo

neck il collo

necklace la collana

necktie la cravatta

need: I need ... ho bisogno di...
o beezon-yo dee

do I need to pay? devo
pagare? dayvo pagaray

needle l'ago *m*

negative (film) la negativa

neither: neither (one) of them
nessuno dei due nays-soono
day doo-ay

neither... nor... né... né... nay

nephew il nipote neepotay

net (in sport) la rete raytay

Netherlands i Paesi Bassi
pa-ayzee

network map la piantina dei
trasporti pubblici poob-bleechee

never mai ma-ee

**have you ever been to
Rome?** è mai stato a
Roma? eh

**no, never; I've never been
there** no, mai; non ci sono
mai stato chee

new nuovo nwovo

news (radio, TV etc) le notizie
noteetzee-ay

newsagent's il giornalaio
jornala-yo

newspaper il giornale jornalay

newspaper kiosk l'edicola *f*

New Year l'anno nuovo *m* nwovo

Happy New Year! felice anno
nuovo! felee-chay

New Year's Eve la notte di
Capodanno, la notte di San

Silvestro not-tay dee

New Zealand la Nuova Zelanda
nwova dzaylanda

**New Zealander: I'm a New
Zealander** sono neozelandese
nay-odzelandayzay

next prossimo

**the next turning/street on
the left** la prossima svolta/
strada a sinistra

at the next stop alla
prossima fermata

next week la settimana
prossima

next to vicino a veecheeno

nice (food) buono bwono

(looks, view etc) bello

(person) simpatico

niece la nipote neepotay

night la notte not-tay

at night di notte

good night buonanotte
bwonanot-tay

**do you have a single room
for one night?** avete una
stanza singola per una
notte? avaytay oona stantza

yes, madam sì, signora

how much is it per night?
quanto si paga per notte?
pair

it's 75 euros for one night
settantacinque euro per
notte set-tantacheenkway
ay-ooro

thank you, I'll take it grazie,
la prendo gratzee-ay

nightclub il night

nightdress la camicia da notte
kam**ee**cha da n**o**t-tay

night porter il portiere di notte
port-y**ai**ray dee

no no

I've no change non ho
spiccioli o speech-yolee

there's no… left non c'è più…
chay p-yoo

no way! assolutam**e**nte no!

oh no! (upset) oh no!

nobody nessuno nes-s**oo**no

there's nobody there non c'è
nessuno chay

noise il rumore room**o**ray

noisy: it's too noisy c'è tr**o**ppo
rumore

non-alcoholic analc**o**lico

none nessuno nes-s**oo**no

nonsmoking compartment la
carrozza per non fumatori kar-
r**o**tza pair non foomat**o**ree

noon mezzogiorno medzoj**o**rno

no-one nessuno nes-s**oo**no

nor: nor do I nemmeno io nem-
m**ay**no **ee**-o

normal normale norm**a**lay

north il nord

in the north al nord

north of Rome a nord di Roma

northern settentrionale set-tentr-
yon**a**lay

Northern Ireland l'Irlanda del
Nord *f* eerl**a**nda

Norway la Norvegia norv**a**yja

nose il naso

nosebleed il sangue dal naso
s**a**ngway

not non

no, I'm not hungry no, non
ho fame o f**a**may

I don't want any, thank you
non ne voglio, gr**a**zie nay v**o**l-yo

it's not necessary non è
necessario ay neches-s**a**r-yo

I didn't know that non lo
sapevo sap**ay**vo

not that one – this one non
quello – questo kw**e**l-lo – kw**e**sto

note (banknote) la bancon**o**ta

notebook il notes

notepaper (for letters) la c**a**rta da
l**e**ttere l**e**t-tairay

nothing niente n-y**e**ntay

nothing for me, thanks per
me niente, gr**a**zie pair may

nothing else nient'altro

novel il romanzo rom**a**ndzo

November novembre nov**e**mbray

now adesso

number il numero n**oo**mairo

I've got the wrong number
ho sbagliato numero o zbal-y**a**to

**what is your phone
number?** qual è il tuo/suo
numero di telefono? kwal ay eel
t**oo**-o/s**oo**-o

number plate la targa

nurse (*male/female*) l'infermiere *m*
enfairm-y**ai**ray/ l'infermi**e**ra *f*

nursery slope la pista per
principianti pair preencheep-
y**a**ntee

nuts le noci n**o**chee

O

o'clock: at 7 o'clock alle sette
al-lay

occupied (toilet) occupato
ok-koopato

October ottobre ot-tobray

odd (strange) strano

of di dee

off (lights) spento

  it's just off corso Europa
è una traversa di corso Europa
ay – travairsa

  we're off tomorrow (leaving)
partiamo domani part-yamo

offensive offensivo

office (place of work) l'ufficio *m*
oof-feecho

officer (said to policeman) agente
ajentay

often spesso

  not often non spesso

  how often are the buses?
ogni quanto passano gli
autobus? on-yee kwanto

oil l'olio *m* ol-yo

ointment l'unguento *m* oongwento

OK d'accordo

  are you OK? tutto bene?
toot-to baynay

  is that OK with you? ti/le va
bene? lay

  is it OK to…? si può…? pwo

  that's OK thanks va bene
così grazie kozee

  I'm OK (nothing for me) io sono
a posto ee-o

  (I feel OK) sto bene

  is this train OK for…? questo
treno va bene per…? kwesto

  I said I'm sorry, OK
ho chiesto scusa, va bene?
ok-yesto skooza

old vecchio vek-yo

DIALOGUE

how old are you? quanti
anni ha? kwantee an-nee a

I'm twenty-five ho
venticinque anni o

and you? e lei? ay lay

old-fashioned fuori moda
fworee

old town (old part of town) la città
vecchia cheet-ta vek-ya

  in the old town nella città
vecchia

olive oil l'olio di oliva *m* ol-yo

olives le olive oleevay

  black/green olives le olive
nere/verdi nairay/vairdee

omelette la frittata

on su soo

  on the street/beach
sulla strada/sulla spiaggia

  is it on this road? è su questa
strada? ay soo kwesta

  on the plane sull'aereo

  on Saturday sabato

  on television alla televisione

  I haven't got it on me non
ce l'ho con me non chay lo kon
may

  this one's on me (drink)
offro io da bere ee-o da bairay

the light wasn't on la luce non era accesa *loochay non aira achayza*

what's on tonight? cosa c'è da vedere stasera? *koza chay da vedairay stasaira*

once (one time) una volta

at once (immediately) immediatamente *eem-med-yatamentay*

one uno *oono*, una *oona*

the white one quello bianco, *kwel-lo*, quella bianca

one-way ticket: a one-way ticket to… un biglietto di sola andata per… *beel-yet-to – pair*

onions le cipolle *cheepol-lay*

online (book, check) on-line

only solo

only one solo uno

it's only 6 o'clock sono solo le sei

I've only just got here sono appena arrivato *ap-payna*

on/off switch l'interruttore *m eentair-root-toray*

open (*adj*) aperto *apairto*

(*verb:* door, of shop) aprire *apreeray*

when do you open? quando aprite? *kwando apreetay*

I can't get it open non riesco ad aprirlo/aprirla *r-yesko ad apreerlo/apreerla*

in the open air all'aria aperta

opening times l'orario di apertura *m orar-yo dee apairtoora*

open ticket il biglietto aperto *beel-yet-to apairto*

opera l'opera *f opaira*

operation (medical) l'operazione *f opairatz-yonay*

opposite: the opposite direction la direzione opposta *deeretz-yonay*

the bar opposite il bar di fronte *frontay*

opposite my hotel di fronte al mio albergo

optician l'ottico *m*

or o

orange (fruit) l'arancia *f arancha* (colour) arancione *aranchonay*

orange juice il succo d'arancia *sook-ko*

(freshly squeezed) la spremuta d'arancia *spremoota*

(fizzy) l'aranciata *f aranchata*

orchestra l'orchestra *f*

order: can we order now? (in restaurant) possiamo ordinare ora? *pos-yamo ordeenaray*

I've already ordered, thanks ho già ordinato, grazie *o ja*

I didn't order this non ho ordinato questo *kwesto*

out of order fuori servizio *fworee sairveetz-yo*

ordinary ordinario

other altro

the other one l'altro, l'altra

the other day l'altro giorno

I'm waiting for the others aspetto gli altri *aspet-to l-yee*

do you have any others?
ne avete degli altri? nay avaytay
dayl-yee

otherwise altrimenti

our il nostro, la nostra
(*plural*) i nostri, le nostre

ours il nostro, la nostra, i nostri,
le nostre

out: he's out è fuori ay fworee

**three kilometres out of
town** tre chilometri fuori città
keelometree fworee cheet-ta

outdoors all'aperto apairto

outside fuori di fworee dee

can we sit outside?
possiamo sedere fuori?
pos-yamo sedairay

oven il forno

over: over here qui kwee

over there lì

over 500 più di cinquecento
p-yoo

it's over è finito/finita ay

**overcharge: you've
overcharged me** c'è un errore
nel conto chay oon air-roray

**overlook: I'd like a room
overlooking the courtyard**
vorrei una stanza che dia sul
cortile vor-ray – kay dee-a sool
korteelay

overcoat il soprabito

overnight (travel) di notte
dee not-tay

overtake sorpassare sorpas-saray

**owe: how much do I owe
you?** quanto le devo? kwanto
lay dayvo

own: my own... il mio...

are you on your own?
è da solo/sola? ay

I'm on my own sono da solo/
sola

owner (*male/female*)
il proprietario propree-etar-yo,
la proprietaria

pack (*verb*) fare le valigie faray lay
valeejay

a pack of... un pacco di...

package (small parcel) il pacco

package holiday la vacanza
organizzata vakantza
organeetzata

packed lunch il pranzo al sacco
prandzo

packet: a packet of cigarettes
un pacchetto di sigarette
pak-ket-to dee seegaret-tay

padlock il lucchetto look-ket-to

Padua Padova padova

page (of book) la pagina pajeena

could you page Mr...?
può far chiamare il signor...?
pwo – k-yamaray

pain il dolore doloray

I have a pain here mi fa male
qui mee fa malay kwee

painful doloroso

painkillers gli analgesici
analjayzeechee

paint la vernice vairneechay

painting il dipinto

pair: a pair of... un paio di... pa-yo

Pakistani pachistano pakeestano

palace il palazzo palatzo

pale pallido

  pale blue blu chiaro k-yaro

pan la pentola

panties le mutande mootanday

pants (underwear: men's/women's) le mutande

  (trousers) i pantaloni

pantyhose il collant kol-lan

paper la carta

  (newspaper) il giornale jornalay

  a piece of paper un pezzo di carta petzo

paper handkerchiefs i fazzoletti di carta fatzolet-tee

parcel il pacco

pardon (me)? (didn't understand/hear) prego? praygo

parents i genitori jeneetoree

parents-in-law i suoceri swochairee

park il parco

  (verb: the car) parcheggiare parkej-jaray

  can I park here? posso parcheggiare qui? kwee

parking lot il parcheggio parkej-jo

part la parte partay

partner (boyfriend, girlfriend etc) il/la partner

party (group) il gruppo groop-po

  (celebration) la festa

pass (in mountains) il passo

passenger (male/female)

il passeggero pas-sej-jairo, la passeggera

passport il passaporto

password la password

past: in the past in passato

  just past the information office appena dopo l'ufficio informazioni ap-payna

path il sentiero sent-yairo

pattern il motivo

pavement il marciapiede marchap-yayday

  on the pavement sul marciapiede

pavement café il caffè all'aperto kaf-fay al-lapairto

pay (verb) pagare pagaray

  can I pay, please? il conto, per favore

  it's already paid for è già pagato ay ja

---

pay phone il telefono pubblico

peaceful tranquillo trankweelo

peach la pesca

peanuts le arachidi arakeedee

pear la perla pairla

peas i piselli

peculiar strano

pedestrian crossing il passaggio pedonale

pas-**saj**-jo peda**nalay**

pedestrian precinct la zona
 pedonale tz**o**na

peg (for washing) la mol**le**tta
 (for tent) il picchetto peek-**ket**-to

pen la p**e**nna

pencil la ma**ti**ta

penfriend il/la corrispondente
 kor-reespon**den**tay

penicillin la penicillina
 peneecheel-**lee**na

penknife il temperino
 tempai**ree**no

pensioner (male/female) il
 pensionato pens-yo**na**to, la
 pensio**na**ta

people la gente j**e**ntay

 **the other people in the
 hotel** le altre persone
 all'albergo lay **a**ltray pai**rso**nay

 too many people troppa
 gente tr**o**p-pa

pepper (spice) il pepe p**ay**pay
 (vegetable) il peperone pepe**ro**nay

peppermint (sweet) la caram**e**lla
 alla m**e**nta

per: per night a notte n**o**t-tay

 how much per day? quanto
 (c**o**sta) al gi**o**rno? kw**a**nto

 per cent per cento pair ch**e**nto

perfect perfetto pair**fe**t-to

perfume il profumo pro**foo**mo

perhaps forse f**o**rsay

 perhaps not forse no

period (of time) il periodo pai**ree**-odo
 (menstruation) le mestruazioni
 mestroo-atz-y**o**nee

perm la permanente pairma**ne**ntay

permit il permesso pair**me**s-so

person la persona pai**rso**na

petrol la benzina bent**zee**na

petrol can la latta di benzina
 bent**zee**na

petrol station la stazione
 di servizio statz-y**o**nay dee
 sair**vee**tz-yo

pharmacy la farmacia
 farma**chee**-a

phone il telefono te**lay**fono
 (verb) telefonare telefo**na**ray

phone book l'elenco
 tele**fo**nico m

phone box la cabina tele**fo**nica

phonecard la scheda telefonica
 sk**ay**da, la c**a**rta telefonica

phone charger il caricatore
 kareeka**to**ray

phone number il numero di
 telefono n**oo**mairo dee te**lay**fono

photo la fotografia fotogra**fee**-a

 **excuse me, could you take
 a photo of us?** scusi, può
 farci una fotografia? sk**oo**zee,
 pwo f**a**rchee

phrasebook il frasario fra**za**r-yo

piano il pianof**o**rte

pickpocket (male/female)
 il borsaiolo borsa-y**o**lo,
 la borsai**o**la

**pick up: will you be there to
 pick me up?** vieni/viene a
 prendermi li? vy**ay**nee/vy**ay**nay a
 pr**e**ndairmee

picnic il picnic

picture (painting) il quadro kw**a**dro
  (photo) la fotografia fotograf**ee**-a
pie (meat) il pasticcio past**ee**cho
  (fruit) la t**o**rta
piece il pezzo p**e**tzo
  a piece of... un pezzo di...
pill la p**i**llola
  I'm on the pill pr**e**ndo la
  pillola
pillow il cuscino koosh**ee**no
pillow case la federa f**a**ydaira
pin lo spillo sp**ee**l-lo
pineapple l'**a**nanas *m*
pineapple juice il succo
  d'ananas s**oo**k-ko
pink r**o**sa
pipe (for smoking) la p**i**pa
  (for water) il tubo t**oo**bo
pipe cleaners gli scovol**i**ni
pity: it's a pity è un pecc**a**to ay

pizza la p**i**zza
place il p**o**sto
  is this place taken?
  è occupato questo posto?
  ay ok-koop**a**to kw**e**sto
  at your place a c**a**sa tua/sua
  t**oo**-a/s**oo**-a
  at his place a c**a**sa sua
plain (not patterned) in t**i**nta unita
  oon**ee**ta
plane l'aereo *m* a-**a**iray-o
  by plane in aereo
plant la pianta p-y**a**nta
plaster cast il gesso j**e**s-so
plasters i cerotti chair**o**t-tee
plastic la pl**a**stica
  (credit card) la carta di credito
  kr**a**yd**e**eto
plastic bag il sacchetto di
  plastica sak-k**e**t-to
plate il piatto p-y**a**t-to

platform il marciapiede
marchapy**ay**day

**which platform is it for
Milan, please?** su quale
binario parte il treno per
Milano, per favore? soo kw**a**lay
beenar-yo p**a**rtay eel tr**a**yno pair

play (*verb:* game, sport) giocare
jok**a**ray

(*instrument*) suonare swon**a**ray

(*noun:* in theatre) la commedia
kom-m**a**yd-ya

playground il parco giochi j**o**kee

pleasant piacevole p-yach**a**yvolay

please per favore pair fav**o**ray

yes please sì, grazie see
gr**a**tzee-ay

could you please…?
potrebbe per favore…? potr**a**yb-
bay

please don't… per favore
non…

pleased to meet you piacere
di conoscerla p-yach**a**iray dee
konosh**a**irla

pleasure il piacere
my pleasure (not at all)
non c'è di che chay dee kay

plenty: plenty of…
molto/molta/molti/molte…

there's plenty of time
c'è (ancora) molto tempo chay

that's plenty, thanks basta
così, grazie koz**ee** gr**a**tzee-ay

pliers le pinze p**ee**ntzay

plug (electrical) la spina
(for car) la candela kand**a**yla

(in sink) il tappo

plumber l'idraulico *m*
eedr**ow**leeko

p.m. del pomeriggio pomair**eej**-jo
(in the evening) di sera s**a**ira

poached egg l'uovo in camicia
m lw**o**vo een kam**ee**cha

pocket la tasca

point: two point five
due virgola cinque

there's no point è inutile
ay een**oo**teelay

points (in car) le puntine poont**ee**nay

poisonous velenoso velen**o**zo

police la polizia poleetz**ee**-a

(military police) i carabinieri
karabeen-y**a**iree

call the police! chiamate la
polizia! k-yam**a**tay

policeman il poliziotto
poleetz-y**o**t-to

police station il commissariato

policewoman la donna
poliziotto poleetz-y**o**t-to

polish il lucido l**oo**cheedo

polite educato edook**a**to

polluted inquinato eenkween**a**to

pony il pony

pool (for swimming) la piscina
peesh**ee**na

poor (not rich) povero p**o**vairo
(quality) scadente skad**e**ntay

Pope il Papa

pop music la musica pop
mooz**ee**ka

pop singer il/la cantante pop
kant**a**ntay

population la popolazione
popolatz-yonay

pork il maiale my-alay

port il porto

porter (in hotel) il portiere
port-yairay

portrait il ritratto

posh chic sheek

possible possibile pos-seebeelay

  is it possible to…?
  è possibile…? ay

  as soon as possible al più
  presto possibile p-yoo

post (mail) la posta

  (*verb*) impostare eempostaray

  could you post this for me?
  potrebbe imbucare questa per
  me? potreb-bay eembookaray
  kwesta pair may

postbox la buca delle lettere
booka del-lay let-tairay

postcard la cartolina

postcode il codice postale
kodeechay postalay

poster il manifesto

post office l'ufficio postale *m*
oof-feecho postalay

poste restante il fermo posta
fairmo

potato la patata

potato chips le patatine
patateenay

pots and pans le pentole pentolay

pottery la ceramica chairameeka

pound (money) la sterlina
stairleena

  (weight) la libbra

power cut l'interruzione della
corrente *f* eentair-rootz-yonay
del-la kor-rentay

power point la presa di corrente
prayza dee

**practise: I want to practise
my Italian** voglio esercitarmi
a parlare italiano vol-yo
esaircheetarmee a parlaray

prawns i gamberetti
gambairet-tee

prefer: I prefer… preferisco…
prefaireesko

pregnant incinta eencheenta

prescription (for medicine)
la ricetta reechet-ta

present il regalo

president (of country) il/la
presidente prezeedentay

pretty grazioso gratz-yozo

  it's pretty expensive
  è piuttosto caro ay p-yootosto

price il prezzo pretzo

priest il sacerdote sachairdotay

prime minister il primo
ministro

printed matter le stampe
stampay

priority (in driving) la precedenza
prechedentza

prison la prigione preejonay

private privato

private bathroom il bagno in
camera ban-yo een kamaira

probably probabilmente
probabeelmentay

problem il problema problayma

no problem! nessun problema

program(me) il programma

promise: I promise prometto

pronounce: how is this pronounced? come si pronuncia? komay see pronooncha

properly (repaired, locked etc) bene baynay

protection factor il fattore di protezione fat-toray dee protetz-yonay

Protestant protestante -tantay

public convenience i gabinetti pubblici poob-bleechee

public holiday la festa nazionale natzyonalay

pudding il dessert des-sair

pull tirare teeraray

pullover il pullover

puncture la foratura foratoora

purple viola v-yola

purse (for money) il portamonete portamonaytay

(US) la borsetta

push spingere speenjairay

pushchair il passeggino pas-sej-jeeno

put mettere met-tairay

where can I put...? dove posso mettere...? dovay

could you put us up for the night? ci può ospitare per una notte? chee pwo ospeetaray pair

pyjamas il pigiama peejama

Q

quality la qualità kwaleeta

quarantine la quarantena kwarantayna

quarter il quarto kwarto

quayside: on the quayside sulla banchina sool-la bankeena

question la domanda

queue la fila

quick veloce velochay

that was quick che velocità kay velocheeta

what's the quickest way there? qual è il modo più rapido per arrivarci? kwal ay eel modo p-yoo rapeedo pair arreevarchee

fancy a quick drink? ti/le va di bere qualcosa rapidamente? lay – bairay kwalkoza rapeedamentay

quickly velocemente velochementay

quiet (place, hotel) tranquillo trankweel-lo

quiet! silenzio! seelentz-yo

quite (fairly) abbastanza ab-bastantza

(very) molto

that's quite right è proprio giusto ay – joosto

quite a lot moltissimo

R

rabbit il coniglio kon**ee**l-yo
race (for runners, cars) la c**o**rsa
racket (tennis, squash) la racchetta rak-ket-ta
radiator il radiatore rad-yat**o**ray
radio la r**a**dio

  on the radio alla radio
rail: by rail in treno tr**a**yno
railway la ferrovia fair-rov**ee**-a
rain la pioggia p-y**o**j-ja

  in the rain s**o**tto la pioggia

  it's raining piove p-y**o**vay
raincoat l'impermeabile *m* eempairmay-ab**ee**lay
randy arrap**a**to
rape lo stupro st**oo**pro
rare (steak) al sangue s**a**ngway
rash (on skin) l'eruzione cutanea *f* erootz-y**o**nay kootan**ay**-a
raspberry il lampone lamp**o**nay
rat il r**a**tto
rate (for changing money) il cambio k**a**mb-yo
rather: it's rather good è piuttosto buono ay p-yoot-tosto bw**o**no

  I'd rather... preferirei... prefaireer**ay**
razor il rasoio ras**o**-yo
razor blades le lamette lam**e**t-tay
read (*verb*) leggere l**e**j-jairay
ready pr**o**nto

  are you ready? sei/è pronto/pronta? say/ay

I'm not ready yet non s**o**no ancora pronto/pronta

real reale ray-**a**lay
really veramente vairam**e**ntay

  I'm really sorry sono veramente spiacente spee-ach**e**ntay

  that's really great è proprio magnifico

  really? davvero? dav-v**a**iro
rearview mirror lo specchietto retrovisore spek-y**e**t-to retroveez**o**ray
reasonable (prices etc) moder**a**to
receipt la ricevuta reechev**oo**ta
recently recentemente rechentem**e**ntay
reception (in hotel) la reception

  (for guests) il ricevimento reecheveem**e**nto

  at reception alla reception
reception desk la reception
receptionist il/la receptionist
recognize riconoscere reekon**o**shairay
recommend: could you recommend...? mi potrebbe consigliare...? mee potr**e**b-bay konseel-y**a**ray

record (music) il disco

red rosso

red wine il vino rosso

refund il rimborso

can I have a refund?
mi può rimborsare?
pwo reemborsaray

region la regione rejonay

registered: by registered mail
(per) raccomandata

registration number il numero
di immatricolazione noomairo
dee eemmatreekolatz-yonay

relative il/la parente parentay

religion la religione releejonay

remember: I don't remember
non ricordo

I remember mi ricordo

do you remember?
ti ricordi/si ricorda?

rent (for apartment etc) l'affitto *m*
(*verb*) noleggiare nolej-jaray

to rent a nolo

rented car la macchina a
noleggio mak-keena a nolej-jo

repair (*verb*) riparare reepararay

can you repair it?
lo/la può riparare? pwo

repeat ripetere repetairay

could you repeat that?
può ripetere? pwo

reservation la prenotazione
prenotatz-yonay

**I'd like to make a
reservation** vorrei prenotare
vor-ray prenotaray

I have a reservation
ho prenotato o

**yes sir, what name
please?** sì, a che nome?
kay nomay

reserve prenotare prenotaray

**can I reserve a table for
tonight?** vorrei prenotare
un tavolo per stasera vor-ray
– un tavolo per stasaira

**yes madam, for how many
people?** sì, signora, per
quante persone? seen-yora,
pair kwantay pairsonay

for two per due

and for what time?
per che ora? pair kay

for eight o'clock
per le otto lay

**and could I have your
name please?** il suo
nome, per favore?
soo-o nomay

see **alphabet** for spelling

rest: I need a rest ho bisogno
di riposarmi o beezon-yo

the rest of the group
il resto del gruppo

restaurant il ristorante
reestorantay

rest room la toilette twalet
see **toilet**

retired: I'm retired sono in
pensione pens-yonay

return (ticket) il biglietto di andata e ritorno beel-yet-to see **ticket**

reverse charge call la telefonata a carico del destinatario

reverse gear la retromarcia retromarcha

revolting disgustoso deezgoostozo

rib la costola

rice il riso reezo

rich (person) ricco reek-ko
(food) sostanzioso sostantz-yozo

ridiculous ridicolo

right (correct) giusto joosto
(not left) destro

    you were right avevi/aveva ragione avayvee/avayva rajonay

    that's right è giusto ay

    this can't be right non è possibile ay pos-seebeelay

    right! d'accordo

    is this the right road for...? è la strada giusta per...? ay – pair

    on the right a destra

    turn right giri a destra jeeree

right-hand drive la guida a destra gweeda

ring (on finger) l'anello *m*

    I'll ring you ti/le telefono lay telayfono

ring back ritelefonare reetelefonaray

ripe (fruit) maturo matooro

rip-off: it's a rip-off è un furto ay oon foorto

rip-off prices i prezzi esorbitanti pretzee

risky rischioso reesk-yozo

river il fiume f-yoomay

road la strada

    is this the road for...? è questa la strada per...? ay kwesta – pair

    down the road in fondo alla strada

road accident l'incidente stradale *m* eencheedentay stradalay

road map la cartina stradale

roadsign il segnale stradale sen-yalay

rob: I've been robbed sono stato derubato/derubata! dairoobato

rock la roccia rocha
(music) il rock

    on the rocks (with ice) con ghiaccio g-yacho

roll (bread) il panino

Roman (*adj*) romano

    the Romans i Romani

Rome Roma

roof il tetto

roof rack il portapacchi portapak-kee

room la camera, la stanza stantza

    in my room nella mia stanza mee-a

room service il servizio in camera sairveetz-yo een

rope la corda

rosé il rosé

roughly (approximately)
grossom**o**do

round: it's my round t**o**cca a
me may

roundabout (for traffic) la
rotat**o**ria

round trip ticket il biglietto di
and**a**ta e rit**o**rno beel-y**e**t-to
see **ticket**

route il tragitto traj**ee**t-to

what's the best route?
qual è il tragitto migliore?
kwal**a**y – meel-y**o**ray

rubber (material) la g**o**mma

(eraser) la g**o**mma (per
cancell**a**re) pair kanchel-l**a**ray

rubber band l'el**a**stico *m*

rubbish (waste) i rifiuti reef-
y**oo**tee

(poor quality goods) la porcheria
porkair**ee**-a

rubbish! (nonsense)
sciocchezze! shok-k**e**tzay

rucksack lo zaino tza-**ee**no

rude sgarb**a**to zgarb**a**to

ruins le rovine rov**ee**nay

rum il rum room

rum and Coke la C**o**ca-Cola
col rum

run (*verb:* person) c**o**rrere k**o**r-rairay

**how often do the buses
run?** ogni quanto t**e**mpo p**a**ssa
l'autobus? **o**n-yee kw**a**nto –
l**o**wtoboos

I've run out of money
s**o**no rim**a**sto senza s**o**ldi s**e**ntza

rush hour l'**o**ra di p**u**nta *f*

S

sad triste tr**ee**stay

saddle (for bike, horse) la s**e**lla

safe (not in danger) sicuro seek**oo**ro

(not dangerous) non pericoloso
pair**ee**kolozo

safety pin la spilla di sicurezza
seekoor**e**tza

sail la vela v**a**yla

sailboard la t**a**vola a vela

sailboarding il windsurf

salad l'insal**a**ta *f*

salad dressing il condim**e**nto
per l'insal**a**ta pair

sale: for sale vendesi vend**e**see

salmon il salmone sal-m**o**nay

salt il sale s**a**lay

same: the same lo st**e**sso

the same as this come
questo k**o**may kw**e**sto

the same again, please
un altro/un'altra, per fav**o**re

it's all the same to me
per me è lo st**e**sso pair may ay

sand la s**a**bbia

sandals i s**a**ndali

sandwich il panino imbott**i**to

sanitary napkins gli assorbenti
igienici as-sorb**e**ntee eej**a**ynee-
chee

sanitary towels gli assorbenti
igienici

sardines le sardine sard**ee**nay

Sardinia la Sardegna sar-d**a**yn-ya

Saturday il s**a**bato

sauce la salsa

saucepan la pentola

saucer il piattino p-yat-teeno

sauna la sauna sowna

sausage la salsiccia salseecha

say: how do you say... in Italian? come si dice... in italiano? komay see deechay... een eetal-yano

what did he/she say? cos'ha detto? koz a

I said... ho detto... o

he/she said... ha detto... a

could you say that again? puoi/può ripetere, per favore? pwoy/pwo reepetairay

scarf (for neck) la sciarpa sharpa (for head) il foulard foolar

scenery il paesaggio pa-ee-zaj-jo

schedule l'orario m

scheduled flight il volo di linea leenay-a

school la scuola skwola

scissors: a pair of scissors un paio di forbici pa-yo dee forbeechee

scooter lo scooter

Scotch lo scotch

Scotch tape lo scotch

Scotland la Scozia skotz-ya

Scottish scozzese skotzayzay

I'm Scottish sono scozzese

scrambled eggs le uova strapazzate wova strapatzatay

scratch il graffio graf-fyo

screw la vite veetay

screwdriver il cacciavite kachaveetay

scrubbing brush (for hands) lo spazzolino per le unghie spatzoleeno pair lay oong-yay

sea il mare maray

by the sea sul mare sool

seafood i frutti di mare froot-tee dee

seafront il lungomare loongomaray

on the seafront sul lungomare sool

seagull il gabbiano gab-yano

search (verb) cercare chairkaray

seashell la conchiglia konkeel-ya

seasick: I feel seasick ho mal di mare o – maray

I get seasick soffro di mal di mare

seaside: by the seaside sul mare sool

seat il posto

is this anyone's seat? è libero questo posto? ay leebairo kwesto

seat belt la cintura di sicurezza cheentoora dee seekooretza

sea urchin il riccio di mare reecho dee maray

seaweed le alghe marine algay mareenay

secluded isolato

second (adj) secondo (of time) il secondo

just a second! un attimo!

second class (travel) in seconda classe klas-say

second floor (UK) il secondo
piano

(US) il primo piano

second-hand di seconda mano

see vedere vedairay

  can I see? posso vedere?

  have you seen…? hai/ha
  visto… a-ee/a

  I see (I understand) capisco

  I saw him this morning
  l'ho visto stamattina lo

self-catering apartment
l'appartamento (per le vacanze)
m pair lay vakantzay

self-service il self-service

sell vendere vendairay

  do you sell…? avete…?
  avaytay

Sellotape lo scotch

send mandare mandaray

  I want to send this to
  England voglio mandare
  questo in Inghilterra vol-yo –
  kwesto een eengeeltair-ra

senior citizen (male/female)
il pensionato, la pensionata

separate separato

separated: I'm separated
sono separato/separata

separately (pay) a parte partay

  (travel) separatamente
  separatamentay

September settembre set-
tembray

septic infetto

serious serio sair-yo

service charge (in restaurant)
il servizio sairveetz-yo

service station la stazione
di servizio statz-yonay dee
sairveetz-yo

serviette il tovagliolo toval-yolo

set menu il menù fisso menoo

several diversi deevairsee

sew cucire koocheeray

  could you sew this back
  on? potrebbe riattaccarlo?
  potreb-bay r-yat-tak-karlo

sex il sesso

  (sexual intercourse) il rapporto
  sessuale ses-swalay

sexy sexy

shade: in the shade all'ombra

shake: to shake hands
stringersi la mano streenjairsee

shallow (water) poco profondo

shame: what a shame!
che peccato! kay

shampoo lo shampoo

  shampoo and set shampoo e
  messa in piega ay – p-yayga

share (verb: room, table etc)
dividere deeveedairay

sharp (knife) tagliente tal-yentay

  (taste) aspro

  (pain) acuto akooto

shattered (very tired) distrutto
deestroot-to

shaver il rasoio razo-yo

shaving foam la schiuma da
barba sk-yooma

shaving point la presa per il
rasoio prayza pair eel razo-yo

she lei lay

  is she here? è qui? ay kwee

sheet (for bed) il lenzuolo lentzwolo

shelf lo scaffale skaf-falay

shellfish i frutti di mare froot-tee
dee maray

sherry lo sherry

ship la nave navay

  by ship con la nave

shirt la camicia kameecha

shit! merda! mairda

shock lo shock

  **I got an electric shock from
the...** ho preso la scossa dal...
o prayzo

shock-absorber
l'ammortizzatore *m*
am-morteetzatoray

shocking scandaloso

shoe la scarpa

  a pair of shoes un paio di
scarpe pa-yo dee skarpay

shoelaces i lacci

shoe polish il lucido per le
scarpe loocheedo pair lay skarpay

shoe repairer il calzolaio
kalzola-yo

shop il negozio negotz-yo

shopping: I'm going shopping
vado a far compere kompairay

shopping centre il centro
commerciale chentro kom-
mairchalay

shop window la vetrina

shore la riva

short (person) basso

  (time) poco

  (journey) corto

shortcut la scorciatoia
skorchato-ya

shorts i calzoncini
kaltzoncheenee

should: what should I do?
cosa dovrei fare?
koza dovray faray

  he shouldn't be long non ci
dovrebbe mettere tanto chee
dovreb-bay met-tairay

  you should have told me
avresti dovuto dirmelo
dovooto deermelo

shoulder la spalla

shout (*verb*) gridare greedaray

show (in theatre) lo spettacolo

  could you show me? mi può
far vedere? mee pwo far vedairay

shower (in bathroom) la doccia
docha

  with shower con doccia

shower gel il gel per la doccia pair

shut (*verb*) chiudere k-yoodairay

  when do you shut? quando
chiudete? kwando k-yoodaytay

Travel tip Most shops and
businesses open Mon–Sat
8am–1pm and 4–7pm,
though many close Saturday
afternoons and Monday
mornings. In the south opening hours can begin and end
an hour later. Traditionally,
everything except bars
and restaurants closes on
Sunday, though in large cities and tourist areas Sunday
shopping is becoming more
common.

---

when do they shut? quando chiudono? k-y**oo**dono

they're shut sono chiusi k-y**oo**see

I've shut myself out mi sono chiuso fuori k-y**oo**zo fw**o**ree

shut up! stai zitto! sty tz**ee**t-to

shutter (on camera) l'otturatore *m* ot-toorat**o**ray

(on window) l'imp**o**sta *f*

shy t**i**mido

Sicily la Sicilia seech**ee**l-ya

sick mal**a**to

I'm going to be sick (vomit) sto per vomitare pair vomeet**a**ray

see **ill**

side il l**a**to

the other side of town l'**a**ltra parte della citt**à** partay del-la cheet-t**a**

side lights le luci di posizione l**oo**chee dee poseetz-y**o**nay

side salad l'insal**a**ta *f*

side street la stradina strad**ee**na

sidewalk il marciapiede marchap-y**ay**day

see **pavement**

sight: the sights of… le attrazioni turistiche di… at-tratz-y**o**nee toor**ee**steekay

sightseeing: we're going sightseeing andiamo a fare un giro turistico and-y**a**mo a f**a**ray oon j**ee**ro

sightseeing tour il giro turistico

sign (roadsign etc) il segnale sen-y**a**lay

signal: he didn't give a signal non ha segnalato a sen-yal**a**to

signature la f**i**rma

signpost il cartello stradale strad**a**lay

silence il silenzio seel**e**ntz-yo

silk la seta s**a**yta

silly sciocco sh**o**k-ko

silver l'argento *m* arj**e**nto

silver foil la stagnola stan-y**o**la

similar simile s**ee**meelay

simple (easy) semplice s**e**mpleechay

since: since yesterday da ieri y**a**iree

since I got here da quando sono arriv**a**to/arriv**a**ta kw**a**ndo

sing cantare kant**a**ray

singer il/la cantante kant**a**ntay

single: a single to… un biglietto di sola andata per… beel-y**e**t-to – pair

I'm single (male/female) sono celibe/n**u**bile ch**a**ylee-bay/n**oo**beelay

single bed il letto a una piazza p-y**a**tza

single room la camera s**i**ngola

sink (in kitchen) l'acquaio *m* akw**a**-yo

sister la sor**e**lla

sister-in-law la cognata kon-y**a**ta

sit: can I sit here? p**o**sso sedere qui? sed**a**iray kwee

is anyone sitting here? è l**i**bero questo posto? ay l**ee**bairo kw**e**sto

sit down sedersi sed**ai**rsee

size la taglia tal-ya

ski lo sci shee

    (*verb*) sciare shee-**a**ray

    a pair of skis un paio di sci
    pa-yo dee

ski boots gli scarponi da sci

skiing lo sci

    we're going skiing andiamo
    a sciare and-yamo a shee-**a**ray

ski instructor (*male/female*)
il maestro di sci m**y**stro dee
shee/la maestra di sci

ski-lift lo ski-lift

skin la pelle p**e**l-lay

skin-diving l'immersione senza
attrezzature *f* eem-mairs-y**o**nay
senza at-trez-zat**oo**ray

skinny mingherlino
meengairl**ee**no

ski-pants i calzoni da sci
kaltz**o**nee da shee

ski-pass lo ski-pass

ski pole la racchetta da sci
rak-k**e**t-ta da shee

skirt la gonna

ski run la pista da sci shee

ski slope il campo da sci

ski wax la sciolina shee-ol**ee**na

sky il cielo ch**a**ylo

sleep (*verb*) dormire dorm**ee**ray

    did you sleep well? hai/ha
    dormito bene? a-ee/a – b**a**ynay

    I need a good sleep ho
    bisogno di fare una buona
    dormita o beez**o**n-yo dee f**a**ray
    oona bw**o**na

sleeper (on train) il vagone letto
vag**o**nay

sleeping bag il sacco a pelo p**a**ylo

sleeping car il vagone letto
vag**o**nay

sleeping pill il sonnifero
son-n**ee**fairo

sleepy: I'm feeling sleepy
ho sonno o

sleeve la manica

slide (photographic) la diapositiva

slip (under dress) la sottoveste
sot-to-v**e**stay

slippery scivoloso sheevol**o**zo

Slovenia la Slovenia slo-v**a**yn-ya

slow lento

    slow down! (driving) rallenta!
    (speaking) parla/parli più
    lentamente! p-yoo lentam**a**ntay

slowly lentamente

    could you say it slowly?
    puoi/può dirlo più lentamente?
    pwoy/pwo d**ee**rlo p-yoo

    very slowly molto lentamente

small piccolo

smell: it smells (smells bad)
puzza p**oo**tza

smile (*verb*) sorridere sor-r**ee**dairay

smoke il fumo f**oo**mo

    do you mind if I smoke?
    ti/le dispiace se fumo? tee/lay
    deesp-y**a**chay say

    I don't smoke non fumo

    do you smoke? fumi/fuma?

snack: I'd just like a snack
vorrei fare uno spuntino vor-**ray**
f**a**ray **oo**no spoon-t**ee**no

sneeze lo sternuto stairn**oo**to

snorkel il respiratore respeerat**o**ray

snow la neve n**a**yvay

  it's snowing nevica n**a**yveeka

so: it's so expensive è così c**a**ro ay

  it's so good è pr**o**prio buono bw**o**no

  not so fast più pi**a**no p-yoo

  so am I anch'io ank**ee**-o

  so do I anch'io

  so-so così così

soaking solution (for contact lenses) la soluzione conservante e disinfettante per le lenti a contatto sol**oo**tz-y**o**nay konsairv**a**ntay ay deeseenfett**a**ntay pair lay

soap il sapone sap**o**nay

soap powder il detersivo (in polvere) detairs**ee**vo een p**o**lvairay

sober s**o**brio

sock il calzino kaltz**ee**no

socket (electrical) la presa pr**a**ysa

soda (water) il seltz

sofa il div**a**no

soft (material etc) m**o**rbido

soft-boiled egg l'uovo alla coque w**o**vo al-la kok

soft drink la bibita (analc**o**lica)

soft lenses le lenti morbide m**o**rbeeday

sole la suola sw**o**la

  could you put new soles on these? può risuolare queste scarpe? pwo reeswol**a**ray kw**e**stay sk**a**rpay

some: can I have some water/rolls? potrei avere

dell'acqua/dei panini?
potray avairay – day

can I have some? posso
averne un po'? avairnay

somebody, someone qualcuno
kwal-koono

something qualcosa kwalkoza

    something to drink qualcosa
    da bere bairay

sometimes qualche volta
kwalkay

somewhere da qualche parte
partay

son il figlio feel-yo

song la canzone kantzonay

son-in-law il genero jaynairo

soon presto

    I'll be back soon torno fra
    poco

    as soon as possible al più
    presto possibile p-yoo – pos-
    seebeelay

sore: it's sore mi fa male malay

sore throat il mal di gola

sorry: (I'm) sorry scusa/mi scusi
skooza/mee skoozee

    sorry? (didn't understand)
    prego? praygo

sort: what sort of…?
che tipo di…? kay

soup la minestra, la zuppa tzoop-pa

sour (taste) aspro

south il sud sood

    in the south al sud

South Africa il Sudafrica
soodafreeka

South African (adj) sudafricano
soodafree-kano

I'm South African (male/female)
sono sudafricano/sudafricana

southeast il sud-est soodest

southwest il sud-ovest soodovest

souvenir il souvenir

spanner la chiave inglese
k-yavay eenglayzay

spare part il pezzo di ricambio
petzo dee reekamb-yo

spare tyre la gomma di scorta

spark plug la candela kandayla

speak: do you speak English?
parla inglese? eenglayzay

    I don't speak… non parlo…

    can I speak to Roberto?
    posso parlare con Roberto?
    parlaray

    who's calling? chi parla? kee

    it's Patricia sono Patricia

    **I'm sorry, he's not in, can
    I take a message?** mi
    dispiace, non c'è; vuole
    lasciare un messaggio?
    mee deesp-yachay, non chay;
    vwolay lasharay oon mes-
    saj-jo

    **no thanks, I'll call back
    later** no, grazie, richiamo
    più tardi reek-yamo p-yoo

    please tell him I called gli
    dica che ho chiamato, per
    favore l-yee – kay o k-yamato

spectacles gli occhiali ok-yalee

speed la velocità velocheeta

speed limit il limite di velocità
leemee-tay dee

speedometer il tachimetro
takeemetro

spell: how do you spell it? come
si scrive? komay see skreevay

see **alphabet**

spend spendere spendairay

spider il ragno ran-yo

spin-dryer la centrifuga
chentreefooga

splinter la scheggia skej-ja

spoke (in wheel) il raggio raj-jo

spoon il cucchiaio kook-ya-yo

sport lo sport

sprain: I've sprained my...
mi sono slogato... zlogato

spring (season) la primavera
preema-vaira

(of car, seat) la molla

square (in town) la piazza p-yatza

stairs le scale skalay

stale (bread) raffermo raf-fairmo

**stall: the engine keeps
stalling** il motore si spegne
in continuazione motoray see
spen-yay een konteenoo-atz-yonay

stamp il francobollo

**a stamp for England,
please** un francobollo per
l'Inghilterra, per favore pair

what are you sending?
per che cosa? kay koza

this postcard per questa
cartolina kwesta

standby (flight) il volo stand-by

star la stella

start l'inizio m eeneetz-yo

(*verb*) cominciare komeencharay

when does it start? quando
comincia? kwando komeencha

the car won't start la
macchina non parte mak-keena

starter (of car) lo starter

(food) l'antipasto m

starving: I'm starving sto
morendo di fame famay

state (in country) lo stato

the States (USA) gli Stati Uniti
l-yee – ooneetee

station la stazione statz-yonay

statue la statua statoo-a

stay: where are you staying?
dov'è alloggiato/alloggiata?
dovay al-loj-jato

I'm staying at... sono
(alloggiato/alloggiata) a...

**I'd like to stay another two
nights** vorrei fermarmi ancora
due notti vor-ray fair-marmee

steak la bistecca

steal rubare roobaray

my bag has been stolen
mi hanno rubato la borsa mee
an-no roobato

steep (hill) ripido

steering lo sterzo stairtzo

step: on the steps sui gradini

stereo lo stereo stairay-o

sterling la sterlina stairleena

steward (on plane) lo steward

stewardess la hostess

sticking plaster il cerotto
chairot-to

still ancora

I'm still waiting sto ancora aspettando

is he still there? è ancora lì? ay

keep still! sta' fermo/ferma! fairmo

sting: I've been stung sono stato punto poonto

stockings le calze kaltzay

stomach lo stomaco

stomach ache il mal di stomaco

stone (rock) la pietra p-yetra

stop (verb) fermare fairmaray

please, stop here (to taxi driver etc) fermi qui, per favore fairmee kwee

do you stop near...? ferma vicino a...? veecheeno

stop doing that! smettila! zmet-teela

stopover la sosta

storm la tempesta

straight: straight ahead avanti diritto

a straight whisky un whisky liscio leesho

straightaway immediatamente eem-med-yatamentay

strange (odd) strano

stranger (male/female) lo straniero stran-yairo/la straniera

I'm a stranger here non sono di qui kwee

strap (on watch) il cinturino cheentooreeno

(on dress) la spallina

(on suitcase) la cinghia cheeng-ya

strawberry la fragola

stream il ruscello rooshel-lo

street la strada

on the street sulla strada sool-la

streetmap la piantina della città p-yanteena del-la cheet-ta

string lo spago

strong forte fortay

stuck bloccato

the key's stuck la chiave si è bloccata k-yavay see ay

student (male/female) lo studente/ la studentessa stoodentay/ stoodentes-sa

stupid stupido stoopeedo

suburb la periferia

subway (US) la metropolitana

suddenly improvvisamente eemprov-veezamentay

suede la pelle scamosciata pel-lay skamo-shata

sugar lo zucchero tzook-kairo

suit il completo komplayto

it doesn't suit me (jacket etc) non mi sta bene baynay

it suits you ti sta bene

suitcase la valigia valeeja

summer l'estate f estatay

in the summer d'estate

sun il sole solay

in the sun al sole

out of the sun all'ombra

sunbathe prendere il sole prendairay eel solay

sunblock (cream) la crema a
protezione totale kr**ay**ma a
protetz-y**o**nay tota**l**ay

sunburn la scottatura skot-tat**oo**ra

sunburnt scott**a**to

Sunday la domenica dom**ay**neeka

sunglasses gli occhiali da sole
ok-y**a**lee da s**o**lay

sun lounger (chair) il lett**i**no

sunny assol**a**to

  it's sunny c'è il sole chay eel s**o**lay

sun roof (in car) il tetto apribile
apr**ee**-beelay

sunset il tram**o**nto

sunshade il parasole paras**o**lay

sunshine la luce del sole l**oo**chay
del s**o**lay

sunstroke il c**o**lpo di sole

suntan l'abbronzatura *f*
ab-brontzat**oo**ra

suntan lotion la lozione solare
lotz-y**o**nay sol**a**ray

suntanned abbronz**a**to
ab-brontz**a**to

suntan oil l'olio solare *m*
ol-yo sol**a**ray

super fant**a**stico

supermarket il supermercato
soopair-mairk**a**to

supper la cena ch**ay**na

supplement (extra charge) il
supplemento soop-plem**e**nto

sure sicuro seek**oo**ro

  are you sure? sei/è sicuro/
sicura? say/ay

  sure! certo! ch**ai**rto

surname il cognome kon-y**o**may

swearword la parolaccia
parol**a**cha

sweater il maglione mal-y**o**nay

sweatshirt la felpa

Sweden la Svezia zv**e**tzee-a

Swedish (*adj*) svedese zved**ay**zay

sweet (taste) dolce d**o**lchay
  (*noun:* dessert) il dolce

sweets le caramelle karam**e**l-lay

swelling il gonfiore gonf-y**o**ray

swim (*verb*) nuotare nwot**a**ray

  I'm going for a swim v**a**do
a fare una nuotata f**a**ray **oo**na
nwot**a**ta

  let's go for a swim andiamo
a fare una nuotata and-y**a**mo

swimming costume il costume
da bagno kost**oo**may da ban-yo

swimming pool la piscina
pee-sh**ee**na

swimming trunks il costume da
bagno kost**oo**may da ban-yo

Swiss svizzero zv**ee**tzairo

switch l'interruttore *m* eentair-
root-t**o**ray

switch off (engine, TV, lights)
spegnere sp**e**n-yairay

switch on (engine, TV, lights)
accendere ach**e**ndairay

Switzerland la Svizzera sv**ee**tzaira

swollen gonfio g**o**nf-yo

T

table il t**a**volo

  a table for two un tavolo per
due pair

table cloth la tovaglia toval-ya

table tennis il ping-pong

table wine il vino da tavola

tailback (of traffic) la coda

tailor il sarto

take (pick up, catch) prendere prendairay

(accept) accettare achetaray

can you take me to the airport? può portarmi all'aeroporto?

do you take credit cards? accettate carte di credito? achet-tatay kartay dee kraydeeto

fine, I'll take it va bene, lo/la prendo baynay

can I take this? (leaflet etc) posso prenderlo/prenderla?

how long does it take? quanto ci vuole? kwanto chee vwolay

it takes three hours ci vogliono tre ore chee vol-yono

is this seat taken? è occupato questo posto? ay ok-koopato kwesto

pizza to take away una pizza da portare via portaray vee-a

can you take a little off here? (to hairdresser) può tagliare un po' qui? pwo tal-yaray oon po kwee

talcum powder il talco

talk (verb) parlare parlaray

tall alto

tampons i tamponi

tan l'abbronzatura f ab-brontzatoora

to get a tan abbronzarsi ab-brontzarsee

tank (of car) il serbatoio sairbato-yo

tap il rubinetto roobeenet-to

tape (cassette) la cassetta

(sticky) il nastro adesivo adezeevo

tape measure il metro a nastro

tape recorder il registratore rejeestratoray

taste il gusto goosto

can I taste it? posso assaggiarlo/assaggiarla? as-saj-jarlo

taxi il taxi

will you get me a taxi? mi può chiamare un taxi? pwo k-yamaray

where can I find a taxi? dove posso prendere un taxi? dovay – prendairay

DIALOGUE

to the airport/to Hotel Centrale please all'aeroporto/all'albergo Centrale, per favore

how much will it be? quanto verrà a costare? kwanto – kostaray

30 euros trenta euro ay-ooro

that's fine, right here, thanks va bene qui, grazie baynay kwee

taxi-driver il tassista

taxi rank il posteggio dei taxi postej-jo day

tea (drink) il tè tay

tea for one/two, please
un/due tè, per favore

teabags le bustine di tè
boosteenay dee tay

teach: could you teach me?
mi puoi/può insegnare?
mee pwoy/pwo eensen-yaray

teacher l'insegnante *m/f*
eensen-yantay

team la squadra skwadra

teaspoon il cucchiaino da tè
kook-kee-a-eeno da tay

tea towel lo strofinaccio
strofeenacho

teenager l'adolescente *m/f*
adoleshentay

telephone
see **phone** *and* **speak**

television la televisione
televeez-yonay

tell: could you tell him…?
potresti/potrebbe dirgli…?
potreb-bay deerl-yee

temperature (weather) la
temperatura tempairatoora
(fever) la febbre feb-bray

temple (building) il tempio

tennis il tennis

tennis ball la palla da tennis

tennis court il campo da tennis

tennis racket la racchetta da
tennis rak-ket-ta

tent la tenda

term (at university, school)
il trimestre treemestray

terminus (rail) il capolinea
kapoleenay-a

terrible terribile tair-reebeelay

terrific fantastico

text (message) il messaggino
mes-saj-jeeno

text (*verb*) mandare un
messaggino a mandaray oon
mes-saj-jeeno

than di dee

smaller than più piccolo di
p-yoo

thanks, thank you grazie
gratzee-ay

thank you very much grazie
mille meel-lay

thanks for the lift grazie del
passaggio

no thanks no grazie

that: that man quell'uomo kwel
womo

that woman quella donna
kwel-la

that one quello/quella lì

I hope that… spero che…
spairo kay

that's nice (food) è buono/
buona bwono

is that…? (quello/quella) è…?

that's it (that's right)
esattamente ezat-tamentay

the il, lo, la eel; (plural) i, gli, le
l-yee, lay

theatre il teatro tay-atro

their(s) il loro, la loro
(*plural*) i loro, le loro

them: for them per loro

  with them con loro

  I gave it to them l'ho dato a
loro lo

  who? – them chi? – loro kee

then (at that time) allora

  (after that) poi poy

there là

  over there laggiù laj-joo

  up there lassù las-soo

  is there…? c'è…? chay

  are there…? ci sono…? chee

  there is… c'è…

  there are… ci sono…

  there you are (giving
something) ecco qua kwa

thermometer il termometro
tairmometro

thermos flask il thermos tairmos

these: these men questi
uomini kwestee

  these women queste donne
kwestay

  can I have these? vorrei
questi/queste vor-ray

they loro

thick spesso

  (stupid) ottuso ot-toozo

thief il ladro

thigh la coscia kosha

thin sottile sot-teelay

  (person) magro

thing la cosa koza

  my things le mie cose lay mee-
ay kozay

think pensare pensaray

  I think so penso di sì

  I don't think so non credo
kraydo

  I'll think about it ci penserò
chee pensairo

third party insurance l'R.C.A.
lair-ray chee a

thirsty: I'm thirsty ho sete
o saytay

this questo, questa kwesto

  this man quest'uomo

  this woman questa donna

  this one questo/questa (qui)
kwee

  this is my wife questa è mia
moglie mol-yay

  is this…? (questo/questa)
è…?

those quelli, quelle kwel-lee/
kwel-lay

  those men quegli uomini
kwayl-yee

  those women quelle donne

  those children quei bambini
kway

  which ones? – those quali?
– quelli/quelle kwalee

thread il filo

throat la gola

throat pastilles le pastiglie per
la gola pasteel-yay pair

through attraverso at-travairso

  does it go through…?
(train, bus) passa per…? pair

throw (*verb*) gettare jet-taray

throw away (*verb*) buttare via
boot-taray

thumb il pollice pol-leechay

thunderstorm il temporale temporal-ay

Thursday il giovedì jovedee

ticket il biglietto beel-yet-to

a return to Rome un biglietto di andata e ritorno per Roma pair

coming back when? il ritorno per quando? kwando

today/next Tuesday oggi/ martedì prossimo oj-jee

that will be 15 euros quindici euro kween-deechee ay-ooro

ticket office la biglietteria beel-yet-tairee-a

tide la marea maray-a

tie (necktie) la cravatta

tight (clothes etc) attillato

it's too tight è troppo stretto ay

tights il collant kol-lan

till la cassa

time il tempo

what's the time? che ore sono? kay oray

this time questa volta kwesta

last time l'ultima volta loolteema

next time la prossima volta

four times quattro volte kwat-tro voltay

timetable l'orario m

tin (can) il barattolo

tinfoil la carta stagnola stan-yola

tin opener l'apriscatole m apree-skatolay

tiny piccolo

tip (to waiter etc) la mancia mancha

tired stanco

I'm tired sono stanco/stanca

tissues i fazzolettini di carta fatzolet-teenee

to: to Naples/London a Napoli/Londra

to Italy/England in Italia/ Inghilterra een eetal-ya/ eengeel-tair-ra

to the post office all'ufficio postale oof-feecho postalay

toast (bread) il pane tostato panay

today oggi oj-jee

toe il dito del piede p-yayday

together insieme eens-yaymay

we're together (in shop etc) siamo insieme s-yamo

can we pay together? possiamo pagare insieme? pos-yamo pagaray

toilet la toilette twalet

where is the toilet? dov'è la toilette? dovay

I have to go to the toilet devo andare alla toilette dayvo andaray

toilet paper la carta igienica eejayneeka

token (for machine) il gettone jet-tonay

tomato il pomodoro

tomato juice il succo di pomodoro sook-ko

tomato ketchup il ketchup

tomorrow domani

tomorrow morning domani mattina

the day after tomorrow dopodomani

toner (cosmetic) il tonico

tongue la lingua leengwa

tonic (water) l'acqua tonica f akwa

tonight (before 10 p.m.) stasera (after 10 p.m.) stanotte stanot-tay

tonsillitis la tonsillite tonseel-leetay

too (excessively) troppo

(also) anche ankay

too hot troppo caldo

too much troppo

me too anch'io ankee-o

tooth il dente dentay

toothache il mal di denti

toothbrush lo spazzolino da denti spatzoleeno

toothpaste il dentifricio denteefreecho

top: on top of... su... soo

at the top in cima cheema

top floor l'ultimo piano oolteemo

topless in topless

torch la torcia elettrica torcha

total il totale totalay

tour (noun) il giro jeero

is there a tour of...? ci sono visite guidate di...? chee – veezeetay gweedatay

tour guide la guida gweeda

tourist il/la turista tooreesta

tourist information office l'ufficio informazioni m oof-feecho eenformatz-yonay

tour operator l'operatore turistico m opairatoray tooreesteeko

towards verso vairso

towel l'asciugamano m ashoogamano

tower la torre tor-ray

town la città cheetta

in town in città

just out of town appena fuori città ap-payna fworee

town centre il centro (della città) chentro del-la cheeta

town hall il municipio mooneecheep-yo

toy il giocattolo jokat-tolo

track (US) il marciapiede marchapyayday

see **platform**

tracksuit la tuta da ginnastica toota da jeennasteeka

traditional tradizionale tradeetz-yonalay

traffic il traffico

traffic jam l'ingorgo m

traffic lights il semaforo

trailer (for carrying tent etc) il rimorchio reemork-yo
(US) la roulotte roolot

trailer park il campeggio per roulotte kampej-jo pair

train il treno trayno

by train in treno

is this train for...? questo
   treno va a…? kwesto
   treno va a…? **kwesto**

sure si

**no, you want that platform
   there** no, deve andare a
   quel binario **day**vay andaray
   a kwel beenar-yo

trainers (shoes) le scarpe
   da ginnastica sk**a**rpay da
   jeennasteeka

train station la stazione
   ferroviaria statz-y**o**nay fair-rov-
   yar-ya

tram il tram

translate tradurre trad**oo**r-ray
   could you translate that?
   puoi/può trad**u**rlo? pwoy/pwo

translation la traduzione
   tradootz-y**o**nay

translator (male/female)
   il tradutt**o**re tradoot-t**o**ray,
   la tradutt**ri**ce tradoot-tr**ee**chay

trashcan la pattumiera
   pat-toom-y**ai**ra

travel viaggiare v-yaj-jaray
   we're travelling around
   stiamo visit**a**ndo la regione
   st-y**a**mo – rej**o**nay

travel agent's l'agenzia di viaggi
   f aj**e**ntz-ya dee vee-aj-jee

traveller's cheque il traveller's
   cheque

tray il vassoio vas-s**o**-yo

tree l'albero m **a**lbairo

tremendous fant**a**stico

trendy alla m**o**da

trim: just a trim please (to
   hairdresser) solo una spuntatina
   per fav**o**re spoontate**e**na

trip (excursion) la gita je**e**ta
   I'd like to go on a trip to...
   vorrei fare una gita a…
   vor-r**ay** faray

trolley il carrello

trouble i problemi probl**ay**mee
   I'm having trouble with...
   ho difficoltà con… o

   sorry to trouble you scusi il
   disturbo sk**oo**zee eel deest**oo**rbo

trousers i pantal**o**ni

true vero v**ai**ro
   that's not true non è vero ay

trunk il bagagliaio bagal-ya-yo

trunks (swimming) il costume da
   bagno kost**oo**may da ban-yo

try (verb) provare provaray
   can I have a try? p**o**sso
   provare?

try on provare
   can I try it on?
   p**o**sso prov**a**rlo/prov**a**rla?

T-shirt la maglietta mal-y**e**t-ta

Tuesday il martedì marted**ee**

tuna il t**o**nno

tunnel il tunnel t**oo**n-nel

Turin Torino tor**ee**no

turn: turn left/right giri a
   sin**i**stra/d**e**stra je**e**ree

turn off: where do I turn off?
   dove devo girare? d**o**vay d**a**yvo
   jeer**a**ray

   **can you turn the heating
   off?** può spegnere il
   riscaldam**e**nto? pwo spen-y**ai**ray

turn on: can you turn the heating on? può accendere il riscaldamento? achendairay

turning (in road) la svolta

Tuscany la Toscana toskana

TV la TV tee voo

tweezers le pinzette peentzet-tay

twice due volte doo-ay voltay

  twice as much il doppio dop-yo

twin beds i letti gemelli jemel-lee

twin room la camera a due letti doo-ay

twist: I've twisted my ankle mi sono slogato la caviglia mee sono zlogato la kaveel-ya

type il tipo

  a different type of... un tipo diverso di... deevairso

typical tipico

tyre lo pneumatico p-nay-oomateeko

Tyrrhenian Sea il Mar Tirreno teer-rayno

U

ugly brutto brootto

ulcer l'ulcera f oolchaira

umbrella l'ombrello m

uncle lo zio tzee-o

unconscious privo di sensi

under (in position) sotto

  (less than) meno di mayno

underdone (meat) al sangue sangway

underground (railway) la metropolitana

underpants le mutande mootanday

understand capire kapeeray

  I understand capisco

  I don't understand non capisco

  do you understand? capisci/capisce? kapeeshee/kapeeshay

unemployed disoccupato deezok-koopato

United States gli Stati Uniti statee ooneetee

university l'università f ooneevairseeta

unleaded petrol la benzina senza piombo bentzeena senza p-yombo

unlimited mileage il chilometraggio illimitato keelometraj-jo

unlock aprire apreeray

unpack disfare le valigie deesfaray lay valeejay

until finché feenkay

unusual insolito

up su soo

  up there lassù las-soo

  he's not up yet (not out of bed) non si è ancora alzato non see ay – altzato

  what's up? che c'è? kay chay

upmarket chic sheek

upset stomach il disturbo di stomaco

upside down sottosopra

upstairs al piano superiore soopair-yoray

urgent urgente oorjentay

us noi noy, ci chee

  with us con noi

  please bring us some water
  ci porti dell'acqua, per favore

USA gli USA oo-sa

use (*verb*) usare oozaray

  may I use…? posso usare…?

useful utile ooteelay

usual solito

  the usual (drink etc) il solito

V

**vacancy: do you have any
vacancies?** (hotel) avete
camere libere? avaytay kamairay
leebairay

vacation la vacanza vakantza

  see **holiday**

  (from university) le vacanze
  vakantzay

vaccination il vaccino vacheeno

vacuum cleaner l'aspirapolvere
m aspeerapolvairay

valid (ticket etc) valido

  how long is it valid for?
  per quanto tempo è valido? pair
  kwanto – ay

valley la valle val-lay

valuable (*adj*) di valore valoray

  **can I leave my valuables
  here?** posso lasciare qui i miei
  oggetti di valore? lasharay kwee
  ee mee-yay oj-jet-tee dee

value il valore valoray

van il furgone foorgonay

vanilla la vaniglia vaneel-ya

  a vanilla ice cream un gelato
  alla vaniglia jelato

vary: it varies dipende
deependay

vase il vaso vazo

Vatican City la Città del
Vaticano cheetta del vateekano

veal il vitello

vegetables la verdura vairdoora

vegetarian (*male/female*)
il vegetariano vejetar-yano,
la vegetariana

vending machine il distributore
automatico deestreebootoray
owtomateeko

Venetian (*adj*) veneziano
venetz-yano

Venice Venezia venaytz-ya

very molto

  very little for me per me
  molto poco pair may

  I like it very much mi piace
  moltissimo mee pee-achay

vest (under shirt) la canottiera
kanot-tyaira

via la via vee-a

video (film) la videocassetta
(recorder) il videoregistratore
veeday-o-rejeestratoray

view la vista

villa la villa

village il paese pa-ayzay

vinegar l'aceto *m* acheto

vineyard la vigna veen-ya

visa il visto

visit (*verb*) visitare veezeetaray

I'd like to visit...
mi piacerebbe visitare...
mee p-yachaireb-bay

vital: it's vital that... è di vitale
importanza che... ay dee
veetalay eemportantza kay

vodka la vodka

voice la voce vochay

volcano il vulcano

voltage il voltaggio voltaj-jo

vomit vomitare vomeetaray

W

waist la vita

waistcoat il gilet jeelay

wait (*verb*) aspettare aspet-taray
  wait for me aspettami/mi
  aspetti

don't wait for me
non aspettarmi/mi aspetti

**can I wait until my wife/
partner gets here?** posso
aspettare fino a quando arriva
mia moglie/la mia partner?
kwando

can you do it while I wait?
può farlo adesso? pwo

**could you wait here for
me?** mi può aspettare qui?
kwee

waiter il cameriere kamair-yairay
  waiter! cameriere!

waitress la cameriera kamair-
  yaira
  waitress! cameriera!

**wake: can you wake me up
at 5.30?** mi può dare la sveglia
alle cinque e mezza? pwo daray
la zvayl-ya

wake-up call la sveglia zvayl-ya

Wales il Galles gal-les

walk: is it a long walk?
ci si mette molto a piedi? chee
see met-tay – p-yayday

it's only a short walk è a due
passi da qui ay a doo-ay – kwee

I'll walk vado a piedi

I'm going for a walk vado a
fare una passeggiata faray oona
pas-sej-jata

wall il muro mooro

wallet il portafoglio porta-fol-yo

**wander: I like just wandering
around** mi piace andarmene in
giro mee pee-achay andarmenay
een jeero

want: I want a… voglio un/uno/
una… vol-yo

I don't want any…
non voglio nessun/nessuno/
nessuna… nes-soon

I want to go home voglio
andare a casa andaray

I don't want to non voglio

he wants to… vuole… vwolay

what do you want? cosa
vuoi/vuole? vwoy

ward (in hospital) la corsia korsee-a

warm caldo

I'm so warm sento molto
caldo

was: he/she/it was… era… aira

wash (verb) lavare lavaray

can you wash these?
può lavare questi/queste?
pwo – kwestee/kwestay

washer (for bolt etc) la rondella

washhand basin il lavabo

washing (clothes) il bucato

washing machine la lavatrice
lavatreechay

washing powder il detersivo
per bucato detairseevo pair

washing-up liquid il detersivo
liquido per i piatti leekweedo
pair ee p-yat-tee

wasp la vespa

watch (wristwatch) l'orologio m
orolojo

**will you watch my things
for me?** può dare un'occhiata
alla mia roba? pwo daray oon
ok-yata alla mee-a

watch out! attenzione!
at-tentz-yonay

watch strap il cinturino
(dell'orologio) cheentooreeno
del orolojo

water l'acqua f akwa

may I have some water?
vorrei un po' d'acqua vor-ray

water bus (in Venice) il vaporetto

waterproof (adj) impermeabile
eempairmay-abeelay

waterskiing lo sci acquatico
shee akwa-teeko

wave (in sea) l'onda f

**way: could you tell me the
way to…?** mi può indicare
come si arriva a…? mee pwo
eendeekaray komay

it's this way da questa parte
kwesta partay

it's that way da quella parte
kwel-la

is it a long way to...?
… è molto lontano/lontana? ay

no way! assolutamente no!
as-solootamentay

DIALOGUE

could you tell me the way to...? come si fa per andare a...? komay – pair andaray

go straight on until you reach the traffic lights vada dritto fino al semaforo

turn left giri a sinistra jeeree

take the first on the right prenda la prima a destra

see where

we noi noy

weak (person, drink) debole daybolay

weather il tempo

DIALOGUE

what's the weather forecast? come sono le previsioni del tempo? komay – lay preveez-yonee

it's going to be fine farà bel tempo

it's going to rain pioverà p-yovaira

it'll brighten up later si rasserenerà più tardi p-yoo

website il sito web seeto

wedding il matrimonio

wedding ring la vera vaira

Wednesday il mercoledì mairkoledee

week la settimana

a week (from) today oggi a otto oj-jee

a week (from) tomorrow domani a otto

weekend il fine settimana feenay

at the weekend durante il fine settimana

weight il peso payzo

weird strano

weirdo il tipo strano

welcome: welcome to... benvenuto a... benvenooto

you're welcome (don't mention it) prego praygo

well: I don't feel well non mi sento bene baynay

she's not well non sta bene

you speak English very well parla inglese molto bene eenglay-zay

well done! bravo!

this one as well anche questo/questa ankay kwesto

well well! (surprise) guarda, guarda! gwarda

DIALOGUE

how are you? come va? komay

very well, thanks benissimo, grazie

– and you? – è lei? ay lay

well-done (meat) ben cotto

Welsh gallese gal-layzay

I'm Welsh sono gallese

were: we were eravamo

west l'ovest m

in the west ad ovest

West Indian (*adj*) delle Indie occidentali del-lay **ee**ndee-ay ocheedent**a**lay

wet umido **oo**meedo, bagnato ban-y**a**to

what? cosa?

  what's that? cos'è? koz**ay**

  what should I do? cosa dovrei fare? dovr**ay** f**a**ray

  what a view! che vista! kay

  what bus is it? che autobus è? kay – ay

wheel la ruota rw**o**ta

wheelchair la sedia a rotelle s**a**yd-ya a rot**e**l-lay

when? quando? kw**a**ndo

  when we get back quando torni**a**mo

  when's the train/ferry? a che **o**ra parte il treno/il traghetto? kay – p**a**rtay

where? dove? d**o**vay

  I don't know where it is non so dov'è dov**ay**

which: which bus? quale autobus? kw**a**lay **ow**toboos

while: while I'm here mentre sono qui m**e**ntray – kwee

whisky il whisky

white bianco b-y**a**nko

white wine il vino bianco

who? chi? kee

  who is it? chi è? ay

  the man who… l'uomo che… lw**o**mo kay

whole: the whole week tutta la settimana t**oo**t-ta

  the whole lot tutto

whose: whose is this? di chi è questo/questa? dee kee ay kw**e**sto

why? perché? pairk**ay**

  why not? perché no?

wide largo

wife la moglie m**o**l-yay

Wi-Fi wi-fi

will: will you do it for me? lo farà per me? pair may

wind il vento

window (of house) la finestra

  (of shop) la vetrina

  near the window vicino alla finestra veech**ee**no

  in the window (of shop) in vetrina

window seat il posto vicino al finestrino veecheeno

windscreen il parabrezza parabretza

windscreen wipers i tergicristalli tairjeekreestal-lee

windsurfing il windsurf

windy: it's windy c'è vento chay

wine il vino

can we have some more **wine?** ancora vino, per favore

wine list la lista dei vini day

winter l'inverno *m* eenvairno

in the winter d'inverno

winter holiday le vacanze invernali vakantzay eenvairnalee

wire il filo di ferro fair-ro

(electric) il filo (elettrico)

wish: best wishes tanti auguri owgooree

with con

I'm staying with... sono ospite di... ospeetay

without senza sentza

witness il/la testimone testeemonay

will you be a witness for **me?** può farmi da testimone? pwo

woman la donna

wonderful meraviglioso mairaveel-yozo

won't: it won't start non parte

wood (material) il legno len-yo

(forest) il bosco

wool la lana

word la parola

work il lavoro

it's not working non funziona foontz-yona

I work in... lavoro a/in...

world il mondo

worry: I'm worried sono preoccupato/preoccupata pray-ok-koopato

worse: it's worse è peggio ay pej-jo

worst il peggio pej-jo

worth: is it worth a visit? vale la pena di visitarlo/visitarla? valay la payna

would: would you give this to...? può dare questo/questa a...? pwo daray kwesto

wrap: could you wrap it up? può incartarlo? pwo

wrapping paper la carta da pacchi pak-kee

wrist il polso

write scrivere skreevairay

could you write it down? può scrivermelo? pwo skreevairmelo

how do you write it? come si scrive? komay see skreevay

writing paper la carta da lettere let-tairay

wrong: it's the wrong key è la chiave sbagliata ay la k-yavay zbal-yata

this is the wrong train questo è il treno sbagliato kwesto

the bill's wrong c'è un errore nel conto chay oon air-roray

sorry, wrong number

mi scusi, ho sbagliato numero
mee skoozee o – noomairo

sorry, wrong room mi scusi,
ho sbagliato camera

**there's something wrong
with...** cè qualcosa che non va
nel/nello/nella... chay kwalkoza
kay

what's wrong? cosa c'è che
non va? koza chay kay

X

X-ray i raggi X raj-jee eeks

Y

yacht lo yacht
yard lo yard
　(backyard etc) il cortile korteelay
year l'anno *m*
yellow giallo jal-lo
yes sì
yesterday ieri yairee
　yesterday morning ieri
　mattina
　the day before yesterday
　l'altro ieri
yet ancora

DIALOGUE

is it here yet? è (già)
　arrivato? ay ja
no, not yet no, non ancora
**you'll have to wait a little
　longer yet** devi/deve
　aspettare ancora un po'
　dayvay aspet-taray

yoghurt lo yogurt yogoort
you (*sing, polite*) lei lay
　(*sing, familiar*) tu
　(*plural*) voi voy
　this is for you questo/questa è
　per te/lei kwesto – ay pair tay/lay
　with you con te/lei
young giovane jovanay
your(s) (*sing, polite*) (il) suo soo-o,
　(la) sua
　(with plural nouns) (i) suoi swoy,
　(le) sue soo-ay
　(*sing, familiar*) (il) tuo too-o, (la)
　tua (i) tuoi twoy, le tue too-ay
　(referring to more than one person)
　(il) vostro, (la) vostra
　(with plural nouns) (i) vostri, (le)
　vostre vostray
youth hostel l'ostello della
　gioventù *m* joventoo

Z

zero lo zero tzairo
zip la cerniera lampo chairn-yaira
　could you put a new zip on?
　potrebbe cambiare la cerniera
　lampo? potreb-bay kamb-yaray
zip code il codice postale
　kodeechay postalay
zoo lo zoo tzo-o

ITALIAN
→ **ENGLISH**

Colloquialisms

The following are words you might well hear. You shouldn't be tempted to use any of the stronger ones unless you are sure of your audience.

accidenti! acheedentee blast!
bestiale! best-yalay great!
cazzate *fpl* katzatay rubbish
cazzo *m* katzo dick
culo koolo arse
che culo! kay koolo lucky bastard!
che fica! kay feeka what a babe!
coglione! kol-yonay bastard!
fatti i cazzi tuoi! fat-tee ee katzee twoy mind your own business!
fico! feeko fantastic!
figlio di puttana! feel-yo dee poot-tana son-of-a-bitch!
finocchio *m* feen-ok-kyo gay
ganzo! gantzo brilliant!
incasinato eenkazeenato messed up
incazzarsi eenkatzarsee to get pissed off
merda! mairda shit!
micidiale meecheed-yalay great!
minchia! meenk-ya fuck!
non me ne fotte niente may nay fot-tay n-yentay I don't give a damn
pezzo di stronzo! petzo dee strontzo you arsehole!

pirla! peerla jerk!
porca puttana! porka poot-tana fuck!
porca troia! porka troy-a fuck!
puttana! poot-tana bitch!
rincoglionito reenkol-yoneeto screwed up
stronzate *fpl* strontzatay rubbish
stronzo *m* strontzo arsehole
testa di cazzo *m* katzo dickhead
troia! troy-a bitch!
va' a farti fottere! fartee fot-tairay fuck off!
va' a quel paese! kwel pa-ayzay fuck off!
vaffanculo! vafankool-lo fuck off!

A

a at; in; to; per
   a persona per person
abbaglianti full beam
abbassare ab-bas-saray to lower, to pull down
abbastanza ab-bastantza enough; quite, rather
abbiamo we have
abbigliamento da bambino *m* ab-beel-yamento children's wear
abbigliamento da donna ladies' wear
abbigliamento da uomo menswear
abbigliamento per signora ladies' clothing
abbonamento *m* ab-bonamento season ticket

abbonamento mensile
menseelay monthly ticket

abbronzante *m* ab-brontzantay
suntan lotion

abbronzarsi ab-brontzarsee
to get a tan

abbronzato ab-brontzato tanned

abbronzatura *f* ab-brontzatoora
suntan

abile abeelay skilful

abitante *m/f* abeetantay
inhabitant

abitare abeetaray to live

abiti *mpl* abeetee clothes

abito *m* abito dress; suit

abitudine *f* abeetoodeenay habit

a.C. (avanti Cristo) B.C.

accanto beside

acceleratore *m* achelairatoray
accelerator

accendere achendairay to switch
on; to light

mi fa accendere? have you
got a light?

accendere i fari switch on
headlights

accendino *m* achendeeno lighter

accensione *m* achens-yonay
ignition

accento *m* achento accent

accessori moda *mpl* fashion
accessories

**accesso riservato ai
viaggiatori muniti di
biglietto** access only for
passengers in possession of
tickets

accettare achet-taray to accept

accettazione *f* achet-tatz-yonay
check-in

acciaio *m* acha-yo steel

accidenti! acheedentee damn!

accomodati come in; take a seat

accomodi: si accomodi
ak-komodee come in; take a seat

accompagnare ak-kompan-yaray
to accompany

accompagnatore *m* ak-kompan-
yatoray, **accompagnatrice** *f*
ak-kompan-yatreechay
tour leader

acconciatore *m* ladies'
hairdresser

accordo *m* agreement

d'accordo all right, OK

essere d'accordo (con)
es-sairay to agree (with)

accreditare ak-kraydeetaray
to credit

acetone *m* achetonay nail polish
remover

**A.C.I. (Automobile Club
d'Italia)** *m* achee Italian
Automobile Association

acqua *f* akwa water

acqua di Colonia dee kolon-ya
eau de Cologne

acquaio *m* akwa-yo sink

acqua potabile potabeelay
drinking water

addormentarsi to fall asleep

addormentato ad-dormentato
asleep

adesso now

adolescente *m/f* adoleshentay
teenager

adulto m adult

aereo m a-**ai**ray-o plane; air (adj)

　andare in aereo to fly

aerobica f a-air**o**beeka aerobics

aeromobile m a-airom**o**beelay
　aeroplane

aeroplano m a-airo**pl**ano
　aeroplane

aeroporto m a-airo**po**rto airport

aerostazione f a-airostatz-**yo**nay
　air terminal

affamato starving

affari mpl business

affermare af-fairm**a**ray
　to maintain

afferrare af-fair-r**a**ray to catch

affettare af-fet-t**a**ray to slice

affittare af-feet-t**a**ray to rent

affittasi to let, to rent

affitto m rent

　dare in affitto to let

　prendere in affitto
　to hire, to rent

affollato crowded

affondare af-fond**a**ray to sink

affrancare af-frank**a**ray to stamp;
　to frank

affrancatura f postage

affrancatura per l'estero
　postage abroad

affrettarsi to hurry

agenda f aj**e**nda diary

agenzia f ajentz**ee**-a agency

agenzia di viaggi(o)
　dee vee-**aj**-jee-o travel agency

agenzia immobiliare eem-
　mobeel-y**a**ray estate agent

agenzia turistica travel agency

aggiungere aj-j**oo**njairay to add

aggiustare aj-joost**a**ray to mend

aggressivo aggressive

agitare prima dell'uso shake
　before use

agitato ajeet**a**to agitated

agli al-yee at the; to the; with

ago m ago needle

agosto m August

agricoltore m agreekolt**o**ray
　farmer

ai a-ee at the; to the; with

ai binari to the platforms/tracks

ai treni to the trains

aiutare a-yoot**a**ray to help

aiuto m a-y**oo**to help

al at the; to the

ala f wing

alba f sunrise

albergo m hotel

albergo a 5/4/3/2 stelle
　5/4/3/2-star hotel

albergo di categoria lusso
　kataygor**ee**-a luxury hotel

albero m **a**lbairo tree

albero a gomiti m crankshaft

alghe marine fpl **a**lgay mar**ee**nay
　seaweed

alimentari mpl groceries

alla at the; to the; with

allacciare le cinture fasten your
　seat belts

allarme m al-l**a**rmay alarm

allattare al-lat-t**a**ray to breastfeed

alle al-lay at the; to the; with

allegria f al-legree-a cheerfulness

allegro cheerful

allenarsi to train

allievo, m **allieva** f al-l-yevo pupil

allo at the; to the

alloggiare al-loj-jaray to stay

alloggio m al-loj-jo accommodation

allora then

   e allora? so what?

allungare al-loongaray to stretch; to extend

almeno al-mayno at least

Alpi fpl alpee Alps

al... piano on/to... floor

alpinismo m alpeeneezmo mountaineering

alpinista m/f mountaineer

al portatore to the bearer

alt stop, halt

alternatore m al-tairnatoray alternator

altitudine f alteetoodeenay altitude

alto high, tall

altopiano m plateau

altra, altri, altre altray other

altrimenti altreementee otherwise

altro other

   un altro another

alunno m, **alunna** f pupil

alzare altzaray to lift, to raise

alzarsi altzarsee to get up, to stand up

amare amaray to love

amaro bitter

ambasciata f ambashata embassy

ambiente m amb-yentay environment

ambulanza f amboolantza ambulance

ambulatorio m amboolator-yo out-patients' department; surgery

americano m, **americana** f American

amico m, **amica** f friend

ammalato ill, sick

ammettere am-met-tairay to admit

ammobiliato am-mobeel-yato furnished

ammortizzatore m am-morteedzatoray shock absorber

amore m amoray love

   fare l'amore faray to make love

ampere: da 15 ampere ampairay 15-amp

anabbaglianti mpl dipped headlights

analgesico m analjayzeeko painkiller

A.N.A.S. f **(Azienda Nazionale Autonoma delle Strade)** national road maintenance authority

anche ankay also; even

   anche a te/lei a tay/lay the same to you

ancora f ankora anchor

ancora ankora still

   ancora più... p-yoo even more...

ancora un/uno/una... another/one more…

ancora (una volta) (once) again

non ancora not yet

andare andaray to go

andarsene andarsenay to go away

andarsene in fretta to rush away

andar via to go away

andate andatay you go

andato gone

andiamo we go

anello *m* ring

angolo *m* corner; angle

animale *m* aneemalay animal

annegare an-negaray to drown

anniversario di matrimonio *m* wedding anniversary

anno *m* year

annoiarsi an-noyarsee to be bored

anno nuovo *m* nwovo New Year

annullare an-nool-laray to cancel

annullato cancelled

antenato *m* ancestor

antenna *f* aerial

antibiotico *m* antibiotic

anticamera *f* waiting room

Antica Roma *f* Ancient Rome

antichità *fpl* anteekeeta antiques

anticipo: in anticipo een anteecheepo in advance; early

antico ancient

antidolorifico *m* painkiller

antigelo *m* anteejelo antifreeze

antiquariato *m* anteekwar-yato antique; antiques shop

antisettico *m* antiseptic

antistaminico *m* antihistamine

aperto open

apparecchio *m* ap-parek-yo phone

apparecchio *m* **acustico** akoosteeko hearing aid

apparire ap-pareeray to appear

appartamento *m* flat, apartment

appartamento ammobiliato furnished flat/apartment

appassionato (di) very keen (on)

appena ap-payna just; hardly, scarcely

appeso ap-payso hanging

appetito *m* ap-peteeto appetite

appoggiato ap-poj-jato leaning

approvare ap-provaray to approve

appuntamento *m* ap-poontamento appointment

apre alle... opens at…

apribottiglie *m* apreebot-teel-yay bottle-opener

aprile *m* apreelay April

aprire apreeray to open

apriscatole *m* apreeskatolay tin opener

AR (andata e ritorno) return (ticket), round trip ticket

AR (avviso di ricevimento) receipt for registered letters which you return to sender

arancione aranchonay orange

arbitro m referee

arco m arch

area di servizio f serveetz-yo
service area

argento m arjento silver

argomento m topic, subject

aria f ar-ya air

avere l'aria... to look…

aria condizionata f kondeetz-
yonata air-conditioning

armadietto m armad-yet-to
locker; cupboard

armadio m armad-yo cupboard;
wardrobe

arrabbiarsi ar-rab-yarsee
to get angry

arrabbiato angry

arrestare ar-restaray to arrest

arrivare ar-reevaray to arrive

arrivederci ar-reevedairchee
goodbye

arrivo m arrival

arrivo previsto per le ore...
expected time of arrival…

arrogante ar-rogantay arrogant

arroganza f ar-rogantza
arrogance

arrostire ar-rosteeray to roast

arte f artay art

articoli da regalo mpl gifts

articoli per la casa
household goods

articoli per la cucina
kitchen articles

articoli sportivi sports gear

artificiale arteefeechalay artificial

artigianato m arteejanato crafts

artista m/f artist

Travel tip Italians are rightly
proud of their arts festivals,
which are spread across the
country but are particularly
strong in the central regions.
Based in ancient amphithea-
tres or within medieval walls,
they occasionally mark the
work of a native composer.
Major concerts and operas
are usually well advertised
but also extremely popu-
lar, so book tickets well in
advance.

ascensore f ashensoray
lift, elevator

asciugacapelli m
ashoogakapel-lee hair dryer

asciugamano m ashoogamano
towel

asciugamano da bagno
bath towel

asciugamano piccolo
hand towel

asciugare ashoogaray to dry

asciugarsi ashoogarsee
to dry oneself

asciugarsi le mani
to dry one's hands

asciugatrice f ashoogatreechay
tumble dryer

asciugatura con fon f
ashoogatoora blow-dry

asciutto ashoot-to dry

ascoltare askoltaray to listen

asilo m *azeelo* nursery school

asilo nido crèche

asino m donkey

asma f *azma* asthma

aspettare *aspet-taray* to wait (for)

aspirapolvere m *aspeerapolvairay* vacuum cleaner

   passare l'aspirapolvere to vacuum

aspirina f *aspeereena* aspirin

aspro sour

assaggiare *as-saj-jaray* to taste

asse da stiro m *as-say da steero* ironing board

assegno m *as-sen-yo* cheque, check

   pagare con un assegno to pay by cheque

assente *as-sentay* absent

assicurata f *as-seekoorata* registered letter

assicurazione f *as-seekooratz-yonay* insurance

assicurazione di viaggio *vee-aj-jo* travel insurance

assistenza auto repairs

associazione f *as-sochatz-yonay* society, association

assolato sunny

assolutamente *as-sloot-amentay* absolutely

assorbente igienico m *as-sorbentay eejeneeko* sanitary towel, sanitary napkin

atlante (geografico) f *atlantay jay-ografeeko* atlas

atlante stradale *stradalay* road atlas

atleta m/f *atlayta* athlete

atletica f *atlayteeka* athletics

attaccapanni m coat rack

attaccato stuck

attenda wait

attenti al cane beware of the dog

attento careful, attentive

attenzione f *at-tentz-yonay* care, attention

   attenzione! look out!; caution!

attenzione: per l'uso leggere attentamente le istruzioni interne warning: before use read instructions inside carefully

atterraggio m *at-tair-raj-jo* landing

atterraggio di fortuna emergency landing

atterrare *at-tair-raray* to land

attillato tight

attimo: un attimo just a minute

attraente *at-tra-entay* attractive

attraversare *at-travairsaray* to go through; to cross

attraverso *at-travairso* through

attrezzatura f *at-tretzatoora* equipment

auguri: tanti auguri *tantee owgooree* best wishes

aula f *owla* classroom

aumentare *owmentaray* to increase

australiano m *owstral-yano*,

australiana *f* Australian

austriaco *m* owstree-ako,
  austriaca *f* Austrian

autentico owtenteeko genuine

autista *m/f* owteesta driver

auto *f* owto car

> Travel tip Cars do not auto-
> matically stop at pedestrian
> crossings in Italy. Even on
> crossings with traffic lights
> you can be subjected to
> some close calls. There may
> be a green light for pedestri-
> ans to go, but it will probably
> be green for one of the lines
> of traffic too.

autoambulanza *f* owtoambulantza
  ambulance

autobus *m* owtoboos bus

autofficina *f* garage (for repairs)

autogrill *m* owtogreel motorway/
  highway restaurant

autolavaggio *m* owtolavaj-jo
  car wash

automobilista *m/f*
  owtomobeeleesta car driver

autonoleggio *m* car rental

autorimessa *f* owtoreemes-sa
  garage

autostop: fare l'autostop
  to hitchhike

autostrada *f* motorway, freeway,
  highway

autunno *m* owtoon-no autumn,
  Fall

avanti come in; cross now

avanti diritto straight ahead

più avanti further on

avere *m* avairay credit

avere to have

avete avaytay you have

avuto had

Avv. (avvocato) lawyer

avventura *f* av-ventoora
  adventure

avviarsi av-vee-arsee to set off

avvicinarsi av-veecheenarsee
  to approach

avviso *m* av-veezo notice

avvocato *m* lawyer

azioni *fpl* atz-yonee shares, stocks

azzurro adzoor-ro sky-blue

B

bacio *m* bacho kiss

baffi *mpl* moustache

bagagli *mpl* bagal-yee luggage,
  baggage

bagagliaio *m* bagal-ya-yo boot,
  trunk; left luggage, baggage
  check

bagaglio a mano *m* bagal-yo
  hand luggage/baggage

bagaglio in eccesso eches-so
  excess baggage

bagnato ban-yato wet

bagnato fradicio fradeecho
  soaked

bagnino *m* ban-yeeno, **bagnina**
  f lifeguard

bagno *m* ban-yo bath; bathroom

andare in bagno to go to the bathroom/toilet/rest room

fare il bagno to have a bath; to have a swim

bagnoschiuma *m* ban-yosk-**yoo**ma bubble bath

baia *f* ba-ya bay

balconata *f* balcony, dress-circle

balcone *m* bal**ko**nay balcony

ballare bal-la**ray** to dance

balletto *m* ballet

ballo *m* dancing; dance

balsamo *m* conditioner

bambino *m*, **bambina** *f* child

bambola *f* doll

banca *f* bank

banchina *f* ban**kee**na platform, track; quayside

banchina non transitabile soft verge

banco *m* desk

banco informazioni eenformatz-**yo**nee information desk

bancomat *m* cash dispenser, ATM

banconota *f* banknote, (US) bill

bandiera *f* band-**yai**ra flag

barare bara**ray** to cheat

barattolo *m* tin

barba *f* beard

farsi la barba to shave

barbiere *m* barb-**yai**ray barber's

barca (a motore) *f* mo**to**ray (motor) boat

barca a remi **ray**mee rowing boat

barca a vela **vay**la sailing boat

basket *m* basketball

basso low

basta (così)! ko**zee** that's enough!

bastare basta**ray** to be enough

battello *m* passenger ferry; steamer

battere bat-tairay to beat

batteria *f* bat-tairee-a battery; drums

beauty-case *m* toilet bag(s)

bebè *m/f* bebay baby

belga *m/f* Belgian

Belgio *m* beljo Belgium

bello beautiful

bene baynay good; fine; well

bene, grazie gratzee-ay fine, thanks

ti sta bene! it serves you right!

va bene! that's fine!, it's OK!; that's right

benissimo! excellent!

benvenuto! benvaynooto welcome!

benzina *f* bendzeena petrol/gas

benzina normale normalay two- or three-star petrol, regular gas

benzina senza piombo sentza p-yombo unleaded petrol/gas

benzina super four-star petrol, premium

benzina verde vairday unleaded petrol/gas

bere bairay to drink

berretto *m* bair-ret-to cap

beve bayvay he/she/it drinks; you drink

bevete bevaytay you drink

bevi bayvee you drink

beviamo we drink

bevo bayvo I drink

bevono they drink

bevuto drank

Travel tip It's cheapest to drink standing at the counter, in which case you pay first at the cash desk, present your receipt to the barperson and give your order. It's customary to leave a small coin as a tip. If there's table service, sit where you like, though bear in mind it'll cost twice as much.

biancheria da bambino *f* b-yankairee-a children's underwear

biancheria da donna ladies' lingerie

biancheria da letto bed linen

biancheria da uomo men's underwear

biancheria intima underwear

biancheria per la casa household linen

bianco b-yanko white

bianco e nero ay nairo black and white

bibita *f* beebeeta soft drink

biblioteca *f* beebl-yoteka library

bicchiere *m* beek-yairay glass

bicicletta *f* beecheeklet-ta bicycle

andare in bicicletta to cycle

bidello *m* beedel-lo, **bidella** *f* caretaker

bigiotteria *f* bijot-tairee-a costume jewellery

biglietttaio *m* beel-yet-ta-yo
conductor

biglietteria *f* beel-yet-tair-**ee**-a
ticket office; box-office

biglietteria automatica
owtom**a**teeka ticket vending
machine

biglietto *m* beel-yet-to ticket;
banknote, (US) bill

biglietto chilometrico
keelom**e**treeko ticket allowing
travel up to a maximum
specified distance

biglietto d'accesso ai treni
dach**e**s-so **a**-ee tr**ay**nee platform
ticket

biglietto da visita business card

biglietto di andata e ritorno
reet**o**rno return (ticket), round
trip ticket

biglietto di auguri owg**oo**ree
(greetings/birthday) card

biglietto di sola andata single
(ticket), one-way ticket

**biglietto per viaggi in
comitiva** vee-**a**j-jee group/
party ticket

biglietto ridotto reed**o**t-to
reduced rate ticket

biglietto valido per più corse
val**ee**do pair p-yoo k**o**rsay
multi-journey ticket

bilancia (pesapersone) *f*
beel**a**nchee-a payzap**ai**rs**o**nay
(bathroom) scales

bilanciatura gomme *f*
beelanchat**oo**ra g**o**m-may
wheel-balancing

binario *m* beenar-yo platform, track

biondo b-y**o**ndo blond

birreria *f* beer-rair**ee**-a
bar specializing in beer

> **Travel tip** Traditional bars
> are functional places and all
> very similar – brightly lit, with
> a counter, a coffee machine
> and a picture of the local
> football team. You'd come
> here for a coffee or a quick
> beer – people don't idle away
> evenings in bars, and in more
> rural areas it's difficult to find
> one open after 8pm.

bisogno: ho bisogno di
o beez**o**n-yo I need

bivio *m* b**ee**v-yo junction

bloccato blocked; stuck

blocchetto di biglietti *m* blok-
k**e**t-to dee beel-yet-tee book of
tickets

boa *f* b**o**-a buoy

bocca *f* mouth

bollire bol-l**ee**ray to boil; to be
boiling

bomba *f* bomb; type of ice
cream; doughnut

bonifico bancario *m* bonee**fee**eeko
bank**a**r-yo credit transfer

bordo: a bordo on board

borgo medioevale *m* med-yo-
ayv**a**lay medieval village

borsa *f* bag

borsa dell'acqua calda del-
l**a**kwa hot-water bottle

borsaiolo *m* borsa-y**o**lo,
borsaiola *f* pickpocket

borsellino *m* purse

borsetta *f* handbag, (US) purse

bosco *m* wood, forest

bottiglia *f* bot-**teel**-ya bottle

bottone *m* bot-**to**nay button

braccialetto *m* brachal**et**-to bracelet

braccio *m* **bra**cho arm

branda *f* campbed

bravo good; skilful

   bravo! well done!

bravura *f* skilfulness

breve **bray**vay short, brief

brillante breel-**lan**tay brilliant

britannico British

brocca *f* jug

bruciare broo**cha**ray to burn

brutto br**oo**t-to ugly

buca delle lettere *f* del-lay let-**tai**ray letter box, mailbox

bucato *f* laundry

   fare il bucato to do the washing

buco *m* hole

buffet *m* snack bar(s); sideboard(s)

buffo b**oo**f-fo funny

buio *m* b**oo**-yo dark

buona fortuna! b**wo**na fort**oo**na good luck!

buonanotte bwona**no**t-tay good night

buon appetito! bwon ap-pet**ee**to enjoy your meal!

buonasera bwonas**ai**ra good evening

buon compleanno!

komplay-**an**-no happy birthday!

buongiorno bwon**jor**no good morning

buono bw**o**no good

buon viaggio! vee-aj-jo have a good trip!

bussola *f* b**oo**s-sola compass

busta *f* b**oo**sta envelope

busta imbottita eembot-t**ee**ta padded envelope

butano *m* boot**a**no camping gas

buttare via boot-**ta**ray v**ee**-a to throw away

C

C (caldo) hot

C (Celsius) C

cabina *f* cabin; beach hut

cabina telefonica telef**o**neeka phone box

caccia *f* **ka**cha hunting

   andare a caccia to go hunting

cacciavite *m* kacha**vee**tay screwdriver

cadere kad**ai**ray to fall

   far cadere to drop

caduta massi falling rocks

caffè *m* kaff**ay** coffee(s); café(s)

caffetteria *f* kaf-fet-tair**ee**-a coffee bar, coffee house

caffettiera *f* kaf-fet-y**ai**ra coffeepot; coffee maker

C.A.I. (Club Alpino Italiano) *m* Italian Alpine Club

calciatore *m* kalchat**o**ray

calciatrice f kalchatreechay
football player

calcio m kalcho football; kick

giocare a calcio jokaray
to play football

> Travel tip Football is the
> national sport, followed fanat-
> ically by millions of Italians,
> and if you're at all interested
> you should try and catch a
> game. The season starts in
> mid-August and finishes in
> June, with matches normally
> played on Sunday after-
> noons, although Saturday,
> Sunday evening and Monday
> games are becoming more
> common.

calcolare kalkolaray to calculate

calcolatore m kalkolatoray
calculator

caldo m heat; warm; hot

avere caldo to be warm

fa caldo it's warm/hot

calendario m kalendar-yo
calendar

calmarsi to calm down

calvo bald

calzature fpl kaltzatooray
footwear

calze fpl kaltzay socks; stockings

calzini mpl kaltzeenee socks

calzolaio m kaltzola-yo shoe
repairer's

calzoleria f kaltzolairee-a
shoe repairer's

calzoncini mpl kaltzoncheenee

shorts

calzoni mpl kaltzonee trousers,
(US) pants

cambiare kamb-yaray to change

cambiarsi kamb-yarsee to change

cambiavalute m kamb-yavalootay
bureau de change

cambio m kamb-yo change;
bureau de change; gears

camera f kamaira room

camera da letto bedroom

camera d'aria dar-ya inner tube

camera doppia dop-ya
double room

**camera doppia con bagno/
servizi** ban-yo/sairveetzee
double room with bathroom

camera doppia senza bagno
sentza double room without
bathroom

camera singola seengola
single room

cameriera f kamair-yaira
maid; waitress

cameriere m kamair-yairay waiter

camiceria f kameechairee-a
shirt shop

camicetta f kamichet-ta blouse

camicia f kameecha shirt

camicia da notte not-tay
nightdress

caminetto m fireplace

camino m chimney

camion m kam-yon lorry

camminare kam-meenaray
to walk

campagna f kampan-ya
countryside; campaign

campana *f* bell (church)

campanello *m* bell; doorbell

campeggio *m* kampej-jo
camping; campsite

campeggio per roulotte roolot
caravan site, trailer park

campionato *m* kamp-yonato
championship

campione senza valore
sample, no commercial value

campo *m* course; court; field

campo da golf golf course

campo da hockey hockey field

campo da tennis tennis court

campo di calcio kalcho
football pitch

campo sportivo sporteevo
sports ground

canadese *m/f* kanadayzay
Canadian

canale *m* kanalay canal; channel

cancellato kanchel-lato cancelled

cancello *m* kanchel-lo gate

candela *f* kandayla
candle; spark plug

candeliere *m* kandel-yairay
candlestick

cane *m* kanay dog

canna da pesca *f* fishing rod

cannuccia *f* kan-noocha straw

canoa *f* kano-a canoe; canoeing

canottaggio *m* kanot-taj-jo
rowing; canoeing

canotto *m* (rubber) dinghy

cantare kantaray to sing

cantina *f* cellar

canto *m* singing

canzone *f* kantzonay song

**C.A.P. (Codice di Avviamento
Postale)** *m* postcode, zip code

cap. (capitolo) chapter

caparra *f* deposit

capelli *mpl* hair

capire kapeeray to understand

capisco: non capisco kapeesko
I don't understand

capitale *f* kapeetalay capital city

capitano *m* captain

capo *m* boss

capolavoro *m* masterpiece

capolinea *m* kapoleenay-a
terminus

cappella *f* chapel

cappello *m* hat

cappotto *m* coat

capra *f* goat

carabinieri *mpl* karabeen-yairee
military police force

carattere *m* karat-tairay character

carburatore *m* karbooratoray
carburettor

carcere *m* karchairay prison

caricatore *m* kareekatoray
charger

carino nice, pleasant

carnevale *m* karnevalay carnival

caro dear, expensive

carreggiata *f* kar-rej-jata roadway

carrello *m* (luggage/baggage)
trolley

carrozza *f* kar-rotza coach,
carriage, car

carrozza cuccette koochet-tay
sleeping car

carrozza letti let-tee sleeping car

carrozza ristorante reestorantay restaurant car

carrozzeria f kar-rotzairee-a car body shop

carrozzina f kar-rotzeena pram

carta f card; paper

carta assegni as-sen-yee cheque/check card

carta da disegno deesen-yo drawing paper

carta da lettere let-tairay writing paper

carta da pacchi pak-kee brown paper

carta d'argento darjento senior citizens' railcard

carta di credito kraydeeto credit card

carta d'identità identity card

carta d'imbarco boarding pass

carta geografica jay-ografeeka map

carta igienica eejeneeka toilet paper

carta verde vairday under-26 reduced fare railcard

carte fpl kartay cards

cartella f school-bag; briefcase

cartina f map

cartoleria f kartolairee-a stationer's

cartolibreria f kartoleebrairee-a stationery and bookshop

cartolina f postcard

cartone m kartonay cardboard

casa f kaza house

casalinga f kazaleenga housewife

casalinghi mpl household goods

cascata f waterfall

caseggiato m kasej-jato block (of apartments)

casella postale f postalay P.O. Box

casello autostradale m kazel-lo owtostradalay motorway/highway toll booth

caserma dei carabinieri f kasairma day karabeen-yairee military police station

caserma dei vigili del fuoco veejeelee del fwoko fire station

caso: per caso pair kazo by chance

in caso di emergenza rompere il vetro in case of emergency break the glass

in caso di sosta in galleria accendere i fari e spegnere il motore if stopping in tunnel, switch on headlights and switch off engine

cassa f kas-sa till, cashdesk, cashier

cassa automatica owtomateeka cash dispenser, automatic teller

cassa continua konteenwa cash dispenser, automatic teller

cassetta f box; cassette

cassetta delle lettere del-lay let-tairay postbox, mailbox

cassetta di sicurezza seekooretza safe-deposit box

cassetto m drawer

cassettone m kas-set-tonay

chest of drawers

cassiere *m* kas-syairay, **cassiera** *f* cashier, teller

castello *m* castle

catena *f* katayna chain

catenaccio *m* katenacho bolt

catino *m* basin

cattedrale *f* kat-taydralay cathedral

cattiveria *f* kat-teevair-ya nastiness; naughtiness

cattivo kat-teevo bad

cattolico Catholic

Travel tip Good Friday is celebrated in many towns and villages, particularly in the south, by parading models of Christ through the streets accompanied by white-robed, hooded figures singing penitential hymns. Many religious processions have strong pagan roots, marking important dates on the calendar and only relatively recently sanctified by the Church.

---

causa *f* kowza cause

cavallo *m* horse

andare a cavallo to go horse riding

cavatappi *m* corkscrew

caviglia *f* kaveel-ya ankle

CC (Carabinieri) military police force

c/c (conto corrente) *m* kor-rentay current account

CE *f* chay EC

c'è chay there is

non c'è he/she/it is not here

non c'è... there is no…

celeste chelestay light blue

celibe chayleebay single (man)

cena *f* chayna supper

cenare chenaray to have dinner

cenno *m* chen-no sign

centinaia *fpl* chenteena-ya hundreds

cento chento hundred

centralino *m* chentraleeno local exchange, operator

centrifuga *f* chentreefooga spin-dryer

centro *m* chentro centre

centro città cheet-ta city centre

centro commerciale kom-merchalay shopping centre

centro culturale kooltooralay arts centre

centro della città cheet-ta city centre

centro (di) informazioni turistiche eenformatz-yonee tooreesteekay tourist information office

centro sportivo sports centre

centro storico old town

ceramica *f* cherameeka pottery

cera per auto *f* chaira pair owto car wax

cercare chairkaray to look for

cerchio *m* chairk-yo circle

cerniera lampo *f* chairn-yaira zip

cerotto *m* cherot-to sticking

plaster, Bandaid

certamente chairtamentay
certainly

cestino *m* chesteeno basket;
wastepaper basket

cfr. (confronta) cf.

charter: il volo charter *m*
charter flight

che kay that, which; than
che? what?

check-in: fare il check-in
to check in

chi? kee who?

chiacchierare k-yak-yairaray
to chat

chiacchierone *m* k-yak-yaironay
chiacchierona *f* chatterbox;
talkative

chiamare k-yamaray to call
come si chiama? komay see
k-yama what's your name?
come ti chiami?
what's your name?

chiamata *f* k-yamata call

**chiamata a carico del
destinatario** kareeko del
desteenatar-yo reverse charge
call

chiamata in teleselezione
teleseletz-yonay direct dialling

chiamata interurbana
eentairoorbana long-distance call

chiamata urbana oorbana
local call

chiaro k-yaro clear; light

chiave *f* k-yavay key; spanner

chiave inglese eenglayzay

wrench

chiavetta *f* k-yavet-ta memory
stick

chiedere k-yaydairay to ask

chiesa *f* k-yayza church

chilo *m* keelo kilo

chilometro *m* keelometro
kilometre

chimica *f* keemeeka chemistry

chiocciola *f* k-yoch-chola @, at
sign

chiodo *m* k-yodo nail (metal)

chirurgia *f* keeroorjee-a surgery

chirurgo *m* keeroorgo surgeon

chitarra *f* keetar-ra guitar

chiude alle... closes at...

chiudere k-yoodairay to close

chiudere a chiave k-yavay
to lock

chiudere bene dopo l'uso
close tightly after use

chiudi il becco! k-yoodee eel
bek-ko shut up!

chiuso (dalle... alle...) k-yoozo
closed (from... to...)

chiuso per ferie closed for
holidays/vacation

chiuso per turno closing day

chiusura settimanale... closed
on...

ci chee here; there; us; each other;
to us; ourselves
ci sono there are

ciao! chow hello!; cheerio!,
goodbye!

ciascuno chaskoono, **ciascuna**
each

cibo *m* cheebo food

ciclismo *m* cheekleesmo cycling

ciclista *m/f* cheekleesta cyclist

cieco chee-ayko blind

cielo *m* chaylo sky

ciglia *fpl* cheel-ya eyelashes

cima: in cima (a) cheema
at the top (of)

cimitero *m* cheemeetairo
cemetery

cinghia della ventola *f*
cheeng-ya fan belt

cinquanta cheenkwanta fifty

cinque cheenkway five

cintura *f* cheentoora belt

cintura di sicurezza dee
seekooretza seat belt

ciò cho this; that

circa cheerka about

circonvallazione *f* cheerkonval-
latz-yonay ring road

**C.I.T. (Compagnia Italiana
Turismo)** *m* cheet Italian
tourist organization

città *f* cheet-ta town(s); city, cities
per la città local mail only

cittadina *f* cheet-tadeena citizen;
city dweller; town

cittadino *m* citizen; city dweller

clacson *m* horn

classe *f* klas-say class; classroom

classe economica economy
class

**clienti: i clienti sono pregati
di lasciare libere le camere
entro le ore 12 del giorno di
partenza** on day of departure,
guests are requested to vacate
rooms before midday

clima *m* climate

clinica *f* clinic

coda *f* tail; queue

coda del treno trayno rear of
the train

code traffic queues ahead

codice della strada *m*
kodeechay highway code

codice di avviamento postale
av-yamento postalay postcode,
zip code

cofano *m* bonnet, hood

cognata *f* kon-yata sister-in-law

cognato *m* brother-in-law

cognome *m* kon-yomay surname

coi koy with the

coiffeur *m* hair stylist

coincidenza *f* ko-eencheedentza
connection (travelling)

col with the

colazione *f* kolatz-yonay breakfast

colla *f* glue

collana *f* necklace

collant *m* kol-lan tights,
pantyhose

collasso *m* collapse

collasso cardiaco heart failure

colle *m* kol-lay hill

collegamenti internazionali
international connections

collegio *m* kol-layjo boarding
school

colletto *m* collar

collezionare kol-letz-yonaray
to collect

collezione *f* kol-letz-yonay
collection

collina *f* hill

collo *m* neck

colloquio *m* kol-lokw-yo
interview; conversation

colonna *f* column

colore *m* koloray colour

colorificio *m* koloreefeecho paint
and dyes shop

colpa: è colpa mia it's my fault

colpi di sole *mpl* solay highlights

colpire kolpeeray to hit; to knock

colpo di sole *m* solay sunstroke

coltello *m* knife

coltello da cucina koocheena
kitchen knife

coltello da pane panay
bread knife

comandante *m/f* komandantay
pilot

comando dei vigili del fuoco
m day veejeelee del fwoko fire
department headquarters

comando dei vigili urbani
oorbanee municipal
headquarters of traffic police

come komay like; as

  come? how?; what?; sorry?,
pardon me?, what did you say?

  come, scusi? skoozee
pardon?, pardon me?

  come stai/sta/state? sta-ee/
sta/statay how are you?

  come va? how are things?

comico *m* komeeko comic;
comedy; comedian

cominciare komeencharay to

start

comitiva *f* group

commedia *f* kom-mayd-ya play;
comedy

commesso *m*, **commessa** *f*
shop assistant

commissariato (di polizia)
m kom-mees-sar-yato dee
poleetzee-a police station

comodo comfortable

compact (disc) *m* compact disc

compagna *f* kompan-ya
schoolfriend; partner

compagnia aerea *f* kompan-
yee-a a-airay-a airline

compagno *m* kompan-yo
schoolfriend; partner

comperare kompairaray to buy

**compere: andare a fare le
compere** kompairay
to go shopping

competizione *f* kompeteetz-yonay
competition; race

compilare kompeelaray to fill in

compleanno *m* komplay-an-no
birthday

completamente kompleta-
mentay completely, entirely

completo *m* komplayto suit;
outfit

completo full; no vacancies

complicato complicated

complimento *m* compliment

comporre kompor-ray to dial

comportamento *m* behaviour

comportarsi to behave

composizione *f* kompozeetz-yonay
composition

comprare kompr**a**ray to buy

compreso kompr**ay**zo included

compressa f tablet

computer portatile m
portat**ee**lay laptop

comune m kom**oo**nay town hall;
municipal district

comunicazione f komooneekatz-
y**o**nay phone call

comunque kom**oo**nkway however

con with

concerto m konch**ai**rto concert

concessionario m konches-
syon**a**r-yo agent, dealer

conchiglia f konk**ee**l-ya shell

condoglianze fpl kondol-y**a**ntzay
condolences

condotta f behaviour

conducente m/f kondooch**e**ntay
driver

conferenza f konfair**e**ntza lecture;
conference

conferma: dare conferma
to confirm

confermare konfairm**a**ray
to confirm

confetto m sugar-coated pill;
sugar-coated almond

confezione f konfetz-y**o**nay pack;
packaging

confine m konf**ee**nay border

confusione f konfooz-y**o**nay
confusion; mess

congelatore m konjelat**o**ray
freezer

congratulazioni! kongratoolatz-
y**o**nee congratulations!

congresso m conference

conoscere kon**o**shairay to know

consegnare konsen-y**a**ray
to deliver

conservare in frigo keep
refrigerated

conservare in luogo asciutto
keep in a dry place

consigliare konseel-y**a**ray
to recommend

consolato m consulate

**consumarsi: da consumarsi
preferibilmente entro...** best
before...

contagioso kontaj**o**zo infectious

contanti mpl cash

pagare in contanti to pay
cash

contare kont**a**ray to count

contascatti *m* kontaskat-tee time-unit counter(s)

contatto: mettersi in contatto con to contact

contenere kontenairay to contain

contento happy; pleased

contenuto *m* kontenooto contents

continuare konteenwaray to continue, to go on

continui konteenwee keep going

continuo konteenwo continuous

conto *m* bill, check

conto corrente kor-rentay current account

conto in banca bank account

contraccettivo *m* kontrachetteevo contraceptive

contraccezione *f* kontra-chetzyonay contraception

contraddire kontrad-deeray to contradict

contrario a kontrar-yo opposed to

contrassegno IVA kontras-senyo eeva proof that VAT has been paid

contro against

controllare kontrol-laray to check

controllo automatico della velocità *m* automatic speed check

controllo bagagli bagal-yee baggage control

controllo biglietti ticket inspection

controllo passaporti passport control

controllo radar della velocità radar speed check

controllore *m* kontrol-loray ticket inspector; bus conductor

conversare konvairsaray to converse

conversazione *f* konvairsatz-yonay conversation

convincente konveenchentay convincing

convincere konveenchairay to convince, to persuade

convinto convinced

coperchio *m* kopairk-yo lid

coperta *f* kopairta blanket

coperto *m* cover charge

  al coperto indoors

coppa *f* cup

copriletto *m* bedspread

coraggioso koraj-jozo brave

corda *f* rope

cordiale kord-yalay friendly

cornice *f* korneechay frame

coro *m* choir

corpo *m* body

corrente *f* kor-rentay current; draught

correnti pericolose *fpl* dangerous currents

correre kor-rairay to run

corridoio *m* kor-reedo-yo corridor; aisle

corridore *m* kor-reedoray runner

corriera *f* kor-ya-ira coach, long-distance bus

corrispondente *m/f* kor-reespondentay penfriend

corrispondenza *f* kor-reespondentza mail;

correspondence

corruzione f kor-rootz-yonay corruption

corsa f race; running

corsa semplice sempleechay one way (ticket)

corsia di emergenza f emairjentza emergency lane

corso m course; main street

corso di lingua leengwa language course

cortile m korteelay courtyard

corto short

cosa f koza thing

  cosa? what?

  cosa hai/ha detto? what did you say?

coscia f kosha thigh

così kozee like this; so

  così grande granday so big

  così così so-so

costa f coast

costare kostaray to cost

costola f rib

costruire kostroo-eeray to build

costume m kostoomay custom

costume da bagno kostoomay da ban-yo swimsuit; swimming trunks

cotone m kotonay cotton

cotone idrofilo eedrofeelo cotton wool

cotto: ben cotto well done

  poco cotto underdone

  troppo cotto overdone

C.P. (Casella Postale) f P.O. Box

cravatta f tie, necktie

credenza f kredentza dresser; cupboard

credere kraydairay to believe, to think

  non posso crederci! kredairchee I can't believe it!

credito m kraydeeto credit

crema f krayma cream; custard

crema detergente detairjentay cleansing cream

crema idratante eedratantay moisturizer

crema solare solaray suntan lotion

cremeria f kremairee-a dairy shop, also selling ice cream and cakes

cretino m idiot, fool; stupid

C.R.I. (Croce Rossa Italiana) f Italian Red Cross

cric m jack

criminalità f crime(s)

crisi f kreezee crisis, crises

critica f criticism

criticare kreeteekaray to criticize

crociera f krochaira cruise

crudele kroodaylay cruel

cruscotto m krooskot-to dashboard

cuccetta f koochet-ta couchette

cucchiaino m kook-ya-eeno teaspoon; coffeespoon

cucchiaio m kook-ya-yo spoon

  un cucchiaio (di) a spoonful (of)

cucina f koocheena kitchen;

cooker; cooking, cookery

cucinare koocheenaray to cook

cucire koocheeray to sew

cuffia da bagno f ban-yo bathing cap

cugino m koojeeno, **cugina** f cousin

cultura f kooltoora culture

cunetta o dosso dips or blind summits

cuoca f kwoka cook

cuocere kwochairay to cook; to bake

cuoco m kwoko cook

cuoio m kwo-yo leather

cuore m kworay heart

cupola m dome, cupola

curioso koor-yozo curious

curva f koorva bend

curva pericolosa dangerous bend

cuscino m koosheeno pillow; cushion

D

da from; by; at; to

dà he/she it gives; you give

da consumarsi entro… use by…

dado m nut (for bolt); dice

dagli dal-yee from the; by the

dai da-ee from the; by the; you give

dallo, dal, dalla, dalle dal-lay from the; by the

dama f draughts

danese m/f danayzay Danish; Dane

Danimarca f Denmark

danneggiare dan-nej-jaray to damage

danno m damage; they give

dappertutto dap-pairtoot-to everywhere

dare m daray to give; debit

data f date

data di nascita nasheeta date of birth

date datay you give

davanti m davantee front (part)

  davanti a in front of

  passare davanti (a) to pass, to go past

da vendersi dietro presentazione di ricetta medica to be sold on prescription only

da vendersi entro… sell by…

davvero dav-vairo really?

  ah, davvero? is it?; do they? etc

d.C. (dopo Cristo) A.D.

debito m daybeeto debt

debole daybolay weak

decidere decheedairay to decide

decimo m daycheemo tenth

decollare dekol-laray to take off

decollo m take-off

degente m/f dejentay in-patient

del, dei day, **degli** dayl-yee some; of the

delfino m dolphin

delicato frail, delicate

delizioso deleetz-**yo**zo lovely,
  delicious; charming

dello, della, delle del-**lay**
  some; of the

deltaplano m hang-gliding

deludere del**oo**dairay
  to disappoint

deluso del**oo**zo disappointed

denaro m money

dente m **den**tay tooth

dentiera f dent-**yai**ra dentures

dentifricio m denteefr**ee**cho
  toothpaste

dentista m/f dentist

dentro inside

dépliant m **day**plee-ant
  brochure(s); leaflet(s)

deposito m dep**o**zeeto deposit

deposito bagagli bag**al**-yee
  left luggage, baggage check

deposito bancario bank**ar**-yo
  deposit account

depresso depressed

deputato m, **deputata** f MP

descrivere desk**ree**vairay
  to describe

desidera? dez**ee**daira what would
  you like?; can I help you?

destinatario m desteen**a**tar-yo
  addressee

destinazione f desteen**a**tz-yonay
  destination

destra f right

  a destra on/to the right

detersivo liquido per i piatti
  m detairs**ee**vo leekw**ee**do pair ee
  p-**yat**-ti washing-up liquid

detersivo per bucato book**a**to
  washing powder

detestare detest**a**ray to hate

deve **day**vay he/she/it must;
  you must

devi **day**vee you must

deviazione f dev-yatz-**yo**nay
  diversion

devo **day**vo I must

devono they must

di of; than

diabetico dee-ab**ay**teeko diabetic

dialetto m dialect

diamante m dee-am**an**tay
  diamond

diamo we give

diapositiva f dee-apozeet**ee**va
  slide

diario m dee-**ar**-yo diary

diarrea f dee-ar-**ray**-a diarrhoea

dibattito m debate

dica? yes?

dice d**ee**chay he/she/it says;
  you say

dicembre m deech**em**bray
  December

dichiarare deek-yar**a**ray
  to declare

dichiarazione f deek-yaratz-**yo**nay
  statement

dici d**ee**chee you say

diciamo deech-**ya**mo we say

diciannove deechan-**no**-vay
  nineteen

diciassette deechas-**set**-tay
  seventeen

diciotto deech**ot**-to eighteen

dico I say

dicono they say

dieci dee-aychee ten

dieta f d-yayta diet

   essere a dieta to be on a diet

dietro m d-yaytro back, rear; at the back

   dietro (a) behind

difendere deefendairay to defend

difettoso deefet-tozo faulty

difficile deef-feecheelay difficult

diligente deeleejentay hard-working

dimenticare deementeekaray to forget

dimenticarsi to forget

diminuire deemeenweeray to lessen

dimostrazione f deemostratz-yonay demonstration

dintorni mpl environs

   nei dintorni di in the vicinity of

Dio m dee-o God

   Dio mio! my God!

dipendere: dipende deependay it depends

dipingere deepeenjairay to paint

dipinto m painting

dire deeray to say; to tell

diretto m direct; through train

direttore m deeret-toray manager; headmaster

direttrice f deeret-treechay manageress; headmistress

direzione f deeretz-yonay direction

disaccordo m deezak-kordo disagreement

disastro m deezastro disaster

discesa f deeshaysa descent; slope; exit

disco m record

discorso m speech

discoteca f disco

discreto deeskrayto discreet

discutere (di) deeskootairay to discuss; to argue

disegnare deesen-yaray to draw

disegno m deesen-yo drawing

disfare: disfare le valigie deesfaray lay valeejay to unpack

disinfettante m deezeenfet-tantay disinfectant, antiseptic

disoccupato deezok-koopato unemployed

disoccupazione f deezok-koopatz-yonay unemployment

disordinato deezordeenato untidy

dispiacere: le dispiace se…? lay deesp-yachay say do you mind if I…?

   mi dispiace (tanto)! I'm (so) sorry!

dispiaciuto deesp-yachooto sorry

disporsi su due file get into two lanes

dispositivo m deespozeeteevo device

dispositivo di emergenza emergency button/handle

distante deestantay far away

distanza f deestantza distance

disteso deestayzo lying down

distinta di versamento *f*
deesteenta dee vairsamento
paying-in slip

distratto absent-minded;
inattentive

distribuire deestreebweeray
to distribute

distribuito da... deestreebweeto
distributed by...

distributore *m* deestreebootoray
distributor, dispenser; petrol
station, gas station

**distributore (automatico) di
biglietti** owtomateeko dee beel-
yet-tee ticket machine

disturbare deestoorbaray
to disturb

disuguale deezoogwalay unequal

ditale *m* deetalay thimble

dite deetay you say

dito *m* deetay finger

dito del piede p-yayday toe

ditta *f* deet-ta firm, company

divano *m* deevano sofa

diversi deevairsee, **diverse**
deevairsay several

diverso different

divertente deevairtentay amusing

divertirsi deevairteersee to enjoy
oneself

dividere deeveedairay to divide

divieto di accesso no entry

**divieto di accesso ai non
addetti ai lavori** no access –
works only

**divieto di accesso – escluso
residenti/bus/taxi**
residents/buses/taxis only

divieto di affissione
stick no bills

divieto di balneazione no
bathing

divieto di fermata no stopping

divieto di pesca no fishing

divieto di sosta no parking

divieto di transito no
thoroughfare

divorziato deevortz-yato divorced

dizionario *m* deetz-yonar-yo
dictionary

do I give

dobbiamo we must

docce *fpl* dochay showers

doccia *f* docha shower

   fare la doccia to have a
   shower

dodici doh-deechee twelve

Dogana *f* Customs

Dogana merci Customs for
freight

Dogana passeggeri passenger
Customs

dolce *m* dolchay sweet; cake

dolci *mpl* dolchee confectionery;
cakes

dollaro *m* dollar

dolore *m* doloray pain

doloroso dolorozo painful

domanda *f* question

domandare domandaray to ask

domani domanee tomorrow

   a domani see you tomorrow

domenica *f* domayneeka Sunday

   la domenica on Sundays

   la domenica e i giorni

festivi Sundays and public holidays

donna *f* woman

donne ladies (toilet), ladies rest room

dopo after; afterwards

dopobarba *m* aftershave

doposciampo *m* doposhampo conditioner

doppio dop-yo double

dormire dormeeray to sleep

   andare a dormire to go to bed

dottore (Dott.) *m* dot-toray doctor

dottoressa (Dott.ssa) *f* doctor

dove? dovay where?

   dove si trova...? where is...?

dovere *m* dovairay to have to, must; to owe; duty

dovete dovaytay you must

dovuto had to

dozzina *f* dodzeena dozen

   (una) dozzina (di) a dozen (of)

drammatico dramatic

dritto straight on

droga *f* drug(s)

drogheria *f* drogairee-a grocer's

dubitare doobeetaray to doubt

due doo-ay two

due pezzi *mpl* petzee bikini

dune *fpl* doonay sand dunes

dunque doonkway therefore, so; well (then)

duomo *m* dwomo cathedral

durante doorantay during

durante la marcia reggersi agli appositi sostegni please hold on while vehicle is in motion

duro dooro hard

E

e ay and

è ay he/she/it is; you are

ebreo ebray-o Jewish

ecc. (eccetera) etc

eccetto echet-to except

ecco ek-ko here is/are; here you are; that's it

   ecco qua! kwa here you are!

edicola *f* newsagent's

edificio *m* edeefeecho building

educato edookato polite

effettua: si effettua dal... al... this service is available from... until...

Egr.Sig. (egregio signore) Mr (in letters)

elastico *m* rubber band; elastic

elenco telefonico *m* telayfoneeko telephone directory

elettrauto *m* elet-trowto workshop for car electrical repairs

elettricista *m* elet-treecheesta electrician

elettricità *f* elet-treecheeta electricity

elettrico elet-treeko electric

elettrodomestici *mpl* elet-trodomesteechee electrical appliances

elicottero *m* helicopter

emergenza *f* emairjentza
emergency; emergency lane

emissione del biglietto
take your ticket here

emozionante emotz-yonantay
exciting

E.N.I.T. (Ente Nazionale Italiano per il Turismo) *m*
eneet Italian national tourist board

enorme enormay enormous

enoteca *f* enotayka
wine-tasting shop

entrare entraray to go in;
to come in

entrata *f* entrance

entrata con abbonamento o biglietto già convalidato
entry for those with season tickets or with validated tickets

entrata libera admission free

entusiasmante entooz-yazmantay
fascinating; exciting

E.P.T. (Ente Provinciale per il Turismo) *m* Italian local tourist board

equipaggio *m* ekeepaj-jo crew

equitazione *f* ekweetatz-yonay
horse riding

equivoco *m* ekweevoko
misunderstanding

erba *f* airba grass

errore *m* er-roray mistake

esagerare esajairaray
to exaggerate

esame *m* esamay examination

esattamente esat-tamentay
exactly

esatto esat-to correct

esaurito sold out

esausto esowsto exhausted

escluso frontisti residents only

escluso sabato e festivi
except Saturdays and Sundays/ holidays

escursione *f* eskoors-yonay
excursion, outing; hike

esempio *m* esemp-yo example

per esempio for example

esente da tasse esentay da
tas-say duty-free

esercizio *m* ezaircheetz-yo
exercise; shop

espresso *m* strong black coffee; express letter; express train

esprimere espreemairay
to express

essere es-sairay to be

esso es-so it

est *m* east

estate *f* estatay summer

estero: all'estero al-lestairo
abroad

estetista *f* beautician

estintore *m* esteentoray fire extinguisher

età *f* ayta age

etichetta *f* eteeket-ta label

etto(grammo) *m* hundred grams

Eurocity *m* international fast train

europeo ay-ooropay-o European

evitare eeveetaray to avoid

F

F (freddo) cold

fa he/she/it does; you do; ago

fabbrica *f* factory

facchino *m* fak-**kee**no porter

faccia *f* facha face

facciamo fachamo we do

faccio facho I do

facile facheelay easy

fai fa-ee you do

fai da te *m* da tay DIY

falso false

fame: avere fame avairay famay
   to be hungry

famiglia *f* fameel-ya family

famoso famous

fanno they do

fantastico *m* terrific; fantasy
   film/movie

fa' pure! pooray do as you
   please!; please, do!

fare faray to make; to do

farfalla *f* butterfly

fari *mpl* headlights

fari posteriori postair-yoree
   rear lights

farmacia *f* farmachee-a chemist's,
   pharmacy

farmacia di turno duty
   chemist's, late-night pharmacy

faro *m* light; lighthouse

fasciatura *f* fashatoora bandage

fastidio *m* fasteed-yo nuisance

fate fatay you do

fatica *f* fateeka hard work; strain

fatto a mano handmade

fattoria *f* farm

fattura *f* fat-toora invoice

favore *m* favoray favour

per favore please

favorevole *a* favorayvolay
   in favour of

fazzolettini di carta *mpl* fatzolet-
   teenee tissues, Kleenex

fazzoletto *m* fatzolet-to
   handkerchief

febbraio *m* feb-bra-yo February

febbre *f* feb-bray temperature

febbre da fieno *f* f-yayno hay
   fever

federa *f* faydaira pillowcase

fegato *m* faygato liver

felice feleechay happy

feriale: giorno feriale
   jorno fair-yalay working day

feriali *mpl* working days

ferita *f* wound

ferito injured

fermare fairm**a**ray to stop

fermarsi to stop

fermata (dell'autobus) *f* fairm**a**ta del-l**ow**toboos (bus) stop

fermata a richiesta reek-y**e**sta request stop

fermata facoltativa fakoltat**ee**va request stop

fermata obbligatoria ob-bleegat**o**r-ya compulsory stop

fermata prenotata bus/tram stopping

fermo! f**ai**rmo don't move!

fermo per manutenzione closed for repairs

fermo posta *m* poste restante

ferragosto *m* August 15th (public holiday)

ferramenta *f* hardware store(s)

ferro *m* f**ai**r-ro iron; knitting needle

ferro da stiro st**ee**ro iron (for ironing)

ferrovia *f* fair-rov**ee**-a railway

Ferrovie dello Stato *fpl* fair-rov**ee**-ay Italian State Railways

festa *f* party; holiday, vacation

festivi *mpl* public holidays

fetta *f* slice

FFSS (Ferrovie dello Stato) *fpl* Italian state railways

fiala *f* f-y**a**la phial

fiammifero *m* f-yam-m**ee**fairo match (light)

fianco *m* f-y**a**nko side; hip

fidanzata *f* feedantz**a**ta fiancée

fidanzato *m* fiancé; engaged

fidarsi to trust

fido *m* credit

fiera *f* f-y**ai**ra funfair; trade fair

fiero proud

figlia *f* f**ee**l-ya daughter

figlio *m* son

figlio di puttana! dee son of a bitch!

fila *f* queue

   fare la fila to queue

film *m* film, movie

filo *m* thread

filo di ferro wire

filtro *m* filter

finale *f* feen**a**lay final

finalmente feenalm**e**ntay at last

finché feenk**ay** until

fine *f* f**ee**nay end; thin; fine (blade, pen etc); refined

fine del tratto autostradale end of motorway/highway

fine settimana set-teem**a**na weekend

finestra *f* window

finestrino *m* window (on plane, train)

finire feen**ee**ray to finish

fino thin; fine (blade, pen etc); even

   fino a until

finocchio *m* feen**o**k-yo fennel

fioraio *m* f-yor**a**-yo florist

fiore *m* f-y**o**ray flower

fiorentino fyor**e**nteeno Florentine

Firenze *f* feer**e**ntzay Florence

firma *f* signature

firmare feermaray to sign

fischio *m* feesk-yo whistle

fisica *f* feezeeka physics

fiume *m* f-yoomay river

flacone *m* flakonay medicine
bottle

foglia *f* fol-ya leaf

folla *f* crowd

fon *m* hair dryer

fondo *m* bottom

in fondo a at the end/bottom
of

fondotinta *m* fondoteenta
foundation cream

fontana *f* fountain

footing *m* jogging

foratura *f* foratoora puncture

forbici *mpl* forbeechee scissors

forchetta *f* forket-ta fork

foresta *f* forest

forfora *f* dandruff

forma *f* form

in forma fit

formato emme-pi-tre *m*
formato em-may pee tray MP3
format

formica *f* formeeka ant

fornaio *m* forna-yo baker's

fornello *m* cooker; hob

fornire forneeray to supply

forniture per ufficio *fpl* office
supplies

forno *m* oven

forno a microonde meekro-
onday microwave (oven)

forse forsay maybe, perhaps

forte fortay strong; loud

fortuna *f* fortoona luck

fortunatamente fortoonatamentay
fortunately

foruncolo *m* spot

fotografare fotografaray
to photograph

fotografia *f* fotografee-a
photograph; photography

fare fotografie fotografee-ay
to take photographs

fotografo *m* photographer

fotoottica *f* camera shop and
optician

foulard *m* foolar headscarf

fra between; in; through

fra l'altro besides

fragile frajeelay frail

francamente frankamentay
frankly

francese *m/f* franchayzay French;
Frenchman; Frenchwoman

Francia *f* francha France

franco *m* franc

francobollo *m* frankobol-lo stamp

frasario *m* frazar-yo phrasebook

frase *f* frazay sentence

fratello *m* brother

frattura *f* frat-toora fracture

frazione *f* fratz-yonay fraction;
administrative division of a
municipality

freccia *f* frecha indicator; arrow

freddo *m* cold

fa freddo it's cold

avere freddo to be cold

freno m frayno brake

freno a mano handbrake

fresco fresh; cool (weather)

friggere freej-jairay to fry

friggitrice f freej-jeetreechay
deep-fat fryer

frigo m fridge

frigobar m minibar

frigorifero m freegoreefairo fridge

frizione f freetz-yonay clutch;
friction

fronte f frontay forehead
di fronte a opposite;
in front of

frontiera f front-yaira border

frullatore m frool-latoray mixer

frusta f whisk

fruttivendolo m froot-teevendolo
greengrocer's

FS (Ferrovie dello Stato) fpl
Italian state railways

f.to (firmato) signed

fucile m foocheelay gun; rifle

fumare foomaray to smoke

fumatori smokers

fumetto m comic; strip cartoon

fumo m foomo smoke

fune f foonay rope

funivia f fooneevee-a cable car

funzionare foontz-yonaray
to work

fuochi d'artificio mpl fwokee
darteefeecho fireworks

fuoco m fwoko fire

fuori fworee outside

fuori servizio out of order

furgone m foorgonay van

furioso foor-yozo furious

fusibile m foozeebeelay fuse

G

gabinetto m gabeenet-to toilet,
rest room
andare al gabinetto to go to
the toilet/rest room

galleria f gal-lair-ee-a tunnel;
balcony; circle

galleria d'arte dartay art gallery

Galles m gal-les Wales

gallese m/f gal-layzay Welsh;
Welshman; Welshwoman

gamba f leg

gara f sporting event; race;
competition

garanzia f garantzee-a guarantee

gasolio m gazol-yo diesel oil

gasolio invernale eenvairnalay
diesel containing anti-freeze

gatto m cat

gelateria f jelatairee-a ice cream
parlour

gelato m jelato ice cream; frozen

gelo m jaylo frost

gelosia f jelozee-a jealousy

geloso jelozo jealous

gemelli mpl jemel-lee twins

generalmente jenairalmentay
generally

genere m jaynairay type
in genere mostly, generally

genero m jaynairo son-in-law

genitori mpl jeneetoree parents

gennaio m jen-na-yo January

Genova *f* jenova Genoa

gente *f* jentay people

gentile jenteelay kind

gentilezza *f* jenteeletza kindness

Germania *f* jerman-ya Germany

gesto *m* jesto gesture

gettare jet-taray to throw

   gettare via to throw away

gettoni *mpl* jet-tonee telephone
   tokens

ghiacciaio *m* g-yacha-o glacier

ghiaccio *m* g-yacho ice

già ja already

giacca *f* jak-ka jacket

giacca a vento anorak

giallo *m* jal-lo yellow; thriller

giardini pubblici *mpl* poob-
   bleechee public gardens

giardino *m* jardeeno garden

ginecologo *m* jeenaykologo
   gynaecologist

Ginevra *f* jeenevra Geneva

ginnastica *f* jeen-nasteeka
   gymnastics; PE

ginocchio *m* jeenok-yo knee

giocare jokaray to play

giocatore *m* jokatoray player

giocatrice *f* jokatreechay player

giocattolo *m* jokat-tolo toy

giochi per il computer *mpl*
   j-yokee computer games

gioco *m* joko game

gioco di società dee socheta
   board game

gioielleria *f* jo-yel-lairee-a
   jeweller's

gioielli *mpl* jo-yel-lee jewellery

gioielliere *m* jo-yel-yairay jeweller

giornalaio *m* jornala-yo
   newsagent's

giornale *m* jornalay newspaper

giornata *f* jornata day

giorni feriali *mpl* weekdays

giorni festivi public holidays

giorno *m* jorno day

giorno di chiusura k-yoozoora
   closing day

giovane *m/f* jovanay young;
   young person

giovedì *m* jovaydee Thursday

giradischi *m* jeeradeeskee
   record player

girare jeeraray to turn

girarsi to turn

giri a destra jeeree turn right

giri a sinistra seeneestra turn left

giro *m* jeero turn; walk, stroll;
   tour

   a giro di posta by return mail

   andare a far un giro to go for
   a stroll/drive

   fare un giro in bicicletta
   beecheeklet-ta to go for a cycle
   ride

giro a piedi p-yaydee walk, stroll

giro in barca boat trip

giro in macchina mak-keena
   drive

gita *f* jeeta excursion, outing; hike

gita in pullman coach trip

gita organizzata organeedzata
   package tour

gita scolastica skol**a**steeka
school trip

giù joo down

**giubbotti salvagente sotto la
poltrona** lifejackets are under
the seat

giugno *m* j**oo**n-yo June

giusto j**oo**sto right, correct; fair

gli l-yee the; to him; to them

goccia *f* go**cha** drop

gola *f* throat

golf *m* golf; jumper

gomito *m* elbow

gomma *f* rubber; tyre

gomma a terra flat tyre

gomma di scorta spare tyre

gommista *m/f* tyre repair
specialist

gommone *m* gom-m**o**nay
(rubber) dinghy

gonfio gonf-yo swollen

gonna *f* skirt

gorgo *m* whirlpool

governativo governmental; state

governo *m* government

gradino *m* step

grado *m* degree, level

grammatica *f* grammar

grammo *m* gramme

Gran Bretagna *f* bretan-ya
Great Britain

granchio *m* grank-yo crab

grande grand**a**y big

grande magazzino *m*
magadz**ee**no department store

grandine *f* grand**ee**nay hail

grasso fat

gratis free

grato grateful

grattacielo *m* grat-tach**a**ylo
skyscraper

grattugiare grat-tooj**a**ray to grate

gratuito grat**oo**-eeto free

grazie gratzee-ay thank you

grazie a Dio! thank God!

grazie, anche a te/lei ankay
a tay/lay thank you, the same to
you

grazie mille meel-lay thank
you very much

grazioso gratz-y**o**zo pretty

Grecia *f* gr**e**cha Greece

greco *m* Greek

gridare greed**a**ray to shout

grigio gr**ee**jo grey

grosso big, large; thick

grotta *f* cave

gruccia *f* gr**oo**cha coathanger

gruppo *m* group

gruppo sanguigno sangw**ee**n-yo
blood group

guancia *f* gw**a**ncha cheek

guanti *mpl* gw**a**ntee gloves

guanto di spugna *m* dee sp**oo**n-
ya flannel

guardare gward**a**ray to look (at)

guardare in su een soo
to look up

guardaroba *m* gwardar**o**ba
wardrobe; cloakroom

guasto *m* gw**a**sto breakdown;
broken, out of order; rotten

guerra *f* gw**air**-ra war

guida *f* gweeda guide; guidebook

guidare gweedaray to lead; to drive

guidare a passo d'uomo dwomo drive at walking speed

guida telefonica *f* gweeda telephone directory

guscio *m* goosho shell

gusto *m* taste

H

ha a he/she it has; you have

hai a-ee you have

hanno an-no they have

ho o I have

I

i ee the

idea *f* eeday-a idea

idiota *m/f* eed-yota idiot

idraulico *m* eedrowleeko plumber

ieri yairee yesterday

il eel the

imbarazzante eembaratzantay embarrassing

imbarazzato eembaratzato embarrassed

imbarazzo *m* eembaratzo embarrassment

imbarcarsi eembarkarsee to board, to embark

imbarco *m* eembarko boarding

imbarco immediato now boarding

imbrogliare eembrol-yaray to cheat

imbucare eembookaray to post, to mail

immediatamente eem-med-yata-mentay immediately

immersione *f* eem-mairs-yonay skin-diving

immigrato *m* eem-meegrato, **immigrata** *f* immigrant

imparare eempararay to learn

impaziente eempatz-yentay impatient

impermeabile *m* eempairmay-abeelay raincoat; waterproof

importante eemportantay important; significant; sizeable

importare: non importa eemporta it doesn't matter

imposta *f* tax

impostare eempostaray to post, to mail

imposte *fpl* eempostay shutters

improvvisamente eemprov-veezamentay suddenly

in in; into; to

in macchina mak-keena by car

incartare eenkartaray to wrap

incassare eenkas-saray to cash

incidente *m* eencheedentay accident

incinta eencheenta pregnant

incontro *m* meeting

incrocio *m* eenkrocho junction; crossroads, intersection

incrocio pericoloso dangerous junction

indicare eendeekaray to indicate;

to point at; to show

indietro eend-**yay**tro behind; back

faccia marcia indietro facha marcha reverse

indirizzo *m* eendee**reet**zo address

indubbiamente eendoob-ya**men**tay undoubtedly

infarto *m* heart attack

infelice eenfelee**chay** unhappy

infermeria *f* eenfairmair**ee**-a infirmary

infermiere *m* eenfairm-**yai**ray, **infermiera** *f* nurse

infezione *f* eenfetz-**yo**nay infection

influenzare eenfloo-entzaray to influence

informare eenformaray to inform

informarsi (su) to get information (about)

informazioni *fpl* eenformatz-**yo**nee (tourist) information

informazioni elenco abbonati directory enquiries

Ing. (ingegnere) engineer

ingannare eengan-**na**ray to deceive

ingegnere *m* eenjen-**yai**ray engineer

ingenuo eenj**ay**nwo naïve

Inghilterra *f* eengeeltair-ra England

inglese *m/f* eengl**ay**zay English; Englishman; Englishwoman

ingoiare eengo-**ya**ray to swallow

ingorgo *m* traffic jam

ingrandimento *m* enlargement

ingrassaggio *m* eengras-**saj**-jo oiling, lubrication

ingresso *m* entrance (hall)

ingresso gratuito/libero admission free

iniezione *f* eenyetz-**yo**nay injection

inizio *m* een**eetz**-yo beginning

innumerevole een-noomair**ay**volay innumerable

inoltrare eenoltraray to forward

inquilino *m* eenkweel**ee**no, **inquilina** *f* tenant

inquinato eenkween**a**to polluted

insegnante *m/f* eensen-**yan**tay teacher

insegnare eensen-**ya**ray to teach

inserire le monete insert coins

insettifugo *m* eenset-t**ee**foogo insect repellent

insetto *m* eenset-to insect

insieme eens-**yay**may together

insistere eensee**stay**ray to insist

insonnia *f* eenson-ya insomnia

interessante eentaires-**san**tay interesting

interessarsi di/a eentaires-sarsee dee to be interested in

internazionale eentairnatz-yon**a**lay international

interno internal; inside

all'interno inside

intero whole

interruttore *m* eentair-root-t**o**ray switch

interruzione della corrente

f eentair-rootz-y**o**nay d**e**l-la kor-
rentay power cut

intervallo *m* eentairval-lo interval;
break; half-time

intervista *f* eentairve**e**sta
interview

intorno (a) around

intossicazione alimentare
f eentos-seekatz-y**o**nay
aleementaray food poisoning

**introdurre un biglietto alla
volta** insert only one ticket at
a time

invalido disabled

per invalidi for disabled
people

inverno *m* winter

investire eenveste**e**ray to invest;
to knock over

inviare eenv-ya**ra**y
to send; to post, to mail

invidioso eenveed-y**o**zo envious

invitare eenveeta**ra**y to invite

invito *m* invitation

io ee-o I

Irlanda *f* eerl**a**nda Ireland

Irlanda del Nord Northern
Ireland

irlandese *m/f* eerland**ay**zay Irish;
Irishman; Irishwoman

isola *f* e**e**zola island

istituto *m* institute; secondary
school; department

istruttore di nuoto *m* eestroot-
t**o**ray dee nw**o**to swimming
instructor

istruttrice di nuoto *f* eestroot-

tr**e**echay swimming instructor

istruzioni per l'uso instructions
for use

Italia *f* eet**a**l-ya Italy

italiano *m* eetal-y**a**no, **italiana** *f*
Italian

itinerario *m* eeteenair**a**r-yo route,
itinerary

**I.V.A. (Imposta sul Valore
Aggiunto)** *f* e**e**va VAT

I.V.A. compresa kompr**a**yza
inclusive of VAT

K

K-way *m* cagoule

L

L pound, £; lira

l (litro) litre

la the; her; it; you

là there

di là dee over there; that way;
in the other room; from there

labbro *m* l**a**b-bro lip

lacca per capelli *f* kap**e**l-lee
hair spray

lacci per le scarpe *mpl* l**a**chee
pair lay sk**a**rpay shoe laces

ladro *m* thief

laggiù laj-j**oo** over there

lago *m* lake

laguna *f* lagoon

lamentarsi to complain

lametta *f* razor blade

lampada *f* lamp

lampada da comodino bedside lamp

lampadina *f* light bulb

lampione *m* lamp-yonay street lamp

lana *f* wool

lanciare lancharay to throw

largo wide

lasciare lasharay to leave; to let, to allow

lassativo *m* laxative

lato *m* side

latte detergente *m* lat-tay detairjentay skin cleanser

latteria *f* lat-tairee-a dairy shop

lattina *f* can

laurea *f* lowray-a degree

lavabo *m* washbasin

lavanderia (automatica) *f* lavandairee-a owtomateeka launderette

lavandino *m* sink

lavare lavaray to wash

lavare a mano wash by hand

lavare a secco dry-clean only

lavare i panni to do the washing

lavare i piatti p-yat-tee to do the washing-up

lavare la biancheria b-yan-kairee-a to do the washing

lavare separatamente wash separately

lavarsi lavarsee to wash, to have a wash

lavarsi i denti to brush one's teeth

lavasecco *m* dry-cleaner's

lavastoviglie *f* lavastoveel-yay dishwasher

lavatrice *f* lavatreechay washing machine

lavorare lavoraray to work

lavori in corso *mpl* roadworks

lavori stradali roadworks

lavoro *m* work

le lay the; to her; to you

legare legaray to tie

legge *f* lej-jay law

leggere lej-jairay to read

leggero lej-jairo light

legno *m* len-yo wood

lei lay she; her; you

lentamente lentamentay slowly

lenti a contatto *fpl* contact lenses

lenti morbide *fpl* morbeeday soft lenses

lenti rigide *fpl* reejeeday hard lenses

lenti semi-rigide *fpl* saymee reejeeday gas permeable lenses

lento slow

lenzuolo *m* lentzwolo sheet

lettera *f* let-taira letter

lettera tassata excess postage to be paid

letti a castello *mpl* bunk beds

lettino *m* cot; sun lounger

lettino pieghevole p-yaygay-volay lounger; campbed

letto *m* bed

  andare a letto to go to bed

(ri)fare il letto to make the bed

letto a due piazze doo-ay p-yatzay double bed

letto a una piazza p-yatza single bed

leva del cambio *f* layva del kamb-yo gear lever

levare layvaray to remove

levata *f* layvata collection

lezione *f* letz-yonay lesson; class

li lee them

lì lee there

libbra *f* pound

libero vacant, free

libertà *f* freedom

libreria *f* leebrairee-a bookshop, bookstore; bookcase

libretto degli assegni *m* daylyee as-sen-yee cheque book, checkbook

libro *m* book

liceo *m* leechay-o secondary school

lima *f* leema file

lima per le unghie oong-yay nailfile

limite delle acque sicure *m* end of safe bathing area

limite di velocità speed limit

linea *f* leenay-a line

linea aerea a-airay-a airline

linea ferroviaria railway line

lingua *f* leengwa tongue; language

liquido tergicristallo *m* leekweedo tairjeekreestal-lo screen wash

liquori *mpl* leekworee spirits

lira sterlina *f* stairleena pound sterling

liscio leesho smooth; neat

lista *f* list; menu

listino dei cambi *m* exchange rates

L(it). (lire italiane) Italian lire

lite *f* leetay fight

litigare leeteegaray to argue, to quarrel

litigio *m* leeteejo argument, quarrel

litro *m* litre

livido *m* bruise

lo the; him; it

località *f* locality

locanda *f* guesthouse, hotel

loggione *m* loj-jonay gallery, the gods

londinese *m/f* londeenayzay

London *(adj)*; Londoner

Londra *f* London

lontano far away

loro they; them; you

  il/la loro their(s); your(s)

lozione idratante *f* lotz-yonay eedratantay moisturizer

lozione solare solaray suntan lotion

L.st. (lira sterlina) pound

luce *f* loochay light

lucidare loocheedaray to polish

luci di posizione *mpl* loochee dee pozeetz-yonay sidelights

lucido per le scarpe *m* loocheedo pair lay skarpay shoe polish

luglio *m* lool-yo July

lui loo-ee he; him

luna *f* loona moon

luna di miele m-yaylay honeymoon

luna park *m* funfair

lunedì *m* loonaydee Monday

lunghezza *f* loongetza length

lungo long; along

lungomare *m* loongomaray esplanade, promenade

luogo di nascita *m* lwogo dee nasheeta place of birth

M

M (Metropolitana) underground, (US) subway

m (metro) metre

ma but

macchia *f* mak-ya stain

macchina *f* mak-keena car; machine

macchina da scrivere skreevairay typewriter

macchina del caffè kaf-fay coffee-maker

macchina fotografica camera

macchina obliteratrice obleetairatreechay ticket-stamping machine

macelleria *f* machel-lairee-a butcher's

macinacaffè *m* macheena-kaf-fay coffee grinder

madre *f* madray mother

maestra *f* mystra primary school teacher; instructor

maestra di sci shee ski instructor

maestro *m* mystro primary school teacher; instructor

maestro di sci shee ski instructor

maggio *m* maj-jo May

maggior: la maggior parte (di) maj-jor partay most (of)

maggiore maj-joray bigger

maglia *f* mal-ya sweater, pullover

  lavoro a maglia *m* knitting

maglietta *f* mal-yet-ta T-shirt

maglione *m* mal-yonay sweater, jumper

mai ma-ee never

malato ill

malattia *f* disease

malattia venerea vaynairay-a VD

maldestro clumsy

mal di denti m dentee toothache

mal di gola sore throat

mal di mare maray seasickness

mal di testa headache

male m malay pain, ache

far male to hurt

male badly

maledetto damned, cursed

maledizione! maledeetz-yonay damn!

maleducato rude

malgrado despite

malinteso m maleentayzo misunderstanding

malizia f maleetz-ya mischief; malice

malizioso maleetz-yozo mischievous

mancia f mancha tip (in restaurant etc)

mancino mancheeno left-handed

mandare mandaray to send

mangiacassette m manjakas-set-tay portable cassette player

mangianastri m manja-nastree cassette player

mangiare manjaray to eat

manica f sleeve

manifesto m poster

maniglia f maneel-ya handle; door knob

mano f hand

di seconda mano second-hand

mansarda f attic room

Mantova f Mantua

manuale di conversazione m manwalay dee konvairsatz-yonay phrasebook

maratona f marathon

Marche fpl markay Marches

marcia a senso unico alternato temporary one way system in operation

marcia normale normal speed lane

marciapiede m marchap-yayday pavement, sidewalk; platform, track

marco m mark

mare m maray sea

sul mare at the seaside

marea f maray-a tide

alta/bassa marea high/low tide

mar Ionio m ee-on-yo Ionian Sea

marito m husband

mar Mediterraneo m medeetair-ranay-o Mediterranean

marmo m marble

marrone mar-ronay brown

martedì m Tuesday

martello m hammer

mar Tirreno m teer-rayno Tyrrhenian Sea

marzo m martzo March

mascella f mashel-la jaw

maschera f maskaira mask

maschilista m maskeeleesta male chauvinist

massa: una massa (di gente) *f*
a crowd (of people)

massimo: al massimo at the
most

materassino (gonfiabile) *m*
gonfee-**a**beelay air mattress, Lilo

materasso *m* mattress

materia *f* mat**air**-ya subject

matita *f* pencil

matrimonio *m* wedding

mattina *f* morning

   la/alla mattina in the
   morning

   ogni mattina **o**n-yee every
   morning

mattino *m* morning

   il/al mattino in the morning

maturo mat**oo**ro ripe

ma va? really?

   ma va! I don't believe it!

mazza *f* m**a**tza club; bat

me may me

meccanico *m* mek-k**a**neeko
mechanic

medaglia *f* med**a**l-ya medal

media *f* m**a**yd-ya average

medicina *f* medeech**e**ena
medicine

medico (di turno) *m* m**a**ydeeko
dee t**oo**rno doctor (on duty)

medio m**a**yd-yo average; medium

Medioevo *m* med-yo-**a**yvo
Middle Ages

Mediterraneo *m* medeetair-
r**a**nay-o Mediterranean

medusa *f* med**oo**za jellyfish

meglio m**a**yl-yo better

meglio così koz**ee** so much
the better

meno (di) m**a**yno dee less (than)

mento *m* chin

mentre m**e**ntray while

menzionare mentz-yon**a**ray
to mention

meraviglioso meraveel-y**o**zo
wonderful

mercato *m* mairk**a**to market

   a buon mercato bwon cheap,
   inexpensive

> **Travel tip** Every large village
> and town has at least one
> weekly market, and though
> these are usually geared
> towards household goods,
> they can be useful for picking
> up cheap clothing, basket-
> ware, ceramics and picnic
> ingredients.

merce *f* m**ai**rchay goods

   **la merce venduta non si
   cambia senza lo scontrino**
   goods are not exchanged
   without a receipt

merceria *f* mairchair**ee**-a
haberdashery, **(US)** notions

mercoledì *m* mairkoled**ee**
Wednesday

merda! m**ai**rda shit!

merenda *f* afternoon snack

   far merenda to have an
   afternoon snack

mese *m* m**a**yzay month

messa *f* mass

messaggio *m* mes-saj-jo message

messa in piega *f* p-yayga set

messa in piega con il fon
blow-dry

mestiere *m* mest-yairay job

mestruazioni *fpl* mestrwatz-yonee
period, menstruation

metà *f* half

  metà prezzo pretzo half price

metallo *m* metal

metro *m* metre

metrò *m* underground, (US)
subway

metropolitana *f* underground,
subway

mettere met-tairay to put

mettersi in viaggio met-tairsee
een v-yaj-jo to set off on a
journey

mezza: mezza dozzina (di)
medza dodzeena dee half a
dozen (of)

mezzanotte *f* medzanot-tay
midnight

mezza pensione *f* medza pens-
yonay half board

mezzo *m* medzo half; middle

  in mezzo a in the middle of

mezzogiorno *m* medzojorno
midday

mezz'ora *f* medzora half an hour

mi mee me; myself; to me

mia mee-a my; mine

mi dica mee deeka yes?; what
would you like?

mie mee-ay my; mine

miei m-yay-ee my; mine

migliaia *fpl* meel-ya-ya thousands

migliorare meel-yoraray to
improve

migliori meel-yoree, **migliore**
meel-yoray best; better

milanese *m/f* meelanayzay
Milanese; person from Milan

milione meel-yonay million

mille meelay thousand

mingherlino meengairleeno
skinny

minimo least, slightest

  come minimo komay at least

ministero *m* ministry; board;
office

minuto *m* minute

mio mee-o my; mine

mirino *m* viewfinder

mi scusi skoozee excuse me;
sorry

mi spiace spee-achay I'm sorry

misto lana meesto wool mixture

misurare meezooraray to measure

mitt. (mittente) sender

mittente *m* meet-tentay sender

mobili *mpl* mobeelee furniture

moda *f* fashion

  di moda fashionable

modulo *m* form

moglie *f* mol-yay wife

molla *f* spring (mechanical)

molletta (da bucato) *f* clothes
peg

molo *m* quay; pier; jetty

molta a lot, much; very

molti, molte moltay a lot; much;
very; many, lots of

molto a lot; much; very

molto bene, grazie baynay very well, thank you

momento: un momento, prego praygo one moment, please

mondo m world

moneta f monayta coin; small change

monolocale m monolokalay studio flat/apartment

montagna f montan-ya mountain

monumento ai caduti war memorial

moquette f moket (fitted) carpet

morbido soft

morbillo m measles

morire moreeray to die

morso m bite

morte f mortay death

morto dead

mosca f fly

moschea f moskay-a mosque

moscone m moskonay twin-hulled rowing boat

mostra f exhibition; show

mostrare mostraray to show

moto f motorbike

motore m motoray engine

motorino m moped

motoscafo m motorboat

movimenti mpl transactions

movimento m movement

mucca m cow

multa f fine

municipio m mooneecheep-yo town hall

munitevi di un carrello/cestino please take a trolley/basket

muovere mwovairay to move

muoversi mwovairsee to move

muoviti! mwoveetee hurry up!

muro m wall

muscolo m muscle

museo m moozay-o museum

> Travel tip When you arrive in a city it's worth checking with the tourist office about any city cards or passes available: as well as being convenient, they often give you other discounts as well as entry to a number of museums or sites.

musica f moozeeka music

mutande fpl mootanday underpants; pants, panties

mutuo m mootwo mortgage; bank loan

N

nafta f diesel oil

napoletano Neapolitan

Napoli f Naples

nascita f nasheeta birth

nascondere naskondairay to hide

nascondersi to hide

naso m nazo nose

nastro m tape; ribbon

nastro adesivo adhesive tape

nastro trasportatore

trasportat<u>o</u>ray conveyor belt

Natale *m* nat<u>a</u>lay Christmas

Buon Natale! bwon
Merry Christmas!

natale native

nato born

natura *f* nature

naturale: al naturale natoor<u>a</u>lay
(food) plain; natural

naturalmente natooralm<u>e</u>ntay
naturally, of course

naturista *m/f* naturist, nudist

nausea: avere la nausea
av<u>ai</u>ray n<u>o</u>wzay-a to feel sick/
queasy

nave *f* n<u>a</u>vay ship

nave di linea l<u>ee</u>n-ya liner

nave passeggeri pas-sej-j<u>ai</u>ree
passenger ship

navigare nav<u>ee</u>garay to sail

nazionale natz-yon<u>a</u>lay national;
domestic

nazionalità *f* natz-yonal<u>ee</u>ta
nationality

nazione *f* natz-y<u>o</u>nay nation

ne nay of him/her/them/it; about
him/her/them/it

non ne ho o I don't have any

prendine prend<u>ee</u>nay take
some

né: né… né… nay neither…
nor…

neanche nay-<u>a</u>nkay not even

nebbia *f* fog

nebbioso neb-y<u>o</u>zo foggy

necessario neches-sar-yo
necessary

negare neg<u>a</u>ray to deny

negli nayl-yee in the

negoziante *m/f* negotz-y<u>a</u>ntay
shopkeeper

negozio *m* neg<u>o</u>tz-yo shop

nello, nel, nella, nei nay, **nelle**
n<u>e</u>l-lay in the

nemmeno nem-m<u>ay</u>no not even

neozelandese *m/f* nay-o-
dzayland<u>ay</u>zay New Zealand
(adj); New Zealander

neppure nep-p<u>oo</u>ray not even

nero *m* n<u>ai</u>ro black; (hair) dark

nervoso nairv<u>o</u>zo nervous

nessun no; not any

nessun dubbio d<u>oo</u>b-yo
no doubt

nessuno, nessuna no; none;
nobody; not any

da nessuna parte p<u>a</u>rtay
nowhere

netto clean

peso netto net weight

neve *f* n<u>ay</u>vay snow

nevica n<u>a</u>yveeka it is snowing

nevicata *f* snowfall

nevischio *m* neve<u>e</u>sk-yo sleet

niente n-y<u>e</u>ntay nothing

di niente don't mention it

nient'altro? n-yental<u>t</u>ro
anything else?

niente pesce oggi no fish
today

non fa niente it doesn't matter

night *m* night club

nipote *m/f* neep<u>o</u>tay nephew/

niece; grandson/granddaughter

no no; not

nocivo noch**ee**vo harmful

nodo *m* knot

noi noy we; us

noioso noy-**o**zo boring

noleggiare nolej-j**a**ray to rent; to hire out

noleggio barche nolej-jo b**a**rkay boat hire

noleggio biciclette beecheekl**e**t-tay cycle hire

noleggio sci shee ski hire

nolo: a nolo for hire, to rent

nome *m* n**o**may name

nome da ragazza rag**a**tza maiden name

nome da sposata married name

nome di battesimo bat-t**ay**zeemo Christian name

non not

non... affatto not... at all

non bucare book**a**ray do not pierce

non capisco kape**e**sko I don't understand

non esporre ai raggi solari do not expose to direct sunlight

non ferma a... does not stop at...

non fumare no smoking

non fumatori nonsmokers

non lo so I don't know

non... mai ma-ee never, not ever

non... mica m**ee**ka not... at all

nonna *f* grandmother

non... neanche nay-**a**nkay not even

non... nemmeno nem-m**ay**no not even

non... né... né nay neither... nor...

non... neppure nep-p**oo**ray not even

non... nessuno nays-s**oo**no no one; not anybody; nobody; not... any; no

non... niente n-y**e**ntay nothing; not anything

nonno *m* grandfather

non... nulla nothing; not anything

nono *m* ninth

non oltrepassare no trespassing

non oltrepassare la dose prescritta do not exceed the stated dose

nonostante nonost**a**ntay despite

non parlare al conducente do not speak to the driver

non... per niente pair n-y**e**ntay not... at all

Travel tip Since 2005 smoking has been largely banned in restaurants and bars across the country; any establishment that wants to allow smoking has to follow very stringent rules in isolating a separate room. This is beyond the pocket of most places and so the majority remain no-smoking throughout.

---

non... più p-yoo no more, no longer, not... any more

non toccare do not touch

nord *m* north

nord-est *m* north-east

norma: a norma di legge in accordance with the law

normale normalay normal; (petrol/gas) 2- or 3-star, regular gas

norvegese *m/f* norvayjayzay Norwegian

Norvegia *f* norveja Norway

nostro, nostra, nostri, nostre nostray our(s)

nota *f* note

notare notaray to note

notificare noteefeekaray to notify

notizie *fpl* noteetz-yay news

noto well-known

notte *f* not-tay night

la/di notte at night

novanta ninety

nove no-vay nine

novellino *m*, **novellina** *f* beginner

novello new

novembre *m* novembray November

nozze *fpl* notz-zay wedding

ns. (nostro) our(s)

nubile noobeelay unmarried (woman)

nudista *m/f* nudist

nudo naked

nulla nothing

numeri di emergenza emergency phone numbers

numeri utili useful numbers

numero *m* noomairo number

numero di telefono phone number

numero di volo flight number

numeroso noomairozo numerous

nuocere nwochairay to harm

nuora *f* nwora daughter-in-law

nuotare nwotaray to swim

nuoto *m* nwoto swimming

Nuova Zelanda *f* nwova dzaylanda New Zealand

nuovo new

di nuovo again

nuvola *f* cloud

nuvoloso noovolozo cloudy

O

O (ovest) West

o or

o... o... either... or...

obbligare ob-bleegaray to oblige; to force

obbligatorio ob-bleegator-yo obligatory

obiettare ob-yet-taray to object

obiettivo *m* lens; objective

obiezione *f* ob-yetz-yonay objection

occasione *f* ok-kas-yonay chance; bargain

d'occasione secondhand; bargain (price)

occhiali *mpl* ok-yalee glasses, eyeglasses; goggles

occhiali da sole solay sunglasses
occhiata f ok-yata glance
occhio m ok-yo eye
 occhio! watch out!
occidentale ocheedentalay western
occorrere ok-kor-rairay to be needed
occupare ok-kooparay to occupy
occuparsi di dee to take care of
occupato ok-koopato engaged, occupied; taken; busy
occupazione f ok-koopatz-yonay occupation
oculista m/f oculist
odiare od-yaray to hate
odierno od-yairno today's; present
odorare odoraray to smell
odore m odoray smell
offendere of-fendairay to offend

offensivo offensive
offerta f of-fairta offer
offesa f of-fayza offence; insult
officina (meccanica) f of-feecheena garage (for car repairs)
offrire of-freeray to offer
oggetti smarriti lost property, lost and found
oggetto m oj-jet-to object; thing
oggi oj-jee today
ogni on-yee each, every; all
ogni abuso sarà punito penalty for misuse
ognuno on-yoono, **ognuna** everyone
oliera f ol-yaira oil and vinegar cruet
olio m ol-yo oil
olio solare solaray suntan oil

oltre oltray beyond

oltre a in addition to

oltremare oltray-maray overseas

oltrepassare oltray-pas-saray to cross; to go beyond; to go past

ombra f shade

ombrello m umbrella

ombrellone m ombrel-lonay sunshade

ombretto m eye shadow

ombroso ombrozo shady

omosessuale m/f omoses-swalay homosexual

omosessualità f omoses-swaleeta homosexuality

On. (onorevole) MP

onda f wave

ondulato wavy

onestà f honesty

onesto honest

ONU f UN

opale m opalay opal

opera d'arte f dartay work of art

operare opairaray to carry out; to operate; to act; to work

operatore m opairatoray operator

operatrice f opairatreechay operator

operoso opairozo hardworking

opposto opposite

oppure op-pooray or

opuscolo m brochure

opzionale optz-yonalay optional

ora f hour; now; in a moment

che ore sono? kay oray what time is it?

ora di punta rush hour

ora locale lokalay local time

orario m orar-yo timetable, (US) schedule

orario degli spettacoli dayl-yee times of performances

orario di apertura opening hours

orario di visita veezeeta visiting hours

orario di volo flight time

orario estivo summer timetable/schedule

orario ferroviario railway timetable/schedule

orario invernale eenvairnalay winter timetable/schedule

ordinare ordeenaray to order

ordinario ordeenar-yo ordinary, usual

ordinato tidy

ordine m ordeenay order

mettere in ordine met-tairay een to tidy up; to put away

orecchini mpl orek-keenee earrings

orecchio m orek-yo ear

organizzare organeetzaray to organize

orgoglioso orgol-yozo proud

oriente m or-yentay east

orlo m edge

ormai orma-ee by now

oro m gold

orologeria f orolojairee-ya watchmaker

orologio m oroloj-yo clock; watch

orribile or-**ree**beelay horrible;
awful

ortografia *f* spelling

ortolano *m* greengrocer

osare oz**a**ray to dare

ospedale *m* ospayd**a**lay hospital

ospitalità *f* hospitality

ospitare ospeet**a**ray to put up (in
accommodation)

ospite *m/f* ospeetay guest; host

osso *m* bone

ostello della gioventù *m*
joven**too** youth hostel

osteria *f* ostair**ee**-a inn

otorinolaringoiatra *m/f*
otoreenolareengo-y**a**tra ear, nose
and throat specialist

ottanta eighty

ottavo *m* eighth

ottenere ot-ten**ai**ray to obtain,
to get

ottica *f* optician's

ottico *m* optician

ottimo excellent

otto eight

ottobre *m* ot-t**o**bray October

otturatore *m* ot-toor**a**toray shutter
(in camera)

otturazione *f* ot-tooratz-y**o**nay
filling (in tooth)

ovest *m* west

ovvio **o**v-yo obvious

ozioso otz-y**o**zo lazy

pacchetto *m* pak-k**e**t-to package,
small parcel; packet
(of cigarettes etc)

pacchi postali *mpl* parcels,
packages

pacco *m* parcel, package

pace *f* p**a**chay peace

padella *f* frying pan

padre *m* p**a**dray father

paesaggio *m* pa-aysaj-jo
landscape

paese *m* pa-**ay**zay country; town;
village

pag. (pagina) p., pp.

pagamento *m* payment

pagare pag**a**ray to pay

pagare alla cassa
pay at the desk

pagare qui pay here

pagina *f* pa**jee**na page

Pagine Gialle *fpl* pa**jee**nay j**a**l-lay
Yellow Pages

paio *m* p**a**-yo pair

palazzo *m* pal**a**tzo palace

palazzo comunale komoon**a**lay
town hall

palco *m* box (in theatre)

paletta *f* spade (beach); dustpan

palla *f* ball

pallacanestro *f* basketball

pallamano *f* handball

pallavolo *f* volleyball

pallone *m* pal-l**o**nay ball

palude *f* pal**oo**day marsh, swamp

panetteria *f* panet-tairee-ya
baker's

paninoteca *f* paneenotayka
bar selling sandwiches

panne: restare in panne
restaray een pan-nay to break
down

panno *m* cloth

pannolino *m* nappy, diaper

pantaloni *mpl* trousers, pants

pantofole *fpl* pantofolay slippers

papà *m* dad

parabrezza *m* parabretza
windscreen

paracadutismo *m*
parakadooteezmo parachuting

paralume *m* paraloomay
lampshade

paraurti *m* para-oortee bumper,
fender

parcheggiare parkej-jaray
to park

parcheggio *m* parkej-jo car park,
parking lot; parking

parcheggio a giorni alterni
parking on alternate days

parcheggio a pagamento
paying car park/parking lot

parcheggio custodito car park/
parking lot with attendant

parcheggio incustodito
unattended car park/parking
lot

parcheggio privato private
parking

**parcheggio riservato agli
ospiti dell'albergo** parking
reserved for hotel guests only

parchimetro *m* parking meter

parco *m* park

parecchi parek-kee, **parecchie**
parek-yay several

parete *f* paraytay wall

Parigi *f* pareejee Paris

parità *f* pareeta equality

parlamento *m* parliament

parlare parlaray to talk; to speak

parola *f* word

parrucchiere *m* par-rook-yairay,
parrucchiera *f* hairdresser

parte *f* partay part (of)

a parte except

d'altra parte however

da qualche altra parte
kwalkay elsewhere

da qualche parte somewhere

una parte (di) a part (of), a
share

partecipare (a) partecheeparay
to take part in

partenza *f* partentza departure

partire parteeray to leave

partita *f* match (sport)

partito politico *m* political party

Pasqua *f* paskwa Easter

passaggio a livello *m* pas-saj-jo
a leevel-lo level/grade crossing

passaggio pedonale pedonalay
pedestrian crossing

passante *m/f* pas-santay
passer-by

passaporto *m* passport

passatempo *m* pastime

passeggero *m* pas-sej-jairo,
passeggera *f* passenger

passeggiata *f* pas-sej-jata walk; stroll

passeggino *m* pas-sej-jeeno pushchair, buggy

passo *m* pass; step

passo carrabile carraio driveway

pasticceria *f* pasteechairee-a cake shop

pastificio *m* pasteefeecho fresh pasta shop

pastiglie per la gola *fpl* pasteel-yay pair throat pastilles

pastiglie per la tosse tos-say cough sweets

pasto *m* meal

patatine patateenay crisps, potato chips

patente *f* patentay driving licence

patria *f* patr-ya native land

pattinaggio su ghiaccio *m* patteenaj-jo soo g-yacho ice skating

pattinare pat-teenaray to skate

pattini *mpl* skates

pattumiera *f* pat-toom-yaira dustbin, trashcan

paura *f* powra fear

pavimento *m* floor

paziente *m/f* patz-yentay patient

pazzia *f* patz-ee-a madness

pazzo patzo mad

sei pazzo? say you must be crazy!

peccato: è un peccato it's a pity

pecora *f* sheep

pedaggio *m* pedaj-jo toll

pedale *m* pedalay pedal

pedalò *m* pedal boat

pedata *f* kick

pedoni *mpl* pedestrians

peggio pej-jo worse

peggiori pej-joree, **peggiore** pej-joray worst; worse

pelle *f* pel-lay skin; leather

pelle scamosciata *f* skamoshata suede

pelletteria *f* pel-let-tairee-a leather goods

pellicceria *f* pel-leechairee-a furrier

pellicola (a colori) *f* (colour) film

pendolare *m/f* pendolaray commuter

pendolino *m* pendoleeno special fast train, first class only

pene *m* paynay penis

penicillina *f* peneecheel-leena penicillin

penisola *f* peneezola peninsula

penna *f* pen-na pen

penna a sfera sfaira ballpoint pen

pennarello *m* pen-narel-lo felt-tip pen

penna stilografica *f* fountain pen

pennello *m* paint brush

pensare pensaray to think

pensilina *f* bus shelter

pensionato *m* pens-yonato, **pensionata** *f* pensioner

pensione *f* pens-yonay
guesthouse

pensione completa komplayta
full board

pentola *f* saucepan

pentolino *f* pentoleeno small
saucepan

per pair for; by; through;
in order to

per aprire svitare
unscrew to open

per cento chento percent

perché pairkay because

  perché? why?

perciò percho therefore

percorso *m* pairkorso route

perdere pairdairay to lose

  perdere un treno
  to miss a train

perdita *f* leak

per favore pair favoray please

perfetto perfect

perfino even

pericolo *m* danger

pericolo di valanghe valangay
danger of avalanches

**pericoloso: è pericoloso
sporgersi** it is dangerous to
lean out of the window

periferia *f* paireefairee-a suburbs,
outskirts

periodo di validità:... valid for/
until:...

permanente *f* pairmanentay perm

permesso *m* permit; allowed;
excuse me

permettere pairmet-tairay to allow

però pairo but

per piacere pair p-yachairay
please

persiane *fpl* pairs-yanay shutters

persino even

perso lost

persona *f* person

persuadere pairswadairay to
persuade

pertosse *f* pairtos-say whooping
cough

per tutte le altre destinazioni
all other destinations

per uso esterno for external
use

per uso interno for internal use

per uso veterinario for
veterinary use

p. es. (per esempio) e.g.

pesante pezantay heavy

pesare pezaray to weigh

pesca *f* fishing; peach

pesce *m* peshay fish

pescecane *m* peshaykanay shark

pescheria *f* peskairee-a
fishmonger's

peso *m* payzo weight

peso netto net weight

peso netto sgocciolato dry
net weight

pettegolare pet-tegolaray to
gossip

pettinarsi to comb one's hair

pettine *m* pet-teenay comb

petto *m* chest; breast

pezzi di ricambio *mpl* petzee dee
reekamb-yo spare parts

pezzo *m* pe**tz**o piece

piacere *m* p-ya**ch**airay pleasure; to like

  per piacere pair please

  piacere di conoscerla konoshairla pleased to meet you

piacevole p-ya**ch**evolay pleasant

pianerottolo *m* landing

pianeta *m* p-yan**ay**ta planet

piangere p-ya**n**jairay to cry

piano *m* floor, storey; quietly; slowly

piano di sopra upstairs

piano di sotto downstairs

piano superiore soopair-y**o**ray upper floor

pianoterra *m* ground floor, (US) first floor

pianta *f* plant; map

pianterreno *m* p-yantair-**ray**no ground floor, (US) first floor

pianura *f* plain

pianura padana Po valley

piastrella *f* tile

piatti: lavare i piatti to do the washing-up

piattino *m* saucer

piatto *m* plate; dish; flat *(adj)*

piatto di portata serving dish

piatto fondo soup plate

piatto piano plate

piazza *f* p-ya**tz**a square

piccante peek-ka**n**tay spicy

piccolo small

piede *m* p-ya**y**day foot

  andare a piedi p-ya**y**dee to walk

  a piedi on foot

  in piedi standing

Piemonte *m* p-yaym**o**ntay Piedmont

pieno p-ya**y**no full

pietra *f* stone

pigiama *m* peejama pyjamas

pigrizia *f* peegree**tz**-ya laziness

pigro lazy

pila *f* torch

pillola *f* pill

pilota *m* pilot

pinacoteca *f* gallery

pinne *fpl* pee**n**-nay flippers

pinze *fpl* pee**n**tzay pliers

pinzette *fpl* peentze**t**-tay tweezers

pioggia *f* p-yo**j**-ja rain

piove p-yo**v**ay it's raining

piovere p-yo**v**airay to rain

pipa *f* pipe

piscina *f* peesheena swimming pool

piscina coperta indoor swimming pool

piscina per bambini paddling pool

piscina scoperta open-air swimming pool

pista *f* slope; rink; track; runway

pista ciclabile cheekla**b**eelay cycle path

pista da fondo cross-country ski track

pista da pattinaggio pat-tee-na**j**-jo ice rink

pista da sci shee ski slope

pista difficile deef-fee**ch**eelay

difficult slope

pista facile facheelay easy slope

pista per slitte sleet-tay toboggan run

pistola *f* gun

pittore *m* peet-toray, **pittrice** *f* peet-treechay painter

pittura *f* painting

più p-yoo more

non... più... no more

più grande granday bigger

più o meno mayno more or less

piumino *m* p-yoomeeno duvet

piuttosto p-yoot-tosto rather

pizzicheria *f* peetzeekairee-a delicatessen

plastica *f* plastic

platea *f* platay-a stalls

p.le (piazzale) Sq., Square

pneumatico *m* p-nay-oomateeko tyre

po': un po' (di) a little bit (of)

poca few

pochi pokee, **poche** pokay few

pochino: un pochino pokeeno a little bit

poco few

fra poco in a little while

poesia *f* po-ezee-a poetry; poem

poi poy then

politica *f* politics

politico *m*, **politica** *f* politician

politico political

polizia *f* poleetzee-a police

polizia stradale stradalay traffic

police

poliziotta *f* poletz-yot-ta policewoman

poliziotto *m* policeman

polleria *f* pol-lairee-a butcher's specializing in poultry

pollice *m* pol-leechay thumb

pollivendolo *m* butcher specializing in poultry

polmoni *mpl* lungs

polmonite *f* polmoneetay pneumonia

polso *m* wrist

poltrona *f* seat in stalls; armchair

pomata *f* cream

pomata cicatrizzante cheekatreetzantay healing cream for cuts

pomeriggio *m* pomaireej-jo afternoon

ponte *m* pontay bridge; deck

pontile *m* ponteelay landing pier, jetty

popolazione *f* popolatz-yonay population

popolo *m* the people

porca miseria! meezair-ya bloody hell!

porcellana *f* porchel-lana porcelain; china

porta *f* door

portabagagli *m* portabagal-yee porter (in station)

portacenere *m* portachenairay ashtray

porta d'ingresso *f* deengres-so front door

portafoglio *m* portafol-yo wallet

portamonete *m* portamonaytay purse

portapacchi *m* portapak-kee roof rack

portare portaray to carry; to take; to bring

portatile portateelay portable

porte-enfant *m* port-anfan carry-cot

portiere (di notte) *m* port-yairee dee not-tay (night) porter, janitor

portinaio *m* porteena-yo, **portinaia** *f* caretaker

porto *m* harbour

porzione per bambini *f* portzyonay pair children's portion

posare posaray to put down

posate *fpl* pozatay cutlery

possiamo we can

posso I can

possono they can

posta *f* mail

posta aerea a-airay-a airmail

posta centrale chentralay main post office

postagiro *m* postajeero postal giro

posteriore: sedile posteriore *m* saydeelay postairee-oray back seat

posti a sedere *mpl* seats

posti in piedi standing room

postino *m* postman

posto *m* place; seat; space; job, post

posto di polizia poleetzee-a police station

posto di telefono pubblico public telephone

posto prenotato prenotato reserved seat

posto riservato a mutilati e invalidi seat reserved for disabled persons only

postumi della sbornia *mpl* zborn-ya hangover

potabile potabeelay drinkable
  acqua potabile akwa drinking water

potere *m* potairay to be able, can; power

potete potaytay you can

potuto been able to

povero poor

povertà *f* poverty

PP.TT. (Poste e Telecomunicazioni) *fpl* Italian Post Office

pranzo *m* prandzo lunch

prato *m* lawn; meadow

prato all'inglese al-leenglayzay lawn

precedenza *f* prechedentza right of way

precipitarsi (in) precheepeetarsee to rush in

preferire prefaireeray to prefer

preferito favourite

prefisso *m* dialling code, area code

pregare pregaray to request
  si prega di (non)… please do (not)…
  si prega di non fumare

please refrain from smoking

si prega di ritirare lo scontrino please get your receipt first

prego praygo please; pardon; you're welcome; after you

prego? pardon?, pardon me?

prelevamenti withdrawals

prelevare dei soldi prelev**a**ray day to withdraw money

prelievo m prel-y**a**yvo withdrawal

premere praymairay to press

premio m praym-yo prize

prenda take

prendere prendairay to take; to catch

prendere il sole so**l**ay to sunbathe

prendere in affitto to rent

prendersi: da prendersi a digiuno to be taken on an empty stomach

da prendersi dopo/prima dei pasti to be taken after/ before meals

da prendersi secondo la prescrizione medica to be taken according to doctor's prescription

da prendersi tre volte al giorno to be taken three times a day

prenotare prenot**a**ray to book, to reserve

prenotato reserved

prenotazione f prenotatz-y**o**nay reservation, booking

prenotazione obbligatoria ob-bleegat**o**r-ya reservation compulsory

preoccuparsi per pray-ok-koop**a**rsee pair to worry about

preparare prepararay to prepare

prepararsi to get ready

prepararsi a scendere
shendairay get ready to alight

presa f praysa socket

presa multipla adaptor

presentare prezentaray
to introduce

presente prezentay present

preservativo m condom

preside m/f prayseeday
headmaster; headmistress

preso prayzo taken

pressione gomme f pres-yonay
gom-may tyre pressure

prestare prestaray to lend

    farsi prestare (da) to borrow
(from)

prestito: prendere in prestito
presteeto to borrow

presto soon; early

prete m praytay priest

pretendere pretendairay to claim;
to demand

previsioni del tempo mpl
preveez-yonee weather forecast

prezzo m pretzo price

prezzo intero full price

prezzo ridotto reduced price

prigione f preejonay prison

prima f first; first gear

    prima di before

prima classe klas-say first class

prima colazione f kolatz-yonay
breakfast

prima qualità high quality

primavera f spring

prima visione first release/
showing

primo m first

primo piano m first floor,
(US) second floor

primo tempo m first half

principale preencheepalay main

principe m preencheepay prince

principessa f preencheepes-sa
princess

principiante m/f preencheep-
yantay beginner

privato preevato private

probabilmente probabeelmentay
probably

prodotto artigianalmente
arteejanalmentay made by
craftsmen

professore (Prof.) m teacher;
professor

professoressa (Prof.essa) f
teacher; professor

profondo deep

profumeria f profoomairee-a
perfume shop

profumo m perfume

pro loco f tourist office in small
town

prolunga f extension lead

promettere promet-tairay to
promise

pronto ready; hello (on telephone)

pronto intervento m emergency
service

pronto soccorso m first aid;
casualty

pronunciare pronooncharay to
pronounce

proprietario *m* propr-yetar-yo,
proprietaria *f* owner

proprio exactly; just; really; own

prosa *f* proza theatre drama

　compagnia di prosa theatre
　company

prossimo next

proteggere protej-jairay to
protect

protestare protestaray to protest

provare provaray to try (on)

　prova! just try!

provincia *f* proveencha district

prudente proodentay cautious

prudenza *f* proodentza caution

prurito *m* itch

P.S. (Pubblica Sicurezza) *f*
Police

**P.T. (Poste e
Telecomunicazioni)** *fpl*
Italian Post Office

pubblico *m* public; audience

pugilato *m* poojeelato boxing

pugno *m* poon-yo fist; punch

　un pugno (di) a handful (of)

pulire pooleeray to clean

pulito clean

pulitura *f* dry-cleaner's

pullman *m* coach, long-distance
bus

pungere poonjairay to sting

punire pooneeray to punish

punteggio *m* poontej-jo score

punto di vista *m* point of view

puntuale poontwalay on time

puntura *f* poontoora bite; injection

può pwo he/she/it can; you can

può darsi maybe, perhaps

puoi pwoy you can

pura lana vergine pure new
wool

pura seta pure silk

puro cotone pure cotton

puro lino pure linen

puzzle *m* jigsaw

puzzo *m* pootzo stink

p.zza (piazza) Square

Q

qua kwa here

　di qua (over) here, this way

quaderno *m* kwadairno exercise
book

quadrato *m* kwadrato square

quadro *m* kwadro painting;
picture

qualche kwalkay some, a few

qualcosa kwalkoza something;
anything

　qualcos'altro kwalkozaltro
　something else

qualcuno kwalkoono somebody

quale kwalay which

qualità *f* kwaleeta quality

quando kwando when

quanta? kwanta how much?

quanti? kwantee, **quante?**
kwantay how many?

quantità *f* kwanteeta quantity

quanto? kwanto how much?

quaranta kwaranta forty

quarta f kwarta fourth (gear)

quartiere m kwart-yairay quarter, area

quarto m kwarto quarter, fourth

tre quarti mpl three quarters

quasi kwazee almost, nearly

quattordici kwat-tor-deechee fourteen

quattro kwat-tro four

quello kwel-lo that (one)

quello lì that (one)

questa kwesta this (one)

queste kwestay these

questi kwestee these

questo kwesto this (one)

questo qui kwee this (one)

qui kwee here

quindi kweendee therefore

quindici kween-deechee fifteen

quinta f kweenta fifth (gear)

quinto m kweento fifth

R

racc. recorded delivery

racchetta (da tennis) f rak-ket-ta (tennis) racket

raccomandata f recorded delivery (mail)

raccomandata con ricevuta di ritorno reechevoota recorded-delivery mail with card sent back to sender on delivery

raccomandata espresso recorded-delivery express mail

raccordo autostradale m owto-stradalay motorway junction, highway intersection

radersi to shave

radiosveglia f rad-yosvayl-ya radio alarm

raffreddore m raf-fred-doray cold (illness)

ragazza f ragatza girl; girlfriend

ragazza alla pari au pair girl

ragazzo m ragatzo boy; boyfriend

raggio m raj-jo spoke

raggi X mpl raj-jee eeks X-ray

ragionevole rajonayvolay reasonable

ragno m ran-yo spider

RAI-TV (Radiotelevisione italiana) f ra-eeteevoo Italian radio and television

rallentare ral-lentaray reduce speed, slow down

rampe rampay ramps

rappresentante m/f rap-prezentantay agent

raramente raramentay seldom

raro rare

rasoio m razoy-o razor; shaver

ratto m rat

razza di idiota! ratza stupid idiot!

re m ray king

recinto m recheento fence

reclamare reklamaray to complain

reclamo m complaint

regalo m present

reggiseno m rej-jeesayno bra

regina *f* rej**ee**na queen

regionale *m* rejon**a**lay local train stopping at all stations

Regno Unito *m* ren-yo United Kingdom

remare rem**a**ray to row

remo *m* r**a**ymo oar

rene *m* r**a**ynay kidney (in body)

Rep. (repubblica) *f* republic

reparto *m* department; ward

respirare respeer**a**ray to breathe

respiratore (a tubo) *m* respeerat**o**ray a t**oo**bo snorkel

responsabile respons**a**beelay responsible

restituire resteetw**ee**ray to give back

resto *m* rest; change (money)

il resto (di) *m* the rest (of)

rete *f* r**a**ytay net; goal; network

retromarcia *f* retrom**a**rcha reverse gear

riagganciare ree-ag-ganch**a**ray to hang up

ribassato reduced

ricambi *mpl* spare parts

ricamo *m* embroidery

ricco reek-ko rich

ricetta *f* reech**e**t-ta recipe; prescription

ricevere reech**a**yvairay to receive

ricevitore *m* reecheve**e**t**o**ray receiver

ricevuta *f* freechev**oo**ta receipt

ricevuta di ritorno acknowledgement of receipt

ricevuta fiscale feesk**a**lay bill,

check (from a restaurant, bar etc)

ricominciare (da capo) reekomeench**a**ray to start again

riconoscere reekon**o**shairay to recognize

ricordarsi (di) to remember

ridere r**ee**dairay to laugh

ridicolo ridiculous

ridiscendere redeesh**e**ndairay to go back down

ridotto reduced

ridurre reed**oo**r-ray to reduce

riduttore *m* reedoot-t**o**ray adaptor

riduzione *f* reedootz-y**o**nay reduction

riempire r-yemp**ee**ray to fill (in)

rientrare r-yentr**a**ray to go/come back (in/home)

rifiuti *mpl* reef-y**oo**tee rubbish

rilassarsi reelas-s**a**rsee to relax

rimandare reemand**a**ray to send back

rimanere reeman**a**iray to stay, to remain

rimborsare reembors**a**ray to refund

rimorchio *m* reem**o**rk-yo trailer

rimozione forzata illegally parked vehicles removed at owner's expense

rinfresco *m* reception, buffet

ringraziare reengratz-y**a**ray to thank

rione *m* ree-**o**nay neighbourhood

riparare reepar**a**ray to repair

riparazioni *fpl* reeparatz-y**o**nee repairs

riparo *m* shelter

ripartire reeparteeray to set off
again

ripetere reepaytairay to repeat

ripido steep

riposarsi to have a rest

riposo *m* reepozo rest

risata *f* reesata laugh

riscaldamento *m* heating

riscuotere un assegno
reeskwotairay oon as-sen-yo
to cash a cheque

riserva *f* reesairva reserve

di riserva spare

riservato reesairvato reserved

**riservato ai clienti
dell'albergo** for hotel guests
only

riservato ai non fumatori
non-smokers only

riservato carico loading only

riservato polizia police only

riservato scarico (merci)
unloading (of goods) only

riservato tram, taxi, bus trams,
taxis, buses only

riservato viacard for magnetic
toll card holders only

risparmi *mpl* savings

rispedire reespedeeray
to send back

rispondere reespondairay to reply

risposta *f* answer

ristorante *m* reestorantay
restaurant

risultato *m* result

ritardo *m* delay

essere in ritardo to be late

in ritardo delayed

ritirata *f* toilet/rest room (on train)

ritiro bagagli *m* bagal-yee
baggage claim

ritornare reetornaray to return, to
come/go back

ritorni go back

ritorno *m* return

riva *f* shore

rivista *f* magazine

rivoltante reevoltantay disgusting

roccia *f* rocha rock; rock climbing

romano Roman

romanzo *m* romandzo novel

rompere rompairay to break

rosa *f* rose; pink

rosolia *f* rozolee-a
German measles

rossetto *m* lipstick

rosso red

rosticceria *f* rosteechairee-a take-
away selling hot meat dishes

rotaie *fpl* rota-yay tracks, rails

rotondo round

rotto broken

roulotte *f* roolot caravan,
(US) trailer

rovesciarsi rovesharsee to
capsize

rovine *fpl* roveenay ruins

R.R. (ricevuta di ritorno)
return receipt for registered
mail

R.U. (Regno Unito) *m* UK

rubare roobaray to steal

rubinetto *m* tap, faucet

rubrica *f* address book

rullino *m* film

rumore *m* roomoray noise

rumoroso roomorozo noisy

ruota *f* rwota wheel

ruscello *m* rooshel-lo stream

S

S. (santo/santa) St., Saint

sabato *m* Saturday

sabbia *f* sab-ya sand

sacchetto (di plastica) *m*
sak-ket-to (plastic) bag

sacco a pelo *m* paylo sleeping
bag

sagra *f* feast; (open air) festival

sala *f* living room

sala da pranzo prandzo
dining room

sala d'aspetto waiting room

sala d'attesa dat-taysa
waiting room

sala d'imbarco deembarko
departure lounge

salato savoury; salty

saldi *mpl* sale

saldi di fine stagione feenay
stajonay end of season sales

sali da bagno *mpl* ban-yo
bath salts

saliera *f* sal-yaira salt cellar

salire saleeray to go up; to get
on/in

salita *f* slope; entry

in salita uphill

salone per uomo womo men's
hairdresser

salotto *m* living room, lounge

saltare saltaray to jump

salto *m* jump

salumaio *m* salooma-yo
delicatessen

salumeria *f* saloomairee-a
delicatessen

salumiere *m* saloom-yairay
delicatessen

salute *f* salootay health

(alla) salute! cheers!

in salute in good health

salute! bless you!

salvagente *m* salvajentay rubber
ring

salve! salvay hi!

salvietta *f* salv-yet-ta napkin

sandali *mpl* sandalee sandals

sangue *m* sangway blood

sanguinare sangweenaray to
bleed

sano healthy

sapere sapairay to know

sapone *m* saponay soap

sapore *m* saporay flavour

Sardegna *f* sardayn-ya Sardinia

sartoria *f* sartoree-a tailor's;
dressmaker's

**S.A.U.B. (Struttura
Amministrativa Unificata di
Base)** *f* Italian national health
service, Italian health care

sbagliato zbal-yato wrong

sbaglio *m* zbal-yo mistake

sbarcare sbarkaray to disembark

sbrigarsi zbreegarsee to hurry

sbrigati! zbreegatee hurry up!

sbucciare zboocharay to peel

scacchi *mpl* skak-kee chess

scadenza *f* skadentza expiry date; deadline

scaffali *mpl* shelves

scala *f* ladder

scala mobile mobeelay escalator

scale *fpl* skalay stairs

scalo *m* stop-over

fare scalo to stop over

scandaloso skandalozo shocking

scandinavo Scandinavian

scapolo *m* bachelor

scaricare skareekaray to download

scarpe *fpl* skarpay shoes

scarpe da ginnastica jeen-nasteeka trainers

scarponi da sci *mpl* da shee ski boots

scatola *f* box

la scatola priva del talloncino non può essere venduta without a coupon this box cannot be sold

scatola del cambio kamb-yo gearbox

scatto *m* unit

scavi *mpl* skavee excavations

scegliere shayl-yairay to choose

scendere shendairay to go down; to get off

scendere le scale skalay to go/come downstairs

scheda *f* skayda card

scheda telefonica phonecard

scherzo *m* skertzo joke

schiaffo *m* sk-yaf-fo slap

schiena *f* sk-yayna back (of body)

schifo: che schifo! kay skeefo it's disgusting!

schifoso skeefozo foul

schiuma da barba *f* sk-yooma shaving foam

schizzare skeetzaray to splash

sci *m* shee ski; skiing

sciacquare shakwaray to rinse

sci acquatico *m* shee akwateeko waterski; waterskiing

sciampo *m* shampo shampoo

sciare shee-aray to ski

andare a sciare to go skiing

sciarpa *f* sharpa scarf

sciatore *m* shee-atoray skier

sciatrice *f* shee-atreechay skier

sci d'acqua *m* shee dakwa water-skiing

sci di fondo cross-country skiing

scienza *f* shee-entza science

sciocco *m* shok-ko idiot; silly

scivolare sheevolaray to skid

scivoloso sheevolozo slippery

scodella *f* bowl

scogliera *f* skol-yaira cliff

scoglio *m* skol-yo rock

scolara *f* schoolgirl

scolaro *m* schoolboy

scommessa *f* bet

scommettere skom-met-tairay to bet; to stake

scomodo uncomfortable

scomparire skompar**ee**ray to disappear

scompartimento *m* compartment

scontento unhappy

sconto *m* discount

scontrino *m* receipt

scontro *m* crash

scopa *f* broom

scorciatoia *f* skorchat**oy**-a shortcut

scorso: l'anno scorso last year

scotch *m* Sellotape, Scotch tape

scottarsi to get sunburnt

scottatura *f* skot-tat**oo**ra sunburn; burn

Scozia *f* sk**o**tzee-a Scotland

scozzese *m/f* skotz**ay**zay Scot; Scottish

scrittura *f* skreet-t**oo**ra writing

scrivere skr**ee**vairay to write

scultura *f* sculpture

scuola *f* skw**o**la school

scuola di lingue l**ee**ngway language school

scuola di sci shee ski school

scuola elementare elementar**ay** primary school

scuola media inferiore m**ay**d-ya eenfair-y**o**ray junior secondary school

scuola media superiore soopair-y**o**ray senior secondary school

scuotere skw**o**tairay to shake

scuro dark

scusa *f* sk**oo**za apology; excuse

scusa! sorry!

scusarsi skooz**a**rsee to apologize

scusi! sk**oo**zee sorry!

come, scusi? k**o**may pardon?, pardon me?

sdraiarsi zdra-y**a**rsee to lie down

se say if

sé say himself; herself; itself; oneself; themselves

sebbene seb-b**ay**nay although

sec. (secolo) century

seccante sek-k**a**ntay annoying

secchiello *m* sek-y**e**l-lo bucket

secchio *m* sek-yo bucket

secco dry

secolo *m* s**ay**kolo century

seconda *f* second (gear)

seconda classe *f* kl**a**s-say second class

seconda visione *f* second release/showing

secondo *m* second

secondo tempo *m* second half

sedere *m* sayd**a**iray bottom (of person)

sedersi to sit down

sedia *f* s**a**yd-ya chair

sedia a rotelle rotel-l**ay** wheelchair

sedia a sdraio zdra-yo deck chair

sedici s**a**y-deechee sixteen

sedile *m* sayd**ee**lay seat; bench

seduto sitting, seated

seg. (seguente) following

sega *f* **say**ga saw

seggiola *f* sej-jola chair

seggiovia *f* sej-jovee-a chairlift

segnale *m* sen-ya**l**ay signal

segnale d'allarme dal-la**r**may
  alarm

segnaletica in rifacimento
  road signs being redone

**segnaletica orizzontale in
  allestimento** road signs being
  painted

segreteria telefonica *f*
  segretai**ree**-a answering
  machine

segreto segra**y**to secret

seguire seg**wee**ray to follow

  segua **say**gwa follow

sei say you are

sei say six

selezionare il numero
  dial the number

sella *f* saddle

semaforo *m* traffic lights

sembrare sembra**r**ay to seem

semiasse *m* semee-**a**ssay
  axle; shaft

seminterrato *m* basement

semplice se**m**pleechay simple

sempre se**m**pray always

  sempre d(i)ritto straight
  ahead, straight on

seno *m* **say**no breast

sensato sensible

sensibile sen**see**beelay sensitive

senso: di buon senso bwon
  sensible

senso dell'umorismo *m* del-

loomo**ree**zmo (sense of) humour

senso unico one way

sentiero *m* sent-ya**i**ro path

sentire sen**tee**ray to feel; to hear;
  to smell

sentirsi (bene) bay**n**ay to feel
  (well)

sentirsi poco bene to feel
  unwell

senza **sent**za without

  senza dubbio doob-yo
  undoubtedly

  senza conservanti no
  preservatives

separatamente separatamentay
  separately

separato separate

sera *f* sa**i**ra evening

  alle 8 di sera at 8 p.m.

  la/di sera in the evening

serbatoio *m* sairbat**oy**-o tank

serio sa**i**r-yo serious

  sul serio sool seriously; really

serpente *m* sairp**e**ntay snake

serratura *f* lock

servire sair**vee**ray to serve

  servitevi help yourselves

  serviti help yourself

  si serva help yourself

servire freddo serve chilled

servizi sair**veet**zee toilets, rest
  room

servizio *m* sair**veet**z-yo service

  il servizio è gratuito free
  service

servizio a bordo in-flight
  service

servizio autotraghetto owtotraget-to car ferry

servizio compreso kompray-zo service charge included

servizio escluso not including service charge

servizio guasti faults service

servizio in camera room service

servizio traghetto traget-to passenger ferry

sessanta sixty

sessista sexist

sesso *m* sex

sesto *m* sixth

seta *f* sayta silk

sete: avere sete avairay saytay to be thirsty

settanta seventy

sette set-tay seven

settembre *m* set-tembray September

settimana *f* week

alla settimana per week

due settimane doo-ay set-teemanay fortnight

settimo *m* seventh

sfacciato sfachato cheeky

sfinito exhausted

sfortunatamente sfortoonatamentay unfortunately

sgabello *m* zgabel-lo stool

sgarbato zgarbato rude

sgradevole zgradayvolay unpleasant

si see himself; herself; itself; themselves

sì see yes

siamo we are

siccome seek-komay as, since

sicuro safe; sure

siete s-yaytay you are

sigaretta *f* cigarette

sigaro *m* cigar

Sigg. (signori) Messrs

sigillare seejeel-laray to seal

significare seen-yeefeekaray to mean

signor (Sig.) seen-yor Mr; Sir

signora (Sig.a) *f* seen-yora lady; Mrs; madam

signore *m* seen-yoray gentleman

signore *fpl* ladies' toilet, rest room

signori *mpl* gents' toilet, rest room

signorina (Sig.na) seen-yoreena Miss

silenzio *m* seelentz-yo silence

simile seemeelay similar

simpatico nice

sinagoga *f* synagogue

sincero seenchairo sincere, frank

singhiozzo *m* seeng-yotzo hiccups

sinistra *f* seeneestra left

a sinistra on/to the left

siringa *f* syringe

sito web *m* seeto website

s.l.m. (sul livello del mare) above sea level

slogarsi zlogarsee to sprain

smalto per le unghie *m* zmalto pair lay oong-yay nail polish

smettere zmet-tairay to stop

sms *m* es-say em-may es-say text

snello znel-lo slim

so: non (lo) so I don't know

sobborghi *mpl* sob-borgee suburbs

soccorso *m* help; assistance

soccorso alpino mountain rescue

soccorso stradale stradalay breakdown service

società *f* sochayta society; company

soffitta *f* loft

soffitto *m* ceiling

soggiorno *m* soj-jorno stay; lounge

sognare son-yaray to dream

sogno *m* son-yo dream

soldi *mpl* soldee money

sole *m* solay sun

soleggiato solej-jato sunny

solito soleeto usual

   di solito usually

sollevare sol-levaray to lift

solo alone; only

solo il sabato/la domenica Saturdays/Sundays only

solo servizio cuccette e letti sleepers/sleeping cars only

soltanto only

soluzione salina per lenti a contatto *f* solootz-yonay – pair soaking solution for contact lenses

somministrazione per via orale to be taken orally

sonnecchiare son-nek-yaray to doze

sonnifero *m* sleeping pill

sonno: avere sonno to be sleepy

sono I am; they are

sopra on; above

   di sopra upstairs

sopracciglio *m* sopracheel-yo eyebrow

soprammobile *m* sopram-mobeelay ornament

soprannome *m* sopran-nomay nickname

sordo deaf

sorella *f* sister

sorgente *f* sorjentay spring

sorpassare sorpas-saray to overtake

sorpasso fast lane, lane for overtaking

sorprendente sorprendentay surprising

sorpresa f sorpraysa surprise

sorridere sor-reedairay to smile

sorriso m smile

sosta autorizzata... parking permitted for...

sosta vietata no parking

sostenere sostenairay to maintain; to uphold

sottile sot-teelay thin

sotto under; below

  di sotto downstairs

sottolineare sot-toleenay-aray to emphasize

sottopassaggio m sot-topas-saj-jo underpass

SP (strada provinciale) f secondary road

Spagna f span-ya Spain

spagnolo m span-yolo, **spagnola** f Spaniard; Spanish

spago m string

spalla f shoulder

sparare spararay to shoot

sparire spareeray to disappear

  sparisci! spareeshee get lost!

spartirsi to share

spaventoso spaventozo appalling, dreadful

spazzare spatzaray to sweep

spazzola f spatzola brush

spazzolino m spatzoleeno brush

specchietto retrovisore m spek-yet-to retroveezoray rearview mirror

specchio m spek-yo mirror

specialista m/f spech-yaleesta specialist

specialità f spech-yaleeta speciality, specialities

> Travel tip In rural areas you can usually pick up basketware, local terracotta or ceramic items as well as a feast of locally produced wine, olive oils, cheeses, hams and salamis. It's worth rooting out the local speciality, even in urban centres: Turin is known for its chocolate, Florence for leather goods, Perugia for ceramics.

specialmente spech-yalmentay especially

spedire spedeeray to send; to post, to mail

spedire per posta to post, to mail

spegnere spen-yairay to switch off

spegnere il motore switch off engine

spendere spendairay to spend

sperare spairaray to hope

spesa f spaysa shopping

spesso often

spettacolo m performance, show

spia f gauge

spiace: mi spiace spee-achay I'm sorry

spiaggia f spee-aj-ja beach

spiccioli mpl speecholee (small) change

spiegare sp-yaygaray to explain

spilla f brooch

spilla di sicurezza seekooretza safety pin

spillo m pin

spina f plug (electrical); thorn

spingere speenjairay to push

spiritoso speereetozo witty

spogliarsi spol-yarsee to undress

spogliatoi mpl spol-yatoy changing rooms

spolverare spolvairaray to dust

sponda f shore; riverbank

sporco dirty

sporco maschilista m maskeeleesta male chauvinist pig

sporgersi (da) sporjairsee to lean (out)

sportello m counter; door (on train)

sportello automatico owtomateeko cash dispenser, ATM

sportello pacchi parcels counter

sport invernali mpl winter sports

sposato married

spugna f spoon-ya sponge

spuntata f trim

spuntino m snack

squadra f skwadra team

squalo m skwalo shark

SS (strada statale) f main road, national road

sta: come sta? komay how are you?

stadio m stad-yo stadium

stagione f stajonay season

stagno m stan-yo pond

stagnola f stan-yola silver foil

stai: come stai? komay sty how are you?

stamattina this morning

stampa f Press

stampe printed matter

stampelle fpl stampel-lay crutches

stanco tired

stanotte stanot-tay tonight

stanza f stantza room

stare staray to be; to stand; to be located; to stay, to remain; to suit

    stare bene baynay to be well

    stare poco bene to be unwell

starter m choke

statale statalay national; state

state: come state? komay statay how are you?

Stati Uniti mpl statee ooneetee United States

stato m state; been

statua f statwa statue

stazione f statz-yonay station

stazione degli autobus dayl-yee owtoboos bus station

stazione della metropolitana underground station, (US) subway station

stazione delle corriere del-lay kor-yairay coach station

stazione di servizio sairveetz-yo petrol/gas station, service station

stazione ferroviaria railway station

steccato *m* fence

stella *f* star

stendersi to lie down

sterlina *f* pound (sterling)

sterzo *m* stertzo steering; steering wheel

stesso, stessa, stessi, stesse stes-say same

stile *m* steelay style

stirare steeraray to iron

stirarsi steerarsee to stretch out

stitico steeteeko constipated

stivali *mpl* steevalee boots

stoffa *f* material, fabric

stomaco *m* stomach

storia *f* stor-ya story; history

storia dell'arte *f* del-lartay history of art

stoviglie *fpl* stoveel-yay crockery

straccio *m* stracho rag; cloth; duster;

strada *f* road

strada a fondo cieco blind alley

strada camionabile route for heavy vehicles

strada dissestata uneven road surface

strada ghiacciata ice on road

strada interrotta road blocked

strada privata private road

strada provinciale secondary road

strada sdrucciolevole slippery road

strada secondaria secondary road

strada senza uscita no thoroughfare, dead end

strada statale main road

straniero *m* stran-yairo **straniera** *f* foreigner

straniero foreign

strano strange

straordinario stra-ordeenar-yo exceptional

stretta del credito *f* kraydeeto credit crunch

stretto narrow

strillare streel-laray to scream

strisce pedonali *fpl* streeshay pedestrian crossing

strofinaccio (da cucina) *m* strofeenacho (da koocheena) tea towel

stronzo *m* bastard

studente *m* stoodentay student

studentessa *f* student

studiare stood-yaray to study

studio *m* study

studioso stood-yozo studious

stufa *f* heater

stupefacente stoopayfachentay astonishing

stupefacenti *mpl* drugs

stupendo! brilliant!

stupro *m* rape

su soo on; up

sua soo-a his; her(s); its; your(s)

subito soobeeto immediately

succedere soochaydairay to

happen

sud *m* south

Sudafrica *f* South Africa

sudafricano *m*, **sudafricana** *f* South African

sudare soo**da**ray to sweat

sud-ovest *m* sood-**o**vest south-west

sue s**oo**-ay his; her(s); its; your(s)

sul sool, **sulla, sullo, sui** s**oo**-ee, **sugli** s**oo**l-yee, **sulle** s**oo**l-lay on the

suo s**oo**-o his; her(s); its; your(s)

suocera *f* sw**o**chaira mother-in-law

suocero *m* sw**o**chairo father-in-law

suoi swoy his; her(s); its; your(s)

suola *f* sw**o**la sole (of shoe)

suonare swon**a**ray to play (instrument); to ring; please ring

superficie *f* soopairf**ee**chay surface; area

supermercato *m* supermarket

superstrada *f* motorway/highway without toll

supplementare soop-plement**a**ray extra

supplemento 3o letto third bed supplement payable

supplemento rapido rap**ee**do supplement for fast train

supporre soop-p**o**r-ray to assume

surf *m* surfboard; surfing

surgelati *mpl* soorjel**a**tee frozen food

surgelato frozen

sussurrare soos-soor-r**a**ray to whisper

svedese *m/f* zved**a**yzay Swedish; Swede

sveglia *f* zv**a**yl-ya alarm clock

svegliare zvayl-y**a**ray to wake

svegliarsi zvayl-y**a**rsee to wake up

sveglio zv**a**yl-yo alert; awake

svendita *f* zvend**ee**ta sale

svenire zven**ee**ray to faint

Svezia *f* zv**e**tzee-a Sweden

sviluppare zveeeloop-p**a**ray to develop

svitato zveet**a**to cracked, nutty

Svizzera *f* zv**ee**tzaira Switzerland

svizzero *m*, **svizzera** *f* Swiss

svuotare zvwot**a**ray to empty

T

T (tabaccheria) tobacconist's

tabaccaio *m* tabak-ka-yo tobacconist's

tabaccheria *f* tabak-kair**ee**-a tobacconist's

tabacchi *mpl* tabak-kee tobacco goods

tabacco *m* tobacco

tabellone *m* indicator board

taccuino *m* tak-kw**ee**no notebook

tachimetro *m* speedometer

taglia *f* t**a**l-ya size

tagliando di controllo *m* tal-y**a**ndo coupon guaranteeing quality; proof of purchase

tagliare tal-ya**ray** to cut

tagliaunghie *m* tal-ya-**oo**ng-yay
nail clippers

taglio *m* tal-yo cut

taglio di capelli haircut

taglio e cucito ay kooch**ee**to
dressmaking

talco *m* talcum powder

tallone *m* tal-l**o**nay heel

tanta a lot; so much

tanti, tante t**a**ntee, t**a**ntay many,
lots of

tanti auguri owg**oo**ree best
wishes

tanto a lot; so much

tapparella *f* blind

tappeto *m* tap-**pay**to carpet

tappezziere *m* tap-petz-y**ai**ray
decorator; upholsterer

tappo *m* cap; plug; cork

tardi late

   a più tardi p-yoo see you later

targa *f* number plate

tariffa *f* fare; charge

tariffa interna eent**ai**rna inland
postage

tariffe postali internazionali *fpl*
tar**ee**f-fay – eentairnatz-yon**a**lee
international postage rates

tariffe postali nazionali natz-
yon**a**lee national postage rates

tasca *f* pocket

tassa *f* tax

tassista *m/f* taxi driver

tasso di cambio *m* kamb-yo
exchange rate

tasso di interesse eentair**e**s-say
interest rate

taverna *f* inn, tavern

tavola *f* t**a**vola table

tavola a vela v**ay**la sailboard

tavola calda snack bar

tavolino *m* coffee table

tavolo *m* table

tazza *f* t**a**tza cup

tazzina da caffè *f* tatz**ee**na
espresso coffee cup

T.C.I. (Touring Club Italiano) *m*
Italian touring club

te tay you

tè *m* tay tea

teatro *m* tay-**a**tro theatre

teatro lirico opera house

tedesco *m/f* ted**e**sko German

TEE *m* Trans-Europe-Express
train

tegame *f* teg**a**may pan

teglia *f* t**a**yl-ya casserole dish

teiera *f* tay-y**a**ira teapot

telefonare telefon**a**ray to phone

telefonata *f* phone call

telefonino *m* telayfon**ee**no mobile
phone, cell phone

telefono *m* tel**a**yfono telephone

telefono a schede sk**a**yday
cardphone

Travel tip Telephone numbers change with amazing
frequency in Italy and codes
are now an integral part of
the number and always need
to be dialled, regardless of
whether or not you are in the
zone you are telephoning.

Telepass electronic toll charge system on motorway

telo da bagno *m* ban-yo bath towel

temperino *m* penknife

tempesta *f* storm

tempo *m* time; weather

tempo libero free time, leisure

tempo limite di accettazione latest check-in time

temporale *m* temporalay thunderstorm

tenda *f* curtain; tent

tenere tenairay to hold; to keep

tenere lontano dalla portata dei bambini keep out of the reach of children

tenere rigorosamente la destra keep to the right

tergicristallo *m* tairjeekreestal-lo windscreen wiper

terminare tairmeenaray to end

termometro *m* thermometer

termosifone *m* termoseefonay radiator

terra *f* earth, soil

terrazzo *m* tair-ratzo (large) balcony; patio

terza *f* tairtza third (gear)

terzo *m* third

tessera di abbonamento *f* season ticket

tesserino *m* travel card

tessuto *m* material, fabric

testa *f* head

testa del treno front of the train

tetto *m* roof

Tevere *m* tevairay Tiber

ti tee you; yourself; to you

tiepido t-yaypeedo lukewarm

tifoso *m*, **tifosa** *f* fan (supporter)

timbro *m* rubber stamp; postmark

timido shy

tinello *m* small dining room

tintoria *f* teentoree-a drycleaner's

tirare teeraray to pull

tiro *m* shooting

titolo *m* title

tizio *m* teetz-yo bloke, guy

toccare tok-karay to touch

tocca a me tok-ka a may this round's on me; it's my turn

togliere tol-yairay to take away; to remove

togliersi: togliti! tol-yeetee get out of the way!

toilette *f* twalet toilet(s), rest room; dressing table

tonnellata *f* ton-nel-lata tonne

tonsillite *f* tonseel-leetay tonsillitis

topo *m* mouse

torcia elettrica *f* torcha torch, flashlight

Torino *f* Turin

tornare tornaray to return, to come back

tornare a casa to go home; to come home

torneo *m* tornay-o tournament, competition

toro *m* bull

torre *f* tor-ray tower

torrefazione *f* tor-refatz-yonay

shop selling coffee

Toscana *f* Tuscany

tosse *f* tos-say cough

tossire tos-seeray to cough

tostapane *m* tostapanay toaster

tostare tostaray to toast

tovagliolo *m* toval-yolo serviette

tra among; between

tradizionale tradeetz-yonalay
traditional

tradurre tradoor-ray to translate

traduzione *f* tradootz-yonay
translation

traffico *m* traffic

traghetto *m* traget-to ferry

tragitto *m* trajeet-to route;
journey

tramonto *m* sunset

trampolino *m* diving board; ski
jump; trampoline

tranne tran-nay except

tranquillo trankweel-lo quiet

**transito con catene o
pneumatici da neve** chains
or snow tyres compulsory

tranviere *m* tranv-yairay tram
driver

trapano *m* drill

trapunta *f* quilt

trascinare trasheenaray to drag

trasferimento bancario *m*
bankar-yo bank transfer

trasmissione *f* trasmees-yonay
transmission; TV/radio
programme

trattoria *f* trat-toree-a restaurant

traversata *f* crossing (sea)

tre tray three

tredici tray-deechee thirteen

treni feriali/festivi trains on
weekdays/holidays

treno *m* trayno train

treno diretto through train

treno espresso long-distance
express train

treno interregionale long-
distance, stopping train

treno merci freight train

treno metropolitano city/
suburban train

treno regionale local train,
stopping at all stations

trenta thirty

tribunale *m* treeboonalay law

courts

tricolore *m* treekol**o**ray Italian flag

trimestre *m* treem**e**stray term

triplo triple, treble

triste tr**ee**stay sad

tritatutto *m* food processor

troppo too; too much

trovare trov**a**ray to find

truccarsi to put on one's make-up

trucco *m* make-up

tu too you

tua t**oo**-a your(s)

tubo *m* t**oo**bo pipe

tubo di scappamento exhaust pipe

tue t**oo**-ay your(s)

tuffarsi to dive

tuffo *m* dive

tuo t**oo**-o, **tuoi** twoy your(s)

tuono *m* tw**o**no thunder

turismo *m* too**ree**zmo tourism

turista *m/f* tourist

tuta da ginnastica *f* jeen-n**a**steeka tracksuit

tutta all; everything

  tutta la... all the...; the whole...

tuttavia however

tutte t**oo**t-tay all; every; everybody

  tutte le direzioni all routes

  tutte le/tutti i... all the... every...

tutti all; every; everybody

  tutti e due ay d**oo**-ay both

tutto all; everything

  in tutto altogether

  tutto il... all the...; the whole...

tutto compreso all inclusive

ubriaco drunk

uccello *m* oochel-lo bird

uccidere ooch**ee**dairay to kill

UE (Unione Europea) *f* oo-ay EU (European Union)

ufficio *m* oof-f**ee**cho office

ufficio cambi k**a**mbee bureau de change

ufficio del turismo too**ree**zmo tourist office

ufficio di informazioni turistiche eenformatz-y**o**nee too**ree**steekay tourist information centre

ufficio informazioni tourist information

ufficio postale post**a**lay post office

ufficio prenotazioni prenotatz-y**o**nee reservations

ufficio prenotazioni merci reservations office for goods

ufficio prenotazioni passeggeri reservations office for passengers

ufficio turistico tourist office

uguaglianza *f* oogwal-y**a**ntza equality

uguale oogw**a**lay equal, same

ultimo oolteemo last

umido oomeedo wet

umore m oomoray mood

umorismo m oomoreezmo
humour

un, una oona a; one

undici oon-deechee eleven

Ungheria f oongairee-a Hungary

unghia f oong-ya fingernail

unguento m oongwento ointment

unico single

Unione Europea f oon-yonay
ay-ooropay-a European Union

unità socio-sanitaria locale f
local health centre

università f ooneevairseeta
university

uno oono a; one

uomini mpl womeenee men; gents'
(toilet), mens' rest room

uomo m womo man

urlare oorlaray to yell

urtare oortaray to hit, to knock

usare oozaray to use

uscire oosheeray to go out

   uscire di casa to leave the
   house

   uscire di nuovo nwovo to go/
   come back out

uscita f oosheeta exit, way out;
gate (airport)

uscita automezzi vehicle exit

uscita camion works exit

uscita d'emergenza emergency
exit

uscita di sicurezza emergency
exit

uscita operai workers' exit

uso e dosi use and dosage

**U.S.S.L. (Unità Socio-
Sanitaria Locale)** f local
health centre

utensili da cucina mpl
koocheena cooking utensils

utile ooteelay useful

V

v. (vedi) see

va he/she/it goes; you go

   come va? komay how are
   things?

   va bene! baynay that's fine!, it's
   OK!; that's right

va' a farti friggere! freej-jairay
go to hell!

va' a quel paese! kwel pa-ayzay
get lost!

vacanze fpl vakanzay holidays,
vacation

vacanze di Natale natalay
Christmas holidays/vacation

Travel tip While it's fun
to stumble across a
local festival, on national
holidays lots of places are
closed. In August, particularly the weeks either side of
Ferragosto (Aug 15), when
most of the country flees to
the coast and mountains,
many towns are left half-
deserted, with shops, bars
and restaurants closed and
a reduced public transport
service.

---

vacanze di Pasqua paskwa
Easter holidays/vacation

vacanze estive esteevay
summer holidays/vacation

vaccinazione f vacheenatz-yonay
vaccination

vaccino m vacheeno vaccination

vada oltre... oltray go past the...

vado I go

vaffanculo! fuck off!

vaglia internazionale m val-ya
eentairnatz-yonalay international
money order

vaglia postale postalay money
order

vaglia telegrafico
telegram money order

vagone m vagonay carriage, car

vagone bagagliaio bagal-ya-yo
luggage/baggage van

vagone letto sleeper, sleeping
car

vagone ristorante reestorantay
restaurant car

vai va-ee you go

valanghe valangay avalanches

validità f validity

valigia f valeeja suitcase
  disfare le valigie deesfaray lay
  valeejay to unpack

valle f val-lay valley

valore: di valore dee valoray
valuable

valuta f currency

valvola f valvola valve

vanga f spade

vanitoso vaneetozo vain

vanno they go

vaporetto m passenger ferry

varechina f varaykeena bleach

variabile varee-abeelay
changeable

vasca da bagno f ban-yo
bathtub

vasellame m vazel-lamay
crockery

vaso m vazo vase; pot

vassoio m vas-soy-o tray

vattene! vat-tenay go away!

vecchia f vek-ya old woman; old

vecchio m old man; old

vedere vedairay to see
  fare vedere to show
  **vedere data sul coperchio/
  sul retro** see date on lid/back

vedi foglio illustrativo see
illustrated instructions leaflet

vedova f vaydova widow

vedovo m widower

vegetariano m vejetar-yano,
vegetariana f vegetarian

veicoli lenti crawler lane

veicolo m vay-eekolo vehicle

vela f vayla sail; sailing

veleno m velayno poison

veliero m vel-yairo sailing ship

veloce velochay fast

velocemente velochaymentay
quickly

velocità f velocheeta speed

vendere vendairay to sell

vendesi for sale

vendita f sale

venerdì *m* Friday

Venezia *f* venetzee-a Venice

veneziane *fpl* venetz-yanay Venetian blinds

veneziano venetz-yano Venetian

vengo I come

vengono they come

veniamo we come

venire veneeray to come

venite veneetay you come

venti twenty

ventilatore *m* venteelatoray fan, ventilator

vento *m* wind

venuto come

veramente vairamentay really

verde vairday green

    al verde broke

vernice *f* vairneechay paint

    vernice fresca wet paint

vero vairo true

vero cuoio kwo-yo real leather

versamenti deposits

versamento (bancario) *m* payment; (bank) giro

versare dei soldi vairsaray day to pay in money

vescica *f* vaysheeka bladder; blister

vespa *f* wasp

vestaglia *f* vestal-ya dressing gown

vestire vesteeray to dress

vestirsi to get dressed

vestito *m* dress

vetro *m* glass (material)

vetta *f* summit, peak

vettura *f* coach, carriage

VF (Vigili del Fuoco) *mpl* fire brigade

vi vee you; yourselves; to you; each other

via *f* vee-a road, street; way; away

via aerea *f* a-airay-a airmail

viacard *f* motorway/highway magnetic card

viaggiare v-yaj-jaray to travel

viaggio *m* v-yaj-jo journey, trip; tour

    fare un viaggio to go on a journey

viaggio d'affari business trip

viaggio organizzato organeedzato package tour

viale *m* vee-alay avenue, boulevard

vialetto *m* v-yalet-to path

vicino *m* veecheeno, **vicina** *f* neighbour

vicino (a) near; nearby

vicolo *m* alleyway

vicolo cieco chayko cul-de-sac, dead end

videoregistratore *m* veeday-o-rejeestratoray video recorder

viene v-yaynay he/she/it comes; you come

vieni v-yaynee you come

vietato v-yaytato forbidden

vietato accendere fuochi no campfires

vietato ai minori di 14 anni no admittance to children

under 14

vietato attraversare i binari do not cross the tracks

vietato bagnarsi no bathing

vietato campeggiare no camping

vietato entrare no entry

vietato fumare no smoking

vietato gettare oggetti dal finestrino do not throw objects out of the window

vietato l'ingresso no entry; no admittance

vietato l'uso dell'ascensore ai minori di anni 12 non accompagnati unaccompanied children under 12 must not use the lift/ elevator

vietato pescare no fishing

vietato sporgersi dal finestrino do not lean out of the window

vietato sputare no spitting

vietato tuffarsi no diving

vietato usare la toilette durante le fermate e nelle stazioni do not use the toilet/ rest room when the train has stopped or is in the station

vigili del fuoco *mpl* veejeelee del fwoko fire brigade

vigili urbani *mpl* traffic police

vigna *f* veen-ya vineyard

villaggio *m* veel-laj-jo village

villetta *f* small detached house

vincere veenchairay to win

vincitore *m* veencheetoray winner

vincitrice *f* veencheetreechay winner

viola v-yola purple

violenza *f* v-yolentza violence

visita *f* veezeeta visit

visita guidata gweedata guided tour

visitare veezeetaray to visit

vista *f* view

visto *m* visa

vita *f* life; waist

vitamine *fpl* vitamins

vitaminico vitamin (-enriched)

vite *f* veetay screw

vivere veevairay to live

vivo alive

v.le (viale) avenue

voce *f* vochay voice

voglia: ho voglia di... o vol-ya I feel like…

vogliamo vol-yamo we want

voglio vol-yo I want

vogliono vol-yono they want

voi voy you

volante *m* volantay steering wheel

volare volaray to fly

voler dire deeray to mean

volere *m* volairay to want; will, wish

volete volaytay you want

volgare volgaray coarse

voli internazionali *mpl* eentairnatz-yonalee international flights

voli nazionali natz-yonalee domestic flights

deliberately

voluto wanted

vomitare vomeetaray to vomit, to be sick

vorrei vor-ray I would like

vostro, vostra, vostri, vostre vostray your(s)

vs. (vostro) your(s)

vulcano *m* voolkano volcano

vuoi vwoy you want

vuole vwolay he/she/it wants; you want

   vuole...? vwolay do you want...?

vuotare vwotaray to empty

vuoto vwoto empty

vuoto a perdere no deposit (on bottle)

vuoto a rendere returnable (bottle)

W

W (viva...!) long live...!

water *m* vatair W.C.

windsurf *m* windsurfing; windsurfing board

Z

zaino *m* dza-eeno rucksack

zanzara *f* dzandzara mosquito

zerbino *m* dzairbeeno doormat

zia *f* tzee-a aunt

zio *m* uncle

zitto tzeet-to quiet; silent

volo *m* flight

volo a vela vayla gliding

volo di linea leenay-a scheduled flight

volo diretto direct flight

volta *f* time

   qualche volta kwalkay sometimes

   una volta once

   una volta scongelato il prodotto non deve essere ricongelato do not refreeze once thawed

voltarsi to turn round

volutamente volootamentay

zitto! shut up!

zona *f* dzona area

zona a traffico limitato
restricted traffic area

zona disco parking discs only

zona pedonale pedestrian
precinct

MENU READER

Food

Essential terms

bread il pane panay
butter il burro boor-ro
cup la tazza tatza
dessert il dessert des-sair
fish il pesce peshay
fork la forchetta forket-ta
glass il bicchiere beek-yairay
knife il coltello
main course la portata
   principale preencheepalay
meat la carne karnay
menu il menù menoo
pepper il pepe paypay
plate il piatto p-yat-to

salad l'insalata f
salt il sale salay
set menu il menù fisso menoo
soup la minestra, la zuppa
   tzoop-pa
spoon il cucchiaio kook-ya-yo
starter l'antipasto m
table il tavolo

another..., please ancora...,
   per favore pair favoray
excuse me! (to call waiter/
   waitress) mi scusi mee skoozee
could I have the bill, please?
   il conto, per favore

A–Z

abbacchio alla romana
ab-bak-yo spring lamb

acciughe achoogay anchovies

acciughe sott'olio sot-tol-yo
anchovies in oil

aceto acheto vinegar

affettato misto variety of cold,
sliced meats such as salami,
ham etc

affogato al caffè kaf-fay
ice cream with hot espresso
poured over it

affumicato smoked

aglio al-yo garlic

agnello an-yel-lo lamb

agnello al forno roast lamb

agnolotti al burro e salvia
an-yolot-tee – ay salv-ya meat-
filled pasta shapes served with
butter and sage

agoni alla graticola grilled
long, narrow fish from
Lake Como

albicocca apricot

alloro laurel

anacardi cashew nuts

ananas pineapple

ananas al maraschino
maraskeeno pineapple with
sweet liqueur

anatra duck

anatra all'arancia arancha duck
à l'orange

anello di riso e piselli rice and

peas cooked in a ring-shaped
mould

anguilla al forno angweel-la
baked eel

anguria water melon

antipasti starters, hors d'oeuvres

antipasti caldi hot starters

antipasti freddi cold starters

antipasti misti variety of
starters

antipasti misti toscani
croutons with liver pâté, salami
and cured ham

antipasto di pesce assortito
peshay mixed seafood starter

arachidi arakeedee peanuts

aragosta spiny lobster

arancia arancha orange

arancini arancheenee fried rice
balls

aringa herring

arista di maiale al forno
my-alay roast chine of pork

arrosto roast

asiago az-yago full-fat white
cheese

asparagi asparajee asparagus

astice asteechay lobster

avocado all'agro avocado pears
with oil, lemon and vinegar
dressing

baccalà dried cod

baccalà alla vicentina
veechenteena dried salted cod
cooked with onions, olive oil,
milk, anchovies, parsley and

parmesan and served
with polenta

bagnacauda ban-yak**ow**da
vegetables, usually raw in an
oil, garlic and anchovy sauce

barbabietole barbab-**yay**tolay
beetroot

basilico baz**ee**leeko basil

bastoncini di pesce
bastonch**ee**nee dee p**e**shay
fish fingers

bavarese bavar**ay**zay (ice-cream)
cake with cream

Bel Paese pa-**ay**zay soft,
full-fat white cheese

besciamella besham**e**l-la
béchamel sauce, white sauce

bignè been-**yay** cream puff

biscotti e verduzzo ay
vaird**oo**tzo home-made biscuits
served with a glass of dry
white wine

biscotto biscuit

bistecca steak

bistecca alla fiorentina
f-yorent**ee**na large charcoal-
grilled beef steak

bistecca di manzo m**a**ndzo
beef steak

bistecca di cavallo horsemeat
steak

bocconcini di manzo e vitello
bok-konch**ee**nee dee m**a**ndzo ay
chopped beef and veal

bollito boiled

bollito misto assorted boiled
meats with vegetables

bomba ice cream bombe;
doughnut

bombolone bombol**o**nay
doughnut

bra full-fat white cheese

braciola di maiale brach**o**la dee
my-**a**lay pork chop

branzino al forno brantz**ee**no
baked sea bass

brasato braz**a**to braised; braised
beef with herbs

brasato al Barolo braised beef
cooked in Barolo wine

bresaola breza-**o**la dried, salted
beef sliced thinly and eaten
cold

brioche bree-**o**sh croissant

broccoletti all'aglio al-lal-yo
broccoli cooked in garlic

brodetto fish casserole

brodo clear broth

brodo di pollo chicken broth

brodo vegetale vejayt**a**lay clear,
vegetable broth

bruschetta alla romana
br**oo**sket-ta toasted bread
rubbed with garlic and
sprinkled with olive oil

bucatini al pomodoro pasta
similar to spaghetti (only
thicker and with a hole
through it) with tomato sauce

budino pudding

burro butter

caciotta kach**o**t-ta type of creamy,
white, medium-soft cheese

caciotta toscana slightly mature, medium-soft cheese from Tuscany

caciucco alla livornese kachook-ko al-la leevornayzay soup made from seafood, tomato and wine served with home-made bread

calamari fritti fried squid

calamari in umido stewed squid

calamaro squid

calzone kaltzonay folded pizza with tomato and mozzarella or ricotta and ham, or other fillings inside

calzone all'amalfitana calzone with cottage cheese, egg, ham and grana cheese

canestrato hard ewes milk cheese

cannella cinnamon

cannelloni al forno rolls of pasta filled with meat and baked in a sauce

cannoli alla siciliana seecheel-yana cylindrical pastries filled with ricotta and candied fruit

cannoncini alla crema kannoncheenee cylindrical pastries filled with custard

cantuccini kantoocheenee almond biscuits

caponata di melanzane melantzanay fried aubergines/eggplants and celery cooked with tomato, capers and olives

cappelle di funghi porcini alla griglia kap-pel-lay dee foongee porcheenee al-la greel-ya grilled boletus mushroom tops

cappelletti small, filled pasta parcels

capperi capers

cappone lesso kap-ponay boiled capon

capretto al forno roast kid

caprino fresh, soft goat's cheese

capriolo in salmì roe deer venison in game sauce

caramella sweet

carciofi karchofee artichokes

carciofini sott'olio karchofeenee sot-tol-yo baby artichokes preserved in oil

carne karnay meat

carne macinata macheenata minced meat

carote karotay carrots

carpaccio karpacho finely sliced raw beef fillets with oil, lemon and grated Parmesan

carré di maiale al forno kar-ray dee my-alay roast loin of pork

carrello dei dolci dolchee dessert trolley

cassata siciliana seecheel-yana Sicilian ice-cream cake with candied fruit, chocolate and ricotta

castagnaccio alla toscana kastan-yacho tart from Tuscany made with chestnut flour

castagne kastan-yay chestnuts

catalogna katalon-ya type of chicory with large leaves

cavoletti di Bruxelles brooksel Brussels sprouts

cavolfiore kavolf-yoray cauliflower

cavolo cabbage

cavolo rosso red cabbage

cazzuola alla milanese katzwola al-la meelanayzay spicy pork sausage, pork and beans stewed in gravy

ceci chaychee chickpeas

cefalo chefalo mullet

cernia chairn-ya grouper (fish)

cervella al burro chairvel-la brains cooked in butter

cetriolo chetree-olo cucumber

charlotte sharlot ice-cream cake with cream, biscuits and fruit

chiacchiere k-yak-yairay sweet pastries fried in lard and sprinkled with fine sugar

chiodi di garofano k-yodee cloves

ciambella chambel-la ring-shaped cake

cicoria cheekoree-a chicory

cicorino cheekoreeno small chicory plants

ciliege cheel-yay-jay cherries

cima alla piemontese cheema al-la p-yaymontayzay baked veal stuffed with chicken and chopped vegetables, served cold

cime di rapa cheemay young leaves of turnip plant

cinghiale in salmì cheeng-yalay wild boar in game sauce

cioccolata chok-kolata chocolate

cioccolata al latte lat-tay milk chocolate

cioccolata fondente fondentay plain chocolate

cioccolato chok-kolato chocolate

cipolle cheepol-lay onions

cocktail di gamberetti prawn cocktail

coda alla vaccinara vacheenara oxtail diced and stewed with vegetables

colomba pasquale paskwalay dove-shaped cake with candied fruit eaten at Easter

conchiglie alla marchigiana konkeel-yay al-la markeejana pasta shells in tomato sauce with celery, carrot, parsley and ham

condimento per l'insalata salad dressing

coniglio koneel-yo rabbit

coniglio in salmì rabbit in game sauce

cono gelato jelato ice-cream cone

contorni vegetable side dishes

coperto cover charge (usually includes bread)

coperto pane e grissini cover charge includes bread and breadsticks

coppa cured neck of pork, finely sliced and eaten cold

cornetto croissant

cosciotto di agnello al forno koshot-to dee an-yel-lo baked leg of lamb

costata alla fiorentina f-yoren-teena Florentine entrecôte

costata (di manzo) mandzo beef entrecôte

costoletta chop

costoletta di vitello alla griglia greel-ya grilled veal chop

cotechino kotekeeno spiced pork sausage, usually boiled

cotoletta veal cutlet

cotoletta alla milanese meelanayzay veal escalope in breadcrumbs

cotoletta alla valdostana veal chop with ham and cheese cooked in breadcrumbs

cotolette di agnello an-yel-lo lamb chops

cotolette di maiale kotolet-tay dee my-alay pork chops

cotto cooked

cozze kotzay mussels

cozze alla marinara mussels in marinade sauce

crauti krowtee white cabbage cut in strips, cooked in vinegar and white wine

crema krayma custard

crema al caffè kaf-fay coffee custard pudding

crema al cioccolato chok-kolato chocolate custard pudding

crema alla vaniglia vaneel-ya vanilla-flavoured custard pudding

crema di... cream of... soup

crema pasticciera pasteechaira confectioner's custard

crêpe krep pancake

crêpe suzette flambéed pancake with orange sauce

crescente kreshentay type of flat, fried Emilian bread

crescenza kreshentza soft, creamy white cheese

crescione kreshonay watercress

crespelle krespel-lay savoury pancakes

crocchette di patate krok-ket-tay dee patatay potato croquettes

crocchette di pesce peshay fish croquettes

crocchette di riso rice croquettes

crostata casalinga kazaleenga home-made lattice pie with jam or custard

crostata di frutta fruit tart

crostata di mele maylay apple
pie

crostini ai funghi a-ee foongee
croutons with mushrooms
cooked in oil with garlic and
parsley

crostini toscani croutons with
liver pâté

crostoni di mozzarella dee
motzarel-la mozzarella and
tomato sauce served hot on
home-made bread

crudo raw

dadi stock cubes

datteri dates

dentice al forno denteechay
baked dentex (type of sea bream)

dolce dolchay dessert

dolci dolchee cakes, gâteaux,
desserts etc

dolci della casa home-made
cakes

endivia belga endeev-ya
Belgian endive

entrecôte (di manzo) mandzo
beef entrecôte

erbe aromatiche airbay
aromateekay herbs

fagiano fajano pheasant

fagioli fajolee beans

fagioli alla messicana type of
chili con carne

fagioli all'olio al-lol-yo beans

with salt, pepper, oil and
vinegar

fagioli borlotti in umido fresh
borlotti beans cooked in
vegetables, herbs and tomato
sauce

fagiolini fajoleenee green beans

fagiolini lessi les-see boiled
French beans

faraona fara-ona guinea fowl

farina flour

fatto in casa kaza home-made

fegatini di pollo chicken livers

fegato faygato liver

fegato alla veneta venayta liver
cooked in butter with onions

ferri: ai ferri a-ee grilled

fetta biscottata slices of crispy
toast-like bread

fettuccine fet-toocheenay ribbon-
shaped pasta

fichi feekee figs

filetti di merluzzo mairlootzo
fillets of cod

filetti di pesce persico peshay
pairseeko fillets of perch

filetto fillet

filetto ai ferri a-ee grilled fillet
of beef

filetto al cognac fillet of beef
in cognac

filetto al pepe verde paypay
vairday fillet of beef with green
pepper

filetto al sangue sangway rare
fillet of beef

filetto a media cottura mayd-ya

medium-done fillet beef

filetto ben cotto well-done fillet of beef

filetto di manzo mandzo fillet of beef

filone (di pane) feelonay dee panay large French stick

finocchi gratinati feenok-kee fennel with melted grated cheese

finocchio feenok-yo fennel

fiori di zucca fritti f-yoree dee tzook-ka fried pumpkin flowers

flan di spinaci speenachee spinach flan

focaccia fokacha flat bread sprinkled with olive oil and baked or grilled

foglie di vite alla greca fol-yay dee veetay Greek-style vine leaves

fondue Bourguignonne boorgeen-yon cubes of fillet steak fried in oil and dipped in various sauces

fonduta fondue made with cheese, milk and eggs

fontina soft, mature cheese often used in cooking

formaggi misti formaj-jee selection of cheeses

formaggio formaj-jo cheese

forno: al forno roast

fragole fragolay strawberries

fricassea di coniglio freekas-say-a dee koneel-yo chopped rabbit cooked in butter and aromatic herbs

frico e polenta ay fried latteria cheese with polenta

frittata type of omelette

frittelle di banane freetel-lay dee bananay banana fritters

frittelle di mele maylay apple fritters

fritto fried

fritto misto mixed seafood in batter

frittura di pesce peshay variety of fried fish

frutta fruit

frutta alla fiamma f-yam-ma flambéd fruit

frutta fresca di stagione stajonay seasonal fruit

frutta secca dried fruit; nuts

frutti di bosco mixture of forest fruits

frutti di mare maray seafood

frutti di mare gratinati seafood au gratin

funghi foongee mushrooms

funghi porcini porcheenee boletus mushrooms

funghi trifolati mushrooms fried in garlic and parsley

fusilli al pomodoro foozeel-lee pasta twirls with tomato sauce

galantina di pollo chicken with spices and herbs served in gelatine

gallina chicken

gamberetti shrimps

gamberetti in salsa rosa roza

shrimps in mayonnaise and ketchup sauce

gamberi crayfish; prawns

gamberoni king prawns

gelatina jelateena gelatine

gelato jelato ice cream

gelato di crema vanilla ice cream

gelato di frutta fruit-flavoured ice cream

ghiacciolo g-yacholo ice lolly

giardiniera di verdure jardeen-yaira dee vairdooray diced, mixed vegetables, cooked and pickled

gnocchetti verdi n-yok-ket-tee vairdee small flour, potato and spinach dumplings sometimes served with melted gorgonzola

gnocchi n-yok-kee small flour

and potato dumplings

gnocchi ai formaggi a-ee formaj-jee potato dumplings with gorgonzola, fontina, mascarpone and Parmesan

gnocchi alla romana small semolina dumplings baked in butter

gnocchi al ragù dumplings with minced meat and tomato sauce

gorgonzola strong, soft blue cheese from Lombardy or Piedmont

grana generic name of cheeses similar to Parmesan

grana padano cheese similar to Parmesan

grancevola granchayvola spiny spider crab

granchio grank-yo crab

grasso fat

gratin di patate grateen dee
  patatay potatoes with grated
  cheese

griglia: alla griglia al-la greel-ya
  grilled

grigliata di pesce greel-yata di
  peshay grilled fish

grigliata mista mixed grill (meat
  or fish)

grissini breadsticks

gruviera groov-yaira Gruyère
  cheese

gulash ungherese oongarayzay
  Hungarian goulash

impanato breaded, in
  breadcrumbs

indivia eendeev-ya endive

insalata salad

insalata caprese kaprayzay
  sliced tomatoes, mozzarella
  and oregano

insalata di carne karnay
  meat salad

insalata di mare maray
  seafood salad

insalata di nervetti sinewy,
  chopped boiled beef or veal,
  served cold with beans and
  pickles

insalata mista mixed salad

insalata russa Russian salad

insalata verde vairday
  green salad

involtini small beef olives

involtini di prosciutto pro-
shoot-to small rolls of sliced
  ham filled with Russian salad

krapfen doughnut

lamponi raspberries

lardo al pepe paypay fatty ham
  with pepper

lasagne al forno lazan-yay
  lasagne

latteria lat-tairee-a full-fat white
  cheese

lattuga lettuce

legumi pulses

lenticchie lenteek-yay lentils

lepre lepray hare

lesso boiled

limone leemonay lemon

lingua leengwa tongue

lingua salmistrata ox tongue
  marinaded in brine then
  cooked

linguine al pesto leengweenay
  kind of flat spaghetti with
  crushed basil, garlic, oil and
  Parmesan dressing

lombatina di vitella ai ferri
a-ee grilled loin of veal

lonza di maiale al latte lontza
  dee my-alay al lat-tay pork loin
  cooked in milk

maccheroni alla siciliana
  mak-kaironee al-la seecheel-yana
  macaroni with tomato sauce and
  grated Sicilian ricotta cheese

maccheroni al ragù macaroni in
  minced beef and tomato sauce

macedonia di frutta machedon-ya fruit salad

macedonia di frutta al maraschino mara-skeeno fruit salad in Maraschino liqueur

maggiorana maj-jorana marjoram

maiale my-alay pork

maionese my-onayzay mayonnaise

mandarancio mandarancho clementine

mandorle mandorlay almonds

mantovana almond cake from Prato

manzo mandzo beef

marinato marinated, soused, pickled

marmellata jam

marmellata d'arance daranchay marmalade

marroni chestnuts

marzapane martzapanay marzipan

mascarpone maskarponay full-fat, cream cheese, often used in desserts

medaglioni di vitello medal-yonee round pieces of veal

mela mayla apple

mela flambé flambéd apple

melanzane melantzanay aubergines/eggplants

melanzane alla piastra p-yastra grilled aubergines/eggplants

melanzane alla siciliana seecheel-yana baked aubergine/eggplant slices with parmesan, tomato sauce and egg

melone melonay melon

melone al porto melon with port

menta mint

menu fisso set menu

menu turistico tourist menu

meringata meringue pie

meringhe con panna maireengay meringues with cream

merluzzo mairlootzo cod

merluzzo alla pizzaiola peetza-yola cod in tomato sauce with anchovies, capers and parsley

merluzzo in bianco b-yanko boiled cod with oil and lemon

messicani in gelatina jelateena rolls of veal in gelatine

miele m-yaylay honey

millefoglie meel-lefol-yay custard slice

minestra di orzo ortzo barley soup

minestra di riso e prezzemolo (in brodo) pretzaymolo parsley and rice soup

minestra di verdure vairdooray vegetable soup

minestra in brodo soup with vegetables and pasta or rice

minestre meenestray soups

minestrone meenestronay thick vegetable broth with rice or thin pasta

mirtilli meerteel-lee bilberries

montasio montaz-yo full-fat white cheese

Montebianco monteb-yanko

puréed chestnut and whipped cream pudding

more moray mulberries, blackberries

mortadella large, mild-flavoured cured sausage, usually served in thin slices

mostarda di Cremona preserve made from candied fruit in grape must or sugar with mustard

mousse al cioccolato chok-kolato chocolate mousse

mozzarella motzarel-la white, mild, slightly rubbery buffalo milk cheese

mozzarella in carrozza een kar-rotza slices of bread and mozzarella coated in flour and fried

nasello nazel-lo hake

naturale: al naturale natooralay plain, natural

nervetti con cipolla cheepol-la chopped, sinewy beef and veal with onions

nocciole nocholay hazelnuts

noccioline nocholeenay peanuts

noce di cocco nochay coconut

noce di vitello ai funghi a-ee foongee veal with mushrooms

noce moscata nutmeg

noci nochee walnuts

nodino veal chop

oca goose

olio ol-yo oil

olio di semi saymee vegetable oil

olio d'oliva olive oil

oliva olive

omelette omelette

orata al forno baked gilthead (fish)

orecchiette al sugo (di pomodoro) orek-yet-tay small pasta shells with tomato sauce

orecchiette con cime di rapa cheemay orecchiette with turnip tops

origano oregano

orzo ordzo barley

ossobuco stewed shin of veal

ostriche ostreekay oysters

paglia e fieno pal-ya ay f-yayno mixture of ordinary and green tagliatelle

pagnotta pan-yot-ta round loaf

paillard di manzo pa-yar dee mandzo slices of grilled beef

paillard di vitello slices of grilled veal

pancetta panchet-ta bacon

pancotto stale bread cooked with tomatoes etc

pan di Spagna span-ya sponge cake

pandoro kind of sponge cake eaten at Christmas

pane panay bread

pane bianco b-yanko white bread

pane integrale eentegralay wholemeal bread

pane tostato toast

pane casereccio kazairecho home-made bread

pane di segale saygalay rye bread

pane e coperto cover charge including bread

pane in cassetta sliced bread

pane nero nairo wholemeal bread

panettone panet-tonay dome-shaped cake with sultanas and candied fruit eaten at Christmas

panforte panfortay nougat-type spiced delicacy from Siena

panini sandwiches; filled rolls

panna cream

panna cotta kind of pudding typical of Tuscany

panna montata whipped cream

panna per cucinare pair koocheenaray cream for cooking

panzanella pantzanel-la Tuscan dish of bread with fresh tomatoes, onions, basil and olive oil

papaia papa-ya papaw, papaya

pappa col pomodoro tomato soup with toasted home-made bread typical of Tuscany

parmigiana di melanzane parmeejana dee melantzanay baked dish of layers of aubergines/eggplants, tomato sauce, mozzarella and Parmesan

parmigiano reggiano parmeejano rej-jano Parmesan cheese

passato di patate patatay cream of potato soup

passato di verdure vairdooray cream of vegetable soup

pasta pasta; cake; pastry

pasta al forno pasta baked in white sauce with grated cheese

pasta alla frutta fruit pastry

pasta e fagioli ay fajolee very thick soup with blended borlotti beans and small pasta

pasta e piselli pasta with peas

pasticcino pasteecheeno small cake

pasticcio di fegato d'oca pasteecho dee faygato baked, pasta-covered dish with goose liver

pasticcio di lepre lepray baked, pasta-covered dish with hare

pasticcio di maccheroni mak-kaironee baked macaroni

pastiera napoletana past-yaira flaky pastry with wheat, ricotta and candied fruit

pastina in brodo noodle soup

patate patatay potatoes

patate al forno baked potatoes

patate arrosto roast potatoes

patate fritte freet-tay chips, French fries

patate in insalata potato salad

patate prezzemolate pretzemo-latay boiled potatoes with oil and parsley

patate saltate saltatay sautéed

potatoes

patatine patateenay crisps, (US) potato chips

patatine fritte freet-tay chips, French fries

pâté di carne karnay pâté

pâté di fegato faygato liver pâté

pâté di pesce peshay fish pâté

pecorino strong, hard ewe's milk cheese

pecorino sardo hard, mature Sardinian ewes cheese

pelati peeled tinned tomatoes

penne pen-nay pasta quills

penne ai quattro formaggi a-ee kwat-tro formaj-jee penne with sauce made from four cheeses

penne all'arrabbiata ar-rab-yata penne with tomato and chili pepper sauce

penne rigate reegatay penne with ridges

pepe paypay pepper (spice)

peperonata peppers cooked in olive oil with onion, tomato and garlic

peperoncino pepaironcheeno chilli pepper

peperone pepaironay pepper (vegetable)

peperoni ripieni (di carne) reep-yaynee dee karnay stuffed peppers (filled with meat)

peperoni sott'olio sot-tol-yo peppers in oil

pera paira pear

pernice pairneechay partridge

pernice alla cacciatora kachatora stewed spiced partridge

pesca peska peach

pesce peshay fish

pesce al cartoccio kartocho fish baked in foil with herbs

pesce in carpione karp-yonay soused fish

pesce spada swordfish

pesche sciroppate peskay sheerop-patay peaches in syrup

petti di pollo alla bolognese bolon-yayzay chicken breasts in breadcrumbs with tomato sauce

petti di pollo impanati chicken breasts in breadcrumbs

piatti di carne p-yat-tee dee karnay meat dishes

piatti di pesce peshay fish dishes

piatto unico freddo p-yat-to cold sliced meat with pickles

piccata di vitello al limone leemonay veal in sour lemon sauce

piccione peechonay pigeon

piccione arrosto roast pigeon

piedini di maiale p-yaydeenee dee my-alay pigs' trotters

pinoli pine nuts

pinzimonio peentzeemon-yo selection of whole, raw vegetables eaten with oil and vinegar dressing

piselli peas

piselli al prosciutto proshoot-
to fresh peas cooked in clear
broth, with butter, ham
and basil

pistacchi peestak-kee pistachios

pizza ai porcini porcheenee
pizza with boletus mushrooms

pizza ai quattro formaggi
kwat-tro formaj-jee pizza with
four cheeses – mozzarella,
gorgonzola, latteria, grana

pizza agli asparagi al-yee
asparajee asparagus pizza

pizza alla diavola d-yavola pizza
with spicy salami

pizza alla marinara pizza with
tomato, oregano, garlic and
anchovies

pizza alla zingara tzeengara
pizza with aubergines/
eggplants, peppers,
mushrooms and olives

pizza al S. Daniele san dan-
yaylay pizza with cured ham

pizza campagnola kampan-yola
pizza with mushrooms and
peppers

pizza capricciosa kapreechosa
pizza with tomato, ham,
mushrooms and artichokes

pizzaiola peetza-ee-ola slices of
cooked beef in tomato sauce,
oregano and anchovies

pizza Margherita margaireeta
pizza with tomato and
mozzarella

pizza napoletana pizza with tomato, mozzarella and anchovies

pizza nordica pizza with chopped salami and frankfurters

pizza orchidea orkeeday-a pizza with peppers and egg

pizza pugliese pool-yayzay tomato and onion pizza

pizza quattro stagioni stajonee pizza with ham, mushrooms, artichokes and anchovies

pizza romana pizza with tomato, mozzarella, anchovies and oregano

pizza siciliana seecheel-yana pizza with anchovies, capers, olives and oregano

pizzetta peetzet-ta small pizza

pizzoccheri alla Valtellinese peetzok-kairee al-la valtel-leenayzay thin, pasta strips with green vegetables, melted butter and cheese

polenta yellow cornmeal porridge, left to set and cut in slices, can be fried or baked

polenta concia koncha sliced polenta baked with garlic, cheese and butter

polenta e osei ozay-ee small birds served with polenta

polenta e uccellini oo-chel-leenee small birds served with polenta

polenta fritta fried polenta

polenta pasticciata pasteechata layers of polenta, tomato sauce and cheese

pollame pol-lamay poultry

pollo chicken

pollo alla cacciatora kachatora chicken chasseur – pieces of fried chicken in a white wine and mushroom sauce

pollo alla diavola dee-avola chicken pieces pressed and fried

polpette polpet-tay meatballs

polpettone polpet-tonay meat-loaf

polpi alla veneziana venetz-yana chopped boiled octopus, seasoned with garlic, lemon juice and parsley

polpo octopus

pomodori tomatoes

pomodori alla maionese my-onay-zay tomatoes with mayonnaise

pomodori pelati peeled tinned tomatoes

pomodori ripieni di riso reep-yaynee tomatoes stuffed with rice

pomodoro tomato

pompelmo grapefruit

porchetta porket-ta roast sucking pig

porchetta allo spiedo sp-yaydo sucking pig on the spit

porro leek

portata course (main course etc)

prezzemolo pretz**ay**molo parsley

primi piatti p-y**at**-tee first courses

prosciutto prosh**oot**-to ham

prosciutto al madera ham with madeira

prosciutto cotto cooked ham

prosciutto crudo dry-cured ham

prosciutto crudo di S. Daniele san dan-y**ay**lay finest quality prosciutto crudo from S. Daniele

prosciutto di Praga type of dry-cured ham

provolone provol**o**nay oval-shaped cheese, with a slight smoked and spicy flavour

prugne pr**oo**n-yay plums

punte di asparagi all'agro p**oo**ntay dee asp**a**rajee asparagus tips in oil and lemon dressing

purè di patate pooray dee pat**a**tay creamed potatoes

quaglie kw**a**l-yay quails

radicchio rad**ee**k-yo chicory

ragù sauce made with minced beef and tomatoes

rapa type of white turnip with flavour similar to radish

ravanelli radishes

ravioli egg pasta filled with meat or cheese

ravioli al pomodoro ravioli in tomato sauce

razza r**a**tza skate

resta di Como speciality of Como, pastry rolled around a stick and baked

ribollita vegetable soup with toasted home-made bread, typical of Tuscany

ricotta soft white cheese, similar to cottage cheese

ricotta piemontese p-yay-mont**ay**zay similar to ricotta romana

ricotta romana soft, white cheese often used in desserts

ricotta siciliana seecheel-y**a**na slightly mature and salty ricotta

rigatoni al pomodoro short, ridged pasta shapes with tomato sauce

ripieno reep-y**ay**no stuffed

risi e bisi risotto with peas and small pieces of ham

riso rice

riso alla greca boiled rice with olives, cheese and tomato

riso in brodo rice in clear broth

riso pilaf rice cooked slowly in the oven with butter and onion

risotto rice simmered slowly in clear broth

risotto al Barolo risotto with Barolo wine

risotto alla castellana risotto with mushroom, ham, cream and cheese sauce

risotto alla marinara seafood risotto

risotto alla milanese (allo zafferano) meelan**ay**zay al-lo tzaf-fair**a**no risotto with saffron

risotto al nero di seppia nairo dee s**e**p-ya risotto with cuttlefish ink

risotto al salto sautéed saffron risotto

risotto con la salsiccia sals**ee**cha risotto with pork sausage

roast-beef all'inglese eengl**ay**zay thin slices of roast beef served cold with lemon

robiola rob-y**o**la soft cheese from Lombardy

rognone trifolato ron-y**o**nay small pieces of kidney in garlic, oil and parsley

rombo turbot

rosetta kind of roll

rosmarino rosemary

rucola rocket

Saint-Honoré santonor**ay** tart with soft, pastry base and small cream éclairs

salame salam**ay** salami

salame di cioccolato dee chok-kol**a**to mixture of broken biscuits and chocolate in the shape of a salami

salatini salat**ee**nee tiny salted crackers, crisps and peanuts (eaten with aperitifs)

sale sal**ay** salt

salmone salm**o**nay salmon

salsa sauce

salsa cocktail mayonnaise and ketchup sauce, served with fish and seafood

salsa di pomodoro tomato sauce

salsa tartara tartar sauce

salsa vellutata white sauce made with clear broth instead of milk

salsa verde va**i**rday sauce made from chopped parsley, anchovies and oil, served with meat

salsiccia sals**ee**cha sausage

saltimbocca alla romana slices of veal rolled up with ham and sage and fried

salvia salv-ya sage

sangue: al sangue s**a**ngway rare

sarago sar**a**go white bream

sarde ai ferri sarday a-ee grilled sardines

scaloppine skalop-peenay veal escalopes

scaloppine al Marsala veal escalopes in Marsala

scamorza affumicata skamortza smoked, soft, oval-shaped cheese

scamorza alla griglia greel-ya grilled soft cheese

scampi crayfish, scampi

scarola type of endive

schiacciata toscana skee-achata bread with fresh oil and rosemary

scorfano scorpion fish

scorpena skorpayna scorpion fish

scorzonera al burro skortzonaira type of root cooked in butter

secondi (piatti) p-yat-tee main courses, second courses

sedano saydano celery

sedano di Verona Veronese celery

sella di cervo chairvo rump of venison

selvaggina selvaj-jeena game

semifreddo ice cream and sponge dessert

senape senapay mustard

seppie in umido sep-yay stewed cuttlefish

sfogliata agli spinaci sfol-yata a-yee speenachee flaky pastry with spinach filling

sfogliata al salmone sal-monay flaky pastry with salmon filling

sofficini al formaggio sof-feecheenee al formaj-jo crispy pancakes with cheese filling

sogliola sol-yola sole

sogliola alla mugnaia moon-ya-ya sole cooked in flour and butter

sorbetto sorbet; soft ice cream

sottaceti sot-tachaytee pickles

soufflé al formaggio formaj-jo cheese soufflé

soufflé al prosciutto pro-shoot-to ham soufflé

spaghetti alla carbonara spaghetti with egg, cheese and diced bacon sauce

spaghetti alla marinara spaghetti with seafood

spaghetti all'amatriciana amatree-chana spaghetti with bacon, onions and tomato sauce

spaghetti alla puttanesca spaghetti with anchovies, capers and black olives in tomato sauce

spaghetti all'arrabbiata al-lar-rab-yata spaghetti with tomato and chilli sauce

spaghetti alle noci nochee spaghetti with fresh cream, grated nuts and cheese

spaghetti alle vongole vongolay spaghetti with clams

spaghetti al nero di seppia

naïro dee sep-ya black spaghetti flavoured with cuttlefish ink

spaghetti al pesto spaghetti in crushed basil, garlic, oil and Parmesan dressing

spaghetti al ragù spaghetti with minced beef and tomato sauce

spalla di maiale al forno my-**a**lay shoulder of roast pork

speck type of dry-cured, smoked ham

spezie spaytz-yay spices

spezzatino di vitello spezzat**ee**no veal stew

spiedini sp-yayd**ee**nee small pieces of a variety of meat or fish roasted on a spit

spiedo: allo spiedo sp-yaydo on a spit

spigola sea bass

spinaci speen**a**chee spinach

spinaci all'agro spinach with oil and lemon

spuma di salmone sp**oo**ma dee salm**o**nay salmon mousse

spuntino snack

stoccafisso dried cod

stracchino strak-k**ee**no soft cheese from Lombardy

stracchino alle fragole al-lay frag**o**lay dessert of strawberries and whipped cream liquidized and frozen

stracciatella stracha-t**e**l-la vanilla ice cream with chocolate chips; beaten eggs cooked in boiling, clear broth

strangolapreti strangolaprayt**ee** little spinach and potato balls

strozzapreti al basilico e pomodoro strotzaprayt**ee** al baz**ee**leeko ay small dumplings with tomato and basil

strudel di mele m**ay**lay apple strudel

stufato stewed

stufato con verdure vaird**oo**ray meat stewed with vegetables and herbs

sugo al tonno tomato sauce with garlic, tuna and parsley

svizzera zv**ee**tzaira hamburger

tacchino tak-k**ee**no turkey

tagliata tal-y**a**ta finely cut beef fillet

tagliatelle tal-yatel-l**ay** thin, flat strips of egg pasta

tagliatelle alla bolognese bolon-y**ay**zay tagliatelle with minced beef and tomato sauce

tagliatelle al ragù tagliatelle with minced beef and tomato sauce

tagliatelle rosse ros-say tagliatelle with chopped red peppers

tagliatelle verdi v**ai**rdee tagliatelle with chopped spinach

taglierini al tartufo tal-yair**ee**nee very thin pasta strips with truffles

taglierini gratinati thin pasta strips au gratin

tagliolini tal-yoleenee thin, soup noodles

tagliolini verdi panna e prosciutto vairdee – ay proshoot-to thin green noodles with cream and ham sauce

taleggio talej-jo full-fat, semi-mature, mild, soft cheese from Northern Italy

tartine tarteenay canapés

tartufo round ice cream sprinkled with cocoa or chocolate powder; truffle (edible fungi)

tavola calda snack bar serving hot dishes

testina di vitello head of small calf

timballo di riso alla finanziera fee-nantz-yaira type of rice pie filled with chicken entrails and crests

timo thyme

tiramisù dessert made of coffee-soaked sponge, eggs, Marsala wine, mascarpone cheese and cocoa powder

toast tost toasted sandwich

tomini sott'olio sot-tol-yo cheese with pepper marinated in oil and herbs

tonno tuna fish

torrone tor-ronay nougat

torta cake; tart; flan

torta della nonna tart with cream and pine nuts

torta di mele maylay apple tart

torta di noci nochee walnut tart

torta di ricotta type of cheesecake

torta gelato jelato ice-cream tart

torta lorenese lorenayzay quiche lorraine

torta pasqualina paskwaleena flaky pastry with spinach, cheese, ham and hard-boiled eggs

tortelli home-made ravioli filled with ricotta and spinach

tortelli di patate patatay home-made ravioli filled with mashed potato and nutmeg

tortellini small pasta filled with pork loin, ham, Parmesan and nutmeg

tortellini al ragù tortellini with minced beef and tomato sauce

tortelloni di magro pasta filled with cheese, parsley and vegetables

tortelloni di ricotta pasta filled with cheese, parsley and vegetables

tortino di asparagi asparajee asparagus pie

tortino di patate patatay potato pie

tournedos toornaydo round, thick slice of beef fillet

tramezzino tramedzeeno sandwich

trancio di coda di rospo trancho angler fish cutlet

trancio di palombo smooth hound slice (fish)

trancio di pesce spada peshay swordfish steak

trenette col pesto trenet-tay type of flat spaghetti with crushed basil, garlic, oil and cheese sauce

triglia treel-ya mullet

trippa tripe

trota trout

uccelletti oochel-let-tee small birds wrapped in bacon on cocktail sticks

umido stewed

uova wova eggs

uova affogate af-fogatay poached eggs

uova all'occhio di bue ok-yo dee boo-ay fried eggs

uova al tegamino con pancetta panchet-ta eggs and bacon

uova farcite farcheetay eggs stuffed with tuna, capers and mayonnaise

uova in camicia kameecha poached eggs

uova in cocotte kokot eggs cooked in a cast-iron pan

uova strapazzate strapatzatay scrambled eggs

uovo wovo egg

uovo alla coque kok boiled egg

uovo sodo hard-boiled egg

uva grapes

uva bianca white grapes

uva nera naira black grapes

valigette verdi al gorgonzola valeejet-tay vairdee large green ravioli filled with gorgonzola cheese

vaniglia vaneel-ya vanilla

vellutata di piselli creamed peas with egg yolks

vellutata al pomodoro cream of tomato soup with fresh cream

vellutata di asparagi asparajee creamed asparagus with egg yolks

veneziana venetz-yana type of small panettone cake sprinkled with sugar

verdura vairdoora vegetables

verdura di stagione stajonay
seasonal vegetables

verdure fresche di stagione
vairdooray freskay seasonal
vegetables

vermicelli vairmeechel-lee pasta
thinner than spaghetti

vitello veal

vitello tonnato sliced veal in
blended tuna, anchovy, oil and
lemon sauce

**vol-au-vent alla crema di
formaggio** krayma dee for-maj-
jo cream cheese vol-au-vent

vongole vongolay clams

würstel voorstel frankfurter

zabaglione/zabaione tzabal-
yonay dessert made from
beaten eggs, sugar and Marsala

zafferano tzaf-fairano saffron

zampone con lenticchie
tzamponay kon lenteek-yay
stuffed pig's trotters with lentils

zucca tzook-ka pumpkin

zucchero tzook-kairo sugar

zucchine tzook-keenay courgettes

zucchine al pomodoro
chopped courgettes in tomato,
garlic and parsley sauce

zuccotto tzook-kot-to ice-cream
cake with sponge, fresh cream
and chocolate

zuppa tzoop-pa soup

zuppa inglese eenglayzay trifle

zuppa pavese pavayzay soup
with home-made bread, grated
cheese and an egg

Drink

Essential terms

beer la birra beer-ra
bottle la bottiglia bot-**teel**-ya
brandy il brandy
coffee il caffè kaf-f**ay**
cup la tazza t**a**tza
a cup of... una tazza di...
gin il gin
gin and tonic un gin t**o**nic
glass il bicchiere beek-y**ai**ray
a glass of... un bicchiere di...
milk il latte l**a**t-tay
mineral water l'acqua minerale f
  akwa meenair**a**lay
orange juice il succo d'arancia
  s**oo**k-ko dar**a**ncha
port il p**o**rto
red wine il v**i**no r**o**sso

rosé il ros**é**
soda (water) il seltz
soft drink la b**i**bita (analc**o**lica)
sugar lo zucchero tz**oo**k-kairo
tea il tè tay
tonic (water) l'acqua t**o**nica f
  akwa
vodka la v**o**dka
water l'acqua f **a**kwa
whisky il whisky
white wine il v**i**no bianco
  b-y**a**nko
wine il v**i**no
wine list la l**i**sta dei v**i**ni day

another ..., please anc**o**ra...,
  per fav**o**re pair fav**o**ray

A–Z

acqua akwa water

acqua minerale meenairalay mineral water

acqua minerale gassata sparkling mineral water

acqua minerale non gassata still mineral water

acqua naturale natooralay still mineral water

acqua tonica tonic water

alcol alcohol

alcolici alkoleechee alcoholic drinks

Amaretto liqueur made from apricot kernels, giving it a strong almond-type flavour

amaro dark, bitter, herbal digestive liqueur

analcolici analkoleechee non-alcoholic drinks

aperitivo aperitif

aranciata aranchata orangeade

Asti Spumante spoomantay sparkling sweet white wine from Asti in Piedmont

Barbaresco dry red wine, typical of the Piedmont region

Barbera barbaira dark dry red wine from Piedmont

Bardolino dry red wine from area around Verona

Bardolino secco dry red wine from the Veneto region

> **Travel tip** An Italian custom – especially in Milan – is the *aperitivo* or pre-dinner drink, usually taken between 6 and 9pm. Another opportunity to preen and pose, *aperitivo* time is also a boon for budget travellers as bar counters are often laden with hot and cold food, all of which is included in the price of your drink.

Barolo dark dry red wine from Piedmont

bevande drinks

bianco b-yanko white

Bianco dei Castelli secco dry white wine from Lazio

bibita analcolica soft drink

birra beer-ra beer

birra alla spina draught beer

birra chiara k-yara amber-coloured light beer, lager

birra grande granday large beer (40 cl, approx. 1 pint)

birra in bottiglia bot-teel-ya bottled beer

birra media mayd-ya medium beer (30 cl)

birra piccola small beer (20cl, approx. 1/2 pint)

birra rossa darker, maltier beer

birra scura skoora beer similar to bitter, darker than birra rossa

bitter bitter-tasting red or orange alcoholic aperitif

Brachetto braket-to sweet

sparkling red wine from Marche or Acqui, Piedmont

Brunello di Montalcino montalcheeno expensive dry red wine, from Montalcino, Tuscany

Cabernet kabairnay dry red wine from Veneto

cacao kaka-o cocoa

caffè kaf-fay coffee; café

caffè corretto espresso coffee with a dash of liqueur or spirit

caffellatte kaf-fel-lat-tay half espresso, half milk

caffè lungo weak black coffee

caffè macchiato mak-yato espresso coffee with a dash of milk

caffè ristretto extra-strong espresso coffee

caffè solubile soloobeelay instant coffee

camomilla camomile tea

cappuccino kap-poocheeno espresso coffee with foaming milk, sprinkled with cocoa/ chocolate powder

Cartizze karteetz-zay sparkling dry white wine from Veneto

Chianti k-yantee dark red Tuscan wine

china keena liqueur made from chinchona bark

chinotto keenot-to sparkling, dark soft drink

cioccolata calda chok-kolata hot chocolate

Cirò cheero slightly sweet, delicate red, rosé or white wine

Coca Cola Coke

Cortese kortayzay dry Piedmontese wine

Corvo di Salaparuta
dry Sicilian red wine

cubetto di ghiaccio g-yacho
ice cube

degustazione (di vini)
degoostatz-yonay wine tasting

denominazione di origine controllata mark guaranteeing the quality of a wine

digestivo deejesteevo digestive liqueur

D.O.C. (Denominazione di Origine Controllata) certifies the origin of a wine

D.O.C.G. (Denominazione di Origine Controllata e Garantita) guarantees the quality of a wine

Dolcetto dolchet-to dry red wine from Piedmont area

espresso strong black coffee

Est-Est-Est dry or sweet white wine from around Montefiascone area in Lazio

frappé frap-pay whisked milkshake or fruit drink with crushed ice

frappé al cioccolato chok-kolato chocolate milkshake with crushed ice

frappé alla banana banana milkshake with crushed ice

frappé alla fragola strawberry milkshake with crushed ice

Frascati dry white wine from area around Rome

Freisa frayza dry red wine from Piedmont region

frizzante freedzantay fizzy

frullato di frutta milkshake with fruit and crushed ice

gazzosa gatz-zoza clear lemonade

ghiaccio g-yacho ice

granita drink with crushed ice

granita di caffè kaf-fay coffee granita

granita di caffè con panna coffee and fresh cream granita

granita di limone leemonay lemon granita

grappa very strong, clear spirit distilled from grape husks

Grignolino green-yoleeno dry red wine, light in colour

Grumello dry, red wine with slight strawberry flavour

> **Travel tip** From sparkling prosecco to deep-red chianti, Italy is renowned for its wines. However, it's rare to find the snobbery often associated with "serious" wine drinking. Light reds such as those made from the dolcetto grape are kept in the fridge in hot weather, while some full-bodied whites are drunk at near room temperature.

Inferno dry red wine from Lombardy

Lambrusco sweet red or white sparkling wine from Emilia Romagna area

latte lat-tay milk

latte macchiato con cioccolato mak-yato kon chok-kolato foaming milk with a sprinkling of cocoa or chocolate powder

Lemonsoda sparkling lemon drink

limonata lemonade; lemon juice

liquore leekworay liqueur

lista dei vini day wine list

Malvasia malvazee-a dry white wine, sometimes slightly sparkling, from Sardinia or Friuli

Marsala thick, very sweet wine similar to sherry

Merlot mairlo very dark red wine with slightly herby flavour, of French origin

Moscato sweet, sparkling fruity wine

Nebbiolo neb-yolo dry red wine from Piedmont region

Oransoda sparkling orange drink

Orvieto orvee-**ay**to crisp white wine, usually dry

> **Travel tip** Although *un mezzo* (half-litre carafe of house wine) is a standard accompaniment to any meal, there's not a great emphasis on dedicated drinking in Italy. You'll rarely see drunks in public, young people don't devote their nights to getting wasted and women, in particular, are frowned upon if they're seen to be overindulging.

Pinot peeno light, dry white wine from the north

Pinot bianco b-yanko dry slightly sparkling white wine from the north

Pinot grigio greejo dry white wine from the north

Pinot nero nairo dry red wine from the north

porto port

prodotto e imbottigliato da... produced and bottled by...

Prosecco sparkling or still white wine from Veneto, can be either sweet or dry

Recioto rechoto sweet sparkling red wine from Veneto

Refosco dry red wine from Friuli

Riesling reezling dry white wine from various Northern regions

rosatello rozatel-lo dry rosé wine

rosato rozato dry rosé wine

rosé rozay rosé wine

rosso red

Sambuca (con la mosca)
aniseed-flavoured liqueur
(served with a coffee bean in
the glass)

Sangiovese sanjovayzay heavy,
dry red wine

Sassella dry, delicate red wine
from Vatellina area

Sauvignon soveen-yon dry white
wine from Veneto

sidro cider

Soave so-avay light, dry white
wine from region around Lake
Garda

spremuta d'arancia darancha
freshly squeezed orange juice

spremuta di limone leemonay
freshly squeezed lemon juice

spumante spoomantay sparkling
wine, like champagne

Strega strayga sweet liqueur
made from a secret recipe

succo sook-ko juice

succo d'arancia darancha
orange juice

succo di albicocca
apricot juice

succo di pera pear juice

succo di pesca peach juice

succo di pompelmo
grapefruit juice

tè tay tea

tè al latte lat-tay tea with milk

tè al limone leemonay lemon tea

Terlano dry white wine from area around Bolzano

Tocai tok-a-ee dry white wine from Veneto and Friuli

Valpolicella valpoleechel-la dry red wine from Veneto region

Verdicchio vairdeek-yo dry white fruity wine from Marche

Vermentino dry wine from Liguria and Sardinia

Vernaccia di S. Gimignano vairnacha dee san jeemeen-yano dry white wine from Tuscany

vino wine

vino bianco b-yanko white wine

vino da dessert des-sair dessert wine

vino da pasto table wine

vino da tavola table wine

vino della casa house wine

Vino Nobile di Montepulciano nobeelay dee montepoolchano high-class Tuscan red wine

vino rosato rozato rosé wine

vino rosé rozay rosé wine

vino rosso red wine

Vin Santo type of dessert wine from Tuscany

Picture credits

Photography by:
Jon Cunningham (pp.67, 213)
Michelle Grant (pp.46, 112, 230, 244, 253, 258)
Chris Hutty (pp.21, 154, 238, 246, 255)
Roger d'Olivere Mapp (pp.5, 25, 36, 58, 76, 202)
Martin Richardson (pp.125, 165, 174)
Natascha Sturny (pp.44, 193)
Karen Trist (pp.28, 46, 85, 94, 103, 138, 184, 220, 226, 250)

Front cover: Chris Hutty
Back cover: Karen Trist

All photos and maps © Rough Guides

ROUGH GUIDES WORLD COVERAGE

ANDORRA Spain
ANTIGUA The Caribbean
ARGENTINA Argentina, Buenos Aires, South America on a Budget
AUSTRALIA Australia, Australia Map, East Coast Australia, Melbourne, Sydney, Tasmania
AUSTRIA Austria, Europe on a Budget, Vienna
BAHAMAS The Bahamas, The Caribbean
BARBADOS The Caribbean
BELGIUM Belgium & Luxembourg, Brussels
BELIZE Belize, Central America On a Budget, Guetemala & Belize Map
BENIN West Africa
BOLIVIA Bolivia, South America on a Budget
BRAZIL Brazil, Rio, South America on a Budget
BRUNEI Malaysia, Singapore & Brunei [1 title], South East Asia on a Budget
BULGARIA Bulgaria, Europe on a Budget
BURKINA FASO West Africa
CAMBODIA Cambodia, South East Asia on a Budget, Vietnam
CAMEROON West Africa
CANADA Canada, Toronto, Toronto Map, Vancouver
CAPE VERDE West Africa
CARIBBEAN The Caribbean
CHILE Chile, South America on a Budget
CHINA Beijing, China, Hong Kong & Macau, Shanghai
COLOMBIA South America on a Budget
COSTA RICA Central America on a Budget, Costa Rica
CROATIA Croatia, Croatia Map, Europe on a Budget
CUBA Cuba, Cuba Map, Havana, The Caribbean
CYPRUS Cyprus
CZECH REPUBLIC The Czech Republic, Czech Republic Map, Europe on a Budget, Prague, Prague Map, Prague Pocket
DENMARK Copenhagen, Denmark, Europe on a Budget, Scandinavia

DOMINICAN REPUBLIC Dominican Republic, Dominican Republic Map, The Caribbean
ECUADOR Ecuador, South America on a Budget
EGYPT Egypt, Cairo & The Pyramids
EL SALVADOR Central America on a Budget
ENGLAND Britain, Camping, Devon & Cornwall, The Cotswolds, Dorset, Hampshire & The Isle of Wight [1 title], England, Europe on a Budget, The Lake District, London, London Pocket, London Map, London Mini Guide, Walks in London & Southeast England, Yorkshire
ESTONIA Europe on a Budget, Estonia, Latvia & Lithuania [1 title]
FIJI Fiji
FINLAND Europe on a Budget, Finland, Scandinavia
FRANCE Brittany & Normandy, Brittany Map, Corsica, Corsica Map, The Dordogne & the Lot, Europe on a Budget, France, Languedoc & Roussillon, The Loire Valley, Paris, Paris Mini Guide, Paris Pocket, Provence & the Cote d'Azur
FRENCH GUIANA South America on a Budget
GAMBIA West Africa
GERMANY Berlin, Europe on a Budget, Germany
GHANA West Africa
GIBRALTAR Spain
GREECE Athens Map, Athens Pocket, Crete, Crete Map, Europe on a Budget, Greece, Greek Islands
GUATEMALA Central America on a Budget, Guatemala, Guatemala & Belize Map
GUINEA West Africa
GUINEA-BISSAU West Africa
GUYANA South America on a Budget
HOLLAND see Netherlands
HONDURAS Central America on a Budget

HUNGARY Budapest, Europe on a Budget, Hungary
ICELAND Iceland, Iceland Map
INDIA Goa, India, Kerala, Rajasthan, Delhi & Agra [1 title]
INDONESIA Bali & Lombok, South East Asia on a Budget
IRELAND Dublin Map, Europe on a Budget, Ireland, Ireland Map
ISRAEL Jerusalem
ITALY Europe on a Budget, Florence & Siena Map, Florence & the best of Tuscany, Italy, Italy Map, The Italian Lakes, Naples & the Amalfi Coast, Rome, Rome Pocket, Sardinia, Sicily, Sicily Map, Tuscany & Umbria, Venice, Venice Pocket
JAMAICA Jamaica, The Caribbean
JAPAN Japan, Tokyo
JORDAN Jordan
KENYA Kenya, Kenya Map
KOREA Korea, Seoul
LAOS Laos, South East Asia on a Budget
LATVIA Europe on a Budget
LESOTHO South Africa
LITHUANIA Europe on a Budget
LUXEMBOURG Belgium & Luxembourg, Europe on a Budget
MALAYSIA Malaysia, Singapore & Brunei [1 title], South East Asia on a Budget
MALI West Africa
MAURITANIA West Africa
MEXICO Mexico, Cancun & The Yucatan, Yucatan Peninsula Map
MONACO France, Provence & the Cote d'Azur
MONTENEGRO Montenegro
MOROCCO Europe on a Budget, Marrakesh Map, Morocco
NEPAL Nepal
NETHERLANDS Amsterdam, Amsterdam Map, Amsterdam Pocket, Europe on a Budget, The Netherlands
NEW ZEALAND New Zealand, New Zealand Map
NICARAGUA Central America on a Budget
NIGER West Africa

OVER 300 DESTINATIONS

NIGERIA West Africa
NORWAY Europe on a Budget, Norway, Scandinavia
OMAN Oman
PANAMA Central America on a Budget, Panama
PARAGUAY South America on a Budget
PERU Peru, Peru Map, South America on a Budget
PHILIPPINES The Philippines, Southeast Asia on a Budget
POLAND Europe on a Budget, Poland
PORTUGAL The Algarve Map, Europe on a Budget, Lisbon Pocket, Portugal
PUERTO RICO The Caribbean, Puerto Rico
ROMANIA Europe on a Budget, Romania
RUSSIA Europe on a Budget, Moscow, St Petersburg
ST LUCIA The Caribbean
SCOTLAND Britain, Camping, Europe on a Budget, Scotland, Scottish Highlands & Islands
SENEGAL West Africa
SERBIA Montenegro, Europe on a Budget
SIERRA LEONE West Africa
SINGAPORE Malaysia, Singapore & Brunei [1 title], Singapore, Southeast Asia on a Budget
SLOVAKIA Czech & Slovak Republics, Europe on a Budget
SLOVENIA Europe on a Budget, Slovenia
SOUTH AFRICA South Africa, South Africa Map
SPAIN Andalucia, Andalucia Map, Barcelona, Barcelona Map, Barcelona Pocket, Europe on a Budget, Mallorca & Menorca, Mallorca Map, Spain
SRI LANKA Sri Lanka, Sri Lanka Map
SURINAME South America on a Budget
SWAZILAND South Africa
SWEDEN Europe on a Budget, Scandinavia, Sweden
SWITZERLAND Europe on a Budget, Switzerland

TAIWAN Taiwan
TANZANIA Tanzania, Zanzibar
THAILAND Bangkok, Southeast Asia on a Budget, Thailand, Thailand Beaches & Islands
TOGO West Africa
TRINIDAD & TOBAGO The Caribbean, Trinidad & Tobago
TUNISIA Tunisia
TURKEY Europe on a Budget, Istanbul, Turkey
TURKS AND CAICOS ISLANDS The Bahamas, The Caribbean
UNITED ARAB EMIRATES Dubai, Dubai & UAE Map [1 title]
UNITED KINGDOM Britain, Devon & Cornwall, England, Europe on a Budget, The Lake District, London, London Map, London Mini Guide, Scotland, Scottish Highlands & Islands, Wales, Walks in London & Southeast England
USA Boston, California, Chicago, Chicago Map, Florida, The Grand Canyon, Hawaii, Las Vegas, Los Angeles & Southern California, Miami & South Florida, Miami Map, New England, New Orleans & Cajun Country, New York City, New York City Mini Guide, New York Pocket, San Francisco, Seattle, Southwest USA, Washington DC, Yellowstone & The Grand Tetons National Park, Yosemite National Park
URUGUAY South America on a Budget
US VIRGIN ISLANDS The Bahamas, The Caribbean
VENEZUELA South America on a Budget
VIETNAM Southeast Asia on a Budget, Vietnam
WALES Britain, Camping, Europe on a Budget, Wales
WORLD COVERAGE Earthbound, Great Escapes, Make the Most of Your Time on Earth, Make the Most of Your Time in Britain Ultimate Adventures

ROUGH GUIDES DON'T JUST TRAVEL

COMPUTING Android Phones, Cloud Computing, Digital Photography, The Internet, iPad, iPhone, iPods & iTunes, Macs & OSX, Saving & Selling Online, Windows 7
FILM Comedy Movies, Cult Movies, Film, Film Musicals, Sci-Fi Movies
LIFESTYLE Babies & Toddlers, Brain Training, Food, Girl Stuff, Green Living, Happiness, Men's Health, Pregnancy & Birth, Psychology, Running, Sex, Weddings
MUSIC The Beatles, The Best Music You've Never Heard, Bob Dylan, Classical Music, Guitar, Jimi Hendrix, Nirvana, Pink Floyd, The Rolling Stones, Velvet Underground, World Music
POPULAR CULTURE Anime, The Best Art You've Never Seen, Classic Novels, Conspiracy Theories, Cult Football, FWD this link, Cult Sport Graphic Novels, Hitchhiker's Guide to the Galaxy, The Lost Symbol, Manga, Nelson Mandela, Next Big Thing, Shakespeare, Surviving the End of the World, True Crime, Unexplained Phenomena, Videogames
SCIENCE The Brain, Climate Change, The Earth, Energy Crisis, Evolution, Future, Genes & Cloning, The Universe

Start your journey at **roughguides.com**

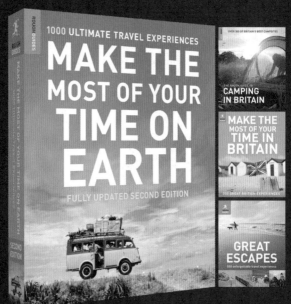